# Familiar Spanish Travels

W. D. Howells

Alpha Editions

This edition published in 2021

ISBN : 9789355756961

Design and Setting By
**Alpha Editions**
www.alphaedis.com
Email - info@alphaedis.com

As per information held with us this book is in Public Domain. This book is a reproduction of an important historical work. Alpha Editions uses the best technology to reproduce historical work in the same manner it was first published to preserve its original nature. Any marks or number seen are left intentionally to preserve its true form.

# Contents

I. AUTOBIOGRAPHICAL APPROACHES — 1 —

II. SAN SEBASTIAN AND BEAUTIFUL BISCAY — 5 —

III. BURGOS AND THE BITTER COLD OF BURGOS — 20 —

IV. THE VARIETY OF VALLADOLID — 35 —

V. PHASES OF MADRID — 54 —

VI. A NIGHT AND DAY IN TOLEDO — 81 —

VII. THE GREAT GRIDIRON OF ST. LAWRENCE — 98 —

VIII. CORDOVA AND THE WAY THERE — 108 —

IX. FIRST DAYS IN SEVILLE — 128 —

X. SEVILLIAN ASPECTS AND INCIDENTS — 148 —

XI. TO AND IN GRANADA — 174 —

XII. THE SURPRISES OF RONDA — 193 —

XIII. ALGECIRAS AND TARIFA — 203 —

# I. AUTOBIOGRAPHICAL APPROACHES

I.

As the train took its time and ours in mounting the uplands toward Granada on the soft, but not too soft, evening of November 6, 1911, the air that came to me through the open window breathed as if from an autumnal night of the middle eighteen-fifties in a little village of northeastern Ohio. I was now going to see, for the first time, the city where so great a part of my life was then passed, and in this magical air the two epochs were blent in reciprocal association. The question of my present identity was a thing indifferent and apart; it did not matter who or where or when I was. Youth and age were at one with each other: the boy abiding in the old man, and the old man pensively willing to dwell for the enchanted moment in any vantage of the past which would give him shelter.

In that dignified and deliberate Spanish train I was a man of seventy-four crossing the last barrier of hills that helped keep Granada from her conquerors, and at the same time I was a boy of seventeen in the little room under the stairs in a house now practically remoter than the Alhambra, finding my unguided way through some Spanish story of the vanished kingdom of the Moors. The little room which had structurally ceased fifty years before from the house that ceased to be home even longer ago had returned to the world with me in it, and fitted perfectly into the first-class railway compartment which my luxury had provided for it. From its window I saw through the car window the olive groves and white cottages of the Spanish peasants, and the American apple orchards and meadows stretching to the primeval woods that walled the drowsing village round. Then, as the night deepened with me at my book, the train slipped slowly from the hills, and the moon, leaving the Ohio village wholly in the dark, shone over the roofs and gardens of Granada, and I was no longer a boy of seventeen, but altogether a man of seventy-four.

I do not say the experience was so explicit as all this; no experience so mystical could be so explicit; and perhaps what was intimated to me in it was only that if I sometime meant to ask some gentle reader's company in a retrospect of my Spanish travels, I had better be honest with him and own at the beginning that passion for Spanish things which was the ruling passion of my boyhood; I had better confess that, however unrequited, it held me in the eager bondage of a lover still, so that I never wished to escape from it, but must try to hide the fact whenever the real Spain fell below the ideal, however I might reason with my infatuation or try to scoff it away. It had once been so inextinguishable a part of me that the record of my journey must be more or less autobiographical; and though I should decently endeavor to keep my past out of it, perhaps I should not try very hard and should not always succeed.

Just when this passion began in me I should not be able to say; but probably it was with my first reading of *Don Quixote* in the later eighteen-forties. I would then have been ten or twelve years old; and, of course, I read that incomparable romance, not only greatest, but sole of its kind, in English. The purpose of some time reading it in Spanish and then the purpose of some time writing the author's life grew in me with my growing years so strongly that, though I have never yet done either and probably never shall, I should not despair of doing both if I lived to be a hundred. In the mean time my wandering steps had early chanced upon a Spanish grammar, and I had begun those inquiries in it which were based upon a total ignorance of English accidence. I do not remember how I felt my way from it to such reading of the language as has endeared Spanish literature to me. It embraced something of everything: literary and political history, drama, poetry, fiction; but it never condescended to the exigencies of common parlance. These exigencies did not exist for me in my dreams of seeing Spain which were not really expectations. It was not until half a century later, when my longing became a hope and then a purpose, that I foreboded the need of practicable Spanish. Then I invoked the help of a young professor, who came to me for an hour each day of a week in London and let me try to talk with him; but even then I accumulated so little practicable Spanish that my first hour, almost my first moment in Spain, exhausted my store. My professor was from Barcelona, but he beautifully lisped his *c's* and *z's* like any old Castilian, when he might have hissed them in the accent of his native Catalan; and there is no telling how much I might have profited by his instruction if he had not been such a charming intelligence that I liked to talk with him of literature and philosophy and politics rather than the weather, or the cost of things, or the question of how long the train stopped and when it would start, or the dishes at table, or clothes at the tailor's, or the forms of greeting and parting. If he did not equip me with the useful colloquial phrases, the fault was mine; and the misfortune was doubly mine when from my old acquaintance with Italian (glib half-sister of the statelier Spanish) the Italian phrases would thrust forward as the equivalent of the English words I could not always think of. The truth is, then, that I was not perfect in my Spanish after quite six weeks in Spain; and if in the course of his travels with me the reader finds me flourishing Spanish idioms in his face he may safely attribute them less to my speaking than my reading knowledge: probably I never employed them in conversation. That reading was itself without order or system, and I am not sure but it had better been less than more. Yet who knows? The days, or the nights of the days, in the eighteen-fifties went quickly, as quickly as the years go now, and it would have all come to the present pass whether that blind devotion to an alien literature had cloistered my youth or not.

I do not know how, with the merciful make I am of, I should then have cared so little, or else ignored so largely the cruelties I certainly knew that the Spaniards had practised in the conquests of Mexico and Peru. I knew of these things, and my heart was with the Incas and the Aztecs, and yet somehow I could not punish the Spaniards for their atrocious destruction of the only American civilizations. As nearly as I can now say, I was of both sides, and wistful to reconcile them, though I do not see now how it could have been done; and in my later hopes for the softening of the human conditions I have found it hard to forgive Pizarro for the overthrow of the most perfectly socialized state known to history. I scarcely realized the base ingratitude of the Spanish sovereigns to Columbus, and there were vast regions of history that I had not penetrated till long afterward in pursuit of Spanish perfidy and inhumanity, as in their monstrous misrule of Holland. When it came in those earlier days to a question of sides between the Spaniards and the Moors, as Washington Irving invited my boyhood to take it in his chronicle of the conquest of Granada, I experienced on a larger scale my difficulty in the case of the Mexicans and Peruvians. The case of these had been reported to me in the school-readers, but here, now, was an affair submitted to the mature judgment of a boy of twelve, and yet I felt as helpless as I was at ten. Will it be credited that at seventy-four I am still often in doubt which side I should have had win, though I used to fight on both? Since the matter was settled more than four hundred years ago, I will not give the reasons for my divided allegiance. They would hardly avail now to reverse the tragic fate of the Moors, and if I try I cannot altogether wish to reverse it. Whatever Spanish misrule has been since Islam was overthrown in Granada, it has been the error of law, and the rule of Islam at the best had always been the effect of personal will, the caprice of despots high and low, the unstatuted sufferance of slaves, high and low. The gloomiest and cruelest error of Inquisitional Spain was nobler, with its adoration of ideal womanhood, than the Mohammedan state with its sensual dreams of Paradise. I will not pretend (as I very well might, and as I perhaps ought) that I thought of these things, all or any, as our train began to slope rather more rapidly toward Granada, and to find its way under the rising moon over the storied Vega. I will as little pretend that my attitude toward Spain was ever that of the impartial observer after I crossed the border of that enchanted realm where we all have our castles. I have thought it best to be open with the reader here at the beginning, and I would not, if I could, deny him the pleasure of doubting my word or disabling my judgment at any point he likes. In return I shall only ask his patience when I strike too persistently the chord of autobiography. That chord is part of the harmony between the boy and the old man who made my Spanish journey together, and were always accusing themselves, the first of dreaming and the last of doddering: perhaps with equal justice. Is there really much difference between the two?

II.

It was fully a month before that first night in Granada that I arrived in Spain after some sixty years' delay. During this period I had seen almost every other interesting country in Europe. I had lived five or six years in Italy; I had been several months in Germany; and a fortnight in Holland; I had sojourned often in Paris; I had come and gone a dozen times in England and lingered long each time; and yet I had never once visited the land of my devotion. I had often wondered at this, it was so wholly involuntary, and I had sometimes suffered from the surprise of those who knew of my passion for Spain, and kept finding out my dereliction, alleging the Sud-Express to Madrid as something that left me without excuse. The very summer before last I got so far on the way in London as to buy a Spanish phrase-book full of those inopportune conversations with landlords, tailors, ticket-sellers, and casual acquaintance or agreeable strangers. Yet I returned once more to America with my desire, which was turning into a duty, unfulfilled; and when once more I sailed for Europe in 1911 it was more with foreboding of another failure than a prescience of fruition in my inveterate longing. Even after that boldly decisive week of the professor in London I had my doubts and my self-doubts. There were delays at London, delays at Paris, delays at Tours; and when at last we crossed the Pyrenees and I found myself in Spain, it was with an incredulity which followed me throughout and lingered with me to the end. "Is this truly Spain, and am I actually there?" the thing kept asking itself; and it asks itself still, in terms that fit the accomplished fact.

## II. SAN SEBASTIAN AND BEAUTIFUL BISCAY

Even at Irun, where we arrived in Spain from Bayonne, there began at once to be temperamental differences which ought to have wrought against my weird misgivings of my whereabouts. Only in Spain could a customs inspector have felt of one tray in our trunks and then passed them all with an air of such jaded aversion from an employ uncongenial to a gentleman. Perhaps he was also loath to attempt any inquiry in that Desperanto of French, English, and Spanish which raged around us; but the porter to whom we had fallen, while I hesitated at our carriage door whether I should summon him as *Mozo* or *Usted*, was master of that *lingua franca* and recovered us from the customs without question on our part, and understood everything we could not, say. I like to think he was a Basque, because I like the Basques so much for no reason that I can think of. Their being always Carlists would certainly be no reason with me, for I was never a Carlist; and perhaps my liking is only a prejudice in their favor from the air of thrift and work which pervades their beautiful province, or is an effect of their language as I first saw it inscribed on the front of the Credit Lyonnais at Bayonne. It looked so beautifully regular, so scholarly, so Latin, so sister to both Spanish and Italian, so richly and musically voweled, and yet remained so impenetrable to the most daring surmise, that I conceived at once a profound admiration for the race which could keep such a language to itself. When I remembered how blond, how red-blond our sinewy young porter was, I could not well help breveting him of that race, and honoring him because he could have read those words with the eyes that were so blue amid the general Spanish blackness of eyes. He imparted a quiet from his own calm to our nervousness, and if we had appealed to him on the point I am sure he would have saved us from the error of breakfasting in the station restaurant at the deceitful *table d'hote*, though where else we should have breakfasted I do not know.

I.

One train left for San Sebastian while I was still lost in amaze that what I had taken into my mouth for fried egg should be inwardly fish and full of bones; but he quelled my anxiety with the assurance, which I somehow understood, that there would be another train soon. In the mean time there were most acceptable Spanish families all about, affably conversing together, and freely admitting to their conversation the children, who so publicly abound in Spain, and the nurses who do nothing to prevent their publicity. There were already the typical fat Spanish mothers and lean fathers, with the slender daughters, who, in the tradition of Spanish good-breeding, kept their black eyes to themselves, or only lent them to the spectators in furtive glances. Both older and younger ladies wore the scanty Egyptian skirt of Occidental civilization, lurking or perking in deep-drooping or high-raking hats, though already here and there was the mantilla, which would more and more prevail as we went southward; older and younger, they were all painted and powdered to the favor that Spanish women everywhere come to.

When the bad breakfast was over, and the waiters were laying the table for another as bad, our Basque porter came in and led us to the train for San Sebastian which he had promised us. It was now raining outside, and we were glad to climb into our apartment without at all seeing what Irun was or was not like. But we thought well of the place because we first experienced there the ample ease of a Spanish car. In Spain the railroad gauge is five feet six inches; and this car of ours was not only very spacious, but very clean, while the French cars that had brought us from Bordeaux to Bayonne and from Bayonne to Irun were neither. I do not say all French cars are dirty, or all Spanish cars are as clean as they are spacious. The cars of both countries are hard to get into, by steep narrow footholds worse even than our flights of steps; in fact, the English cars are the only ones I know which are easy of access. But these have not the ample racks for hand-bags which the Spanish companies provide for travelers willing to take advantage of their trust by transferring much of their heavy stuff to them. Without owning that we were such travelers, I find this the place to say that, with the allowance of a hundred and thirty-two pounds free, our excess baggage in two large steamer-trunks did not cost us three dollars in a month's travel, with many detours, from Irun in the extreme north to Algeciras in the extreme south of Spain.

II.

But in this sordid detail I am keeping the reader from the scenery. It had been growing more and more striking ever since we began climbing into the Pyrenees from Bayonne; but upon the whole it was not so sublime as it was beautiful. There were some steep, sharp peaks, but mostly there were grassy valleys with white cattle grazing in them, and many fields of Indian corn, endearingly homelike. This at least is mainly the trace that the scenery as far as Irun has left among my notes; and after Irun there is record of more and more corn. There was, in fact, more corn than anything else, though there were many orchards, also endearingly homelike, with apples yellow and red showing among the leaves still green on the trees; if there had been something more wasteful in the farming it would have been still more homelike, but a traveler cannot have everything. The hillsides were often terraced, as in Italy, and the culture apparently close and conscientious. The farmhouses looked friendly and comfortable; at places the landscape was

## II. SAN SEBASTIAN AND BEAUTIFUL BISCAY

Even at Irun, where we arrived in Spain from Bayonne, there began at once to be temperamental differences which ought to have wrought against my weird misgivings of my whereabouts. Only in Spain could a customs inspector have felt of one tray in our trunks and then passed them all with an air of such jaded aversion from an employ uncongenial to a gentleman. Perhaps he was also loath to attempt any inquiry in that Desperanto of French, English, and Spanish which raged around us; but the porter to whom we had fallen, while I hesitated at our carriage door whether I should summon him as *Mozo* or *Usted*, was master of that *lingua franca* and recovered us from the customs without question on our part, and understood everything we could not, say. I like to think he was a Basque, because I like the Basques so much for no reason that I can think of. Their being always Carlists would certainly be no reason with me, for I was never a Carlist; and perhaps my liking is only a prejudice in their favor from the air of thrift and work which pervades their beautiful province, or is an effect of their language as I first saw it inscribed on the front of the Credit Lyonnais at Bayonne. It looked so beautifully regular, so scholarly, so Latin, so sister to both Spanish and Italian, so richly and musically voweled, and yet remained so impenetrable to the most daring surmise, that I conceived at once a profound admiration for the race which could keep such a language to itself. When I remembered how blond, how red-blond our sinewy young porter was, I could not well help breveting him of that race, and honoring him because he could have read those words with the eyes that were so blue amid the general Spanish blackness of eyes. He imparted a quiet from his own calm to our nervousness, and if we had appealed to him on the point I am sure he would have saved us from the error of breakfasting in the station restaurant at the deceitful *table d'hote*, though where else we should have breakfasted I do not know.

I.

One train left for San Sebastian while I was still lost in amaze that what I had taken into my mouth for fried egg should be inwardly fish and full of bones; but he quelled my anxiety with the assurance, which I somehow understood, that there would be another train soon. In the mean time there were most acceptable Spanish families all about, affably conversing together, and freely admitting to their conversation the children, who so publicly abound in Spain, and the nurses who do nothing to prevent their publicity. There were already the typical fat Spanish mothers and lean fathers, with the slender daughters, who, in the tradition of Spanish good-breeding, kept their black eyes to themselves, or only lent them to the spectators in furtive glances. Both older and younger ladies wore the scanty Egyptian skirt of Occidental civilization, lurking or perking in deep-drooping or high-raking hats, though already here and there was the mantilla, which would more and more prevail as we went southward; older and younger, they were all painted and powdered to the favor that Spanish women everywhere come to.

When the bad breakfast was over, and the waiters were laying the table for another as bad, our Basque porter came in and led us to the train for San Sebastian which he had promised us. It was now raining outside, and we were glad to climb into our apartment without at all seeing what Irun was or was not like. But we thought well of the place because we first experienced there the ample ease of a Spanish car. In Spain the railroad gauge is five feet six inches; and this car of ours was not only very spacious, but very clean, while the French cars that had brought us from Bordeaux to Bayonne and from Bayonne to Irun were neither. I do not say all French cars are dirty, or all Spanish cars are as clean as they are spacious. The cars of both countries are hard to get into, by steep narrow footholds worse even than our flights of steps; in fact, the English cars are the only ones I know which are easy of access. But these have not the ample racks for hand-bags which the Spanish companies provide for travelers willing to take advantage of their trust by transferring much of their heavy stuff to them. Without owning that we were such travelers, I find this the place to say that, with the allowance of a hundred and thirty-two pounds free, our excess baggage in two large steamer-trunks did not cost us three dollars in a month's travel, with many detours, from Irun in the extreme north to Algeciras in the extreme south of Spain.

II.

But in this sordid detail I am keeping the reader from the scenery. It had been growing more and more striking ever since we began climbing into the Pyrenees from Bayonne; but upon the whole it was not so sublime as it was beautiful. There were some steep, sharp peaks, but mostly there were grassy valleys with white cattle grazing in them, and many fields of Indian corn, endearingly homelike. This at least is mainly the trace that the scenery as far as Irun has left among my notes; and after Irun there is record of more and more corn. There was, in fact, more corn than anything else, though there were many orchards, also endearingly homelike, with apples yellow and red showing among the leaves still green on the trees; if there had been something more wasteful in the farming it would have been still more homelike, but a traveler cannot have everything. The hillsides were often terraced, as in Italy, and the culture apparently close and conscientious. The farmhouses looked friendly and comfortable; at places the landscape was molested by some sort of manufactories which could not conceal their tall chimneys, though they kept the secret of their industry. They were never, really, very bad, and I would have been willing to let them pass for fulling-mills, such as I was so familiar with in *Don Quixote,* if I had thought of these in time. But one ought to be honest at any cost, and I must own that the Spain I was now for the first time seeing with every-day eyes was so little like the Spain of my boyish vision that I never once recurred to it. That was a Spain of cork-trees, of groves by the green margins of mountain brooks, of habitable hills, where shepherds might feed their flocks and mad lovers and maids forlorn might wander and maunder; and here were fields of corn and apple orchards and vineyards reddening and yellowing up to the doors of those comfortable farmhouses, with nowhere the sign of a Christian cavalier or a turbaned infidel. As a man I could not help liking what I saw, but I could also grieve for the boy who would have been so disappointed if he had come to the Basque provinces of Spain when he was from ten to fifteen years old, instead of seventy-four.

It took our train nearly an hour to get by twenty miles of those pleasant farms and the pretty hamlets which they now and then clustered into. But that was fast for a Spanish way-train, which does not run, but, as it were, walks with dignity and makes long stops at stations, to rest and let the locomotive roll itself a cigarette. By the time we reached San Sebastian our rain had thickened to a heavy downpour, and by the time we mounted to our rooms, three pair up in the hotel, it was storming in a fine fury over the bay under them, and sweeping the curving quays and tossing the feathery foliage of the tamarisk-shaded promenade. The distinct advantage of our lofty perch was the splendid sight of the tempest, held from doing its worst by the mighty headlands standing out to sea on the right and left. But our rooms were cold with the stony cold of the south when it is cooling off from its summer, and we shivered in the splendid sight.

III.

The inhabitants of San Sebastian will not hesitate to say that it is the prettiest town in Spain, and I do not know that they could be hopefully contradicted. It is very modern in its more obvious aspects, with a noble thoroughfare called the Avenida de Libertad for its principal street, shaded with a double row of those feathery tamarisks, and with handsome shops glittering on both sides of it. Very easily it is first of the fashionable watering-places of Spain; the King has his villa there, and the court comes every summer. But they had gone by the time we got there, and the town wore the dejected look of out-of-season summer resorts; though there was the apparatus of gaiety, the fine casino at one end of the beach, and the villas of the rich and noble all along it to the other end. On the sand were still many bathing-machines, but many others had begun to climb for greater safety during the winter to the street above. We saw one hardy bather dripping up from the surf and seeking shelter among those that remained, but they were mostly tenanted by their owners, who looked shoreward through their open doors, and made no secret of their cozy domesticity, where they sat and sewed or knitted and gossiped with their neighbors. Good wives and mothers they doubtless were, but no doubt glad to be resting from the summer pleasure of others. They had their beautiful names written up over their doors, and were for the service of the lady visitors only; there were other machines for gentlemen, and no doubt it was their owners whom we saw gathering the fat seaweed thrown up by the storm into the carts drawn by oxen over the sand. The oxen wore no yokes, but pulled by a band drawn over their foreheads under their horns, and they had the air of not liking the arrangement; though, for the matter of that, I have never seen oxen that seemed to like being yoked.

When we came down to dinner we found the tables fairly full of belated visitors, who presently proved tourists flying south like ourselves. The dinner was good, as it is in nearly all Spanish hotels, where for an average of three dollars a day you have an inclusive rate which you must double for as good accommodation in our States. Let no one, I say, fear the rank cookery so much imagined of the Peninsula, the oil, the pepper, the kid and the like strange meats; as in all other countries of Europe, even England itself, there is a local version, a general convention of the French cuisine, quite as good in Spain as elsewhere, and oftener superabundant than subabundant. The plain water is generally good, With an American edge of freshness; but if you will not trust it (we had to learn to trust it) there are agreeable Spanish mineral waters, as well as the Apollinaris, the St. Galmier, and the Perrier of other civilizations, to be had for the asking, at rather greater cost than the good native wines, often included in the inclusive rate.

Besides this convention of the French cuisine there is almost everywhere a convention of the English language in some one of the waiters. You must not stray far from the beaten path of your immediate wants, but in this you are safe. At San Sebastian we had even a wider range with the English of the little intellectual-looking, pale Spanish waiter, with a fine Napoleonic head, who came to my help when I began to flounder in the language which I had read so much and spoken so little or none. He had been a year in London, he said, and he took us for English, though, now he came to notice it, he perceived we were Americans because we spoke "quicklier" than the English. We did not protest; it was the mildest criticism of our national accent which we were destined to get from English-speaking Spaniards before they found we were not the English we did not wish to be taken for. After dinner we asked for a fire in one of our grates, but the maid declared there was no fuel; and, though the hostess denied this and promised us a fire the next night, she forgot it till nine o'clock, and then we would not have it. The cold abode with us indoors to the last at San Sebastian, but the storm (which had hummed and whistled theatrically at our windows) broke during the first night, and the day followed with several intervals of sunshine, which bathed us in a glowing-expectation of overtaking the fugitive summer farther south.

IV.

In the mean time we hired a beautiful Basque cabman with a red Basque cap and high-hooked Basque nose to drive us about at something above the legal rate and let us not leave any worthy thing in San Sebastian unseen. He took us, naturally, to several churches, old and new, with their Gothic and rococo interiors, which I still find glooming and glinting among my evermore thickening impressions of like things. We got from them the sense of that architectural and sculptural richness which the interior of no Spanish church ever failed measurably to give; but what their historical associations were I will not offer to say. The associations of San Sebastian with the past are in all things vague, at least for me. She was indeed taken from the French by the English under Wellington during the Peninsular

War, but of older, if not unhappier farther-off days and battles longer ago her history as I know it seems to know little. It knows of savage and merciless battles between the partisans of Don Carlos and those of Queen Isabella so few decades since as not to be the stuff of mere pathos yet, and I am not able to blink the fact that my beloved Basques fought on the wrong side, when they need not have fought at all. Why they were Carlists they could perhaps no more say than I could. The monumental historic fact is that the Basques have been where they are immeasurably beyond the memories of other men; what the scope of their own memories is one could perhaps confidently say only in Basque if one could say anything. Of course, in the nature of things, the Phoenicians must have been there and the Greeks, doubtless, if they ever got outside of the Pillars of Hercules; the Romans, of course, must have settled and civilized and then Christianized the province. It is next neighbor to that province of Asturias in which alone the Arabs failed to conquer the Goths, and from which Spain was to live and grow again and recover all her losses from the Moors; but what the share of San Sebastian was in this heroic fate, again I must leave the Basques to say. They would doubtless say it with sufficient self-respect, for wherever we came in contact that day with the Basque nature we could not help imagining in it a sense of racial merit equaling that of the Welsh themselves, who are indeed another branch of the same immemorial Iberian stock, if the Basques are Iberians. Like the Welsh, they have the devout tradition that they never were conquered, but yielded to circumstances when these became too strong for them.

Among the ancient Spanish liberties which were restricted by the consolidating monarchy from age to age, the Basque *fueros*, or rights, were the oldest; they lasted quite to our own day; and although it is known to more ignorant men that these privileges (including immunity from conscription) have now been abrogated, the custodian of the House of Provincial Deputies, whom our driver took us to visit, was such a glowing Basque patriot that he treated them as in full force. His pride in the seat of the local government spared us no detail of the whole electric-lighting system, or even the hose-bibs for guarding the edifice against fire, let alone every picture and photograph on the wall of every chamber of greater or less dignity, with every notable table and chair. He certainly earned the peseta I gave him, but he would have done far more for it if we had suffered him to take us up another flight of stairs; and he followed us in our descent with bows and adieux that ought to have left no doubt in our minds of the persistence of the Basque *fueros*.

V.

It was to such a powerful embodiment of the local patriotism that our driver had brought us from another civic palace overlooking the Plaza de la

Constitution, chiefly notable now for having been the old theater of the bull-fights. The windows in the houses round still bear the numbers by which they were sold to spectators as boxes; but now the municipality has built a beautiful brand-new bull-ring in San Sebastian; and I do not know just why we were required to inspect the interior of the edifice overlooking this square. I only know that at sight of our bewilderment a workman doing something to the staircase clapped his hands orientally, and the custodian was quickly upon us in response to a form of summons which we were to find so often used in Spain. He was not so crushingly upon us as that other custodian; he was apologetically proud, rather than boastfully; at times he waved his hands in deprecation, and would have made us observe that the place was little, very little; he deplored it like a host who wishes his possessions praised. Among the artistic treasures of the place from which he did not excuse us there were some pen-drawings, such as writing-masters execute without lifting the pen from the paper, by a native of South America, probably of Basque descent, since the Basques have done so much to people that continent. We not only admired these, but we would not consent to any of the custodian's deprecations, especially when it came to question of the pretty salon in which Queen Victoria was received on her first visit to San Sebastian. We supposed then, and in fact I had supposed till this moment, that it was Queen Victoria of Great Britain who was meant; but now I realize that it must have been the queen consort of Spain, who seems already to have made herself so liked there.

She, of course, comes every summer to San Sebastian, and presently our driver took us to see the royal villa by the shore, withdrawn, perhaps from a sense of its extreme plainness, not to say ugliness, among its trees and vines behind its gates and walls. Our driver excused himself for not being able to show us through it; he gladly made us free of an unrestricted view of the royal bathing-pavilion, much more frankly splendid in its gilding, beside the beach. Other villas ranked themselves along the hillside, testifying to the gaiety of the social life in summers past and summers to come. In the summer just past the gaiety may have been interrupted by the strikes taking in the newspapers the revolutionary complexion which it was now said they did not wear. At least, when the King had lately come to fetch the royal household away nothing whatever happened, and the "constitutional guarantees," suspended amidst the ministerial anxieties, were restored during the month, with the ironical applause of the liberal press, which pretended that there had never been any need of their suspension.

## VI.

All pleasures, mixed or unmixed, must end, and the qualified joy of our drive through San Sebastian came to a close on our return to our hotel well within the second hour, almost within its first half. When I proposed paying our driver for the exact time, he drooped upon his box and, remembering my remorse in former years for standing upon my just rights in such matters, I increased the fare, peseta by peseta, till his sinking spirits rose, and he smiled gratefully upon me and touched his brave red cap as he drove away. He had earned his money, if racking his invention for objects of interest in San Sebastian was a merit. At the end we were satisfied that it was a well-built town with regular blocks in the modern quarter, and not without the charm of picturesqueness which comes of narrow and crooked lanes in the older parts. Prescient of the incalculable riches before us, we did not ask much of it, and we got all we asked. I should be grateful to San Sebastian, if for nothing else than the two very Spanish experiences I had there. One concerned a letter for me which had been refused by the bankers named in my letter of credit, from a want of faith, I suppose, in my coming. When I did come I was told that I would find it at the post-office.

That would be well enough when I found the post-office, which ought to have been easy enough, but which presented certain difficulties in the driving rain of our first afternoon. At last in a fine square I asked a fellow-man in my best conversational Spanish where the post-office was, and after a moment's apparent suffering he returned, "Do you speak English?" "Yes." I said, "and I am so glad you do." "Not at all. I don't speak anything else. Great pleasure. There is the post-office," and it seemed that I had hardly escaped collision with it. But this was the beginning, not the end, of my troubles. When I showed my card to the *poste restante* clerk, he went carefully through the letters bearing the initial of my name and denied that there was any for me. We entered into reciprocally bewildering explanations, and parted altogether baffled. Then, at the hotel, I consulted with a capable young office-lady, who tardily developed a knowledge of English, and we agreed that it would be well to send the *chico* to the post-office for it. The *chico*, corresponding in a Spanish hotel to a *piccolo* in Germany or a page in England, or our own now evanescing bell-boy, was to get a *peseta* for bringing me the letter. He got the *peseta*, though he only brought me word that the authorities would send the letter to the hotel by the postman that night. The authorities did not send it that night, and the next morning I recurred to my bankers. There, on my entreaty for some one who could meet my Spanish at least half-way in English, a manager of the bank came out of his office and reassured me concerning the letter which I had now begun to imagine the most important I had ever missed. Even while we talked the postman came in and owned having taken the letter back to the office. He voluntarily promised to bring it to the bank at one o'clock, when I hastened to meet him. At that hour every one was out at lunch; I came again at four, when everybody had returned, but the letter was not delivered; at five, just before the bank closed, the letter, which had now grown from a *carta* to a *cartela*, was still on its way. I left San Sebastian without it; and will it be credited that when it was forwarded to me a week later at Madrid it proved the most fatuous missive imaginable, wholly concerning the writer's own affairs and none of mine?

I cannot guess yet why it was withheld from me, but since the incident brought me that experience of Spanish politeness, I cannot grieve for it. The young banker who left his region of high finance to come out and condole with me, in apologizing for the original refusal of my letter, would not be contented with so little. Nothing would satisfy him but going with me, on my hinted purpose, and inquiring with me at the railroad office into the whole business of circular tickets, and even those kilometric tickets which the Spanish railroads issue to such passengers as will have their photographs affixed to them for the prevention of transference. As it seemed advisable not to go to this extreme till I got to Madrid, my kind young banker put himself at my disposal for any other service I could imagine from him; but I searched myself in vain for any desire, much less necessity, and I parted from him at the door of his bank with the best possible opinion of the Basques. I suppose he was a Basque; at any rate, he was blond, which the Spaniards are mostly not, and the Basques often are. Now I am sorry, since he was so kind, that I did not get him to read me the Basque inscription on the front of his bank, which looked exactly like that on the bank at Bayonne; I should not have understood it, but I should have known what it sounded like, if it sounded like anything but Basque.

Everybody in San Sebastian seemed resolved to outdo every other in kindness. In a shop where we endeavored to explain that we wanted to get a flat cap which should be both Basque and red, a lady who was buying herself a hat asked in English if she could help us. When we gladly answered that she could, she was silent, almost to tears, and it appeared that in this generous offer of aid she had exhausted her whole stock of English. Her mortification, her painful surprise, at the strange catastrophe, was really pitiable, and we hastened to escape from it to a shop across the street. There instantly a small boy rushed enterprisingly out and brought back with him a very pretty girl who spoke most of the little French which has made its way in San Sebastian against the combined Basque and Spanish, and a cap of the right flatness and redness was brought. I must not forget, among the pleasures done us by the place, the pastry cook's shop which advertised in English "Tea at all Hours," and which at that hour of our afternoon we now found so opportune, that it seemed almost personally attentive to us as the only Anglo-Saxon visitors in town. The tea might have been better, but it was as good as it knew how; and the small boy who came in with his mother (the Spanish mother seldom fails of the company of a small boy) in her moments of distraction succeeded in touching with his finger all the pieces of pastry except those we were eating.

VII.

The high aquiline nose which is characteristic of the autochthonic race abounds in San Sebastian, but we saw no signs of the high temper which is said to go with it. This, indeed, was known to me chiefly from my first reading in *Don Quixote,* of the terrific combat between the squire of the Biscayan ladies whose carriage the knight of La Mancha stopped after his engagement with the windmills. In their exchange of insults incident to the knight's desire that the ladies should go to Toboso and thank Dulcinea for his delivery of them from the necromancers he had put to flight in the persons of two Benedictine monks, "'Get gone,' the squire called, in bad Spanish and worse Biscayan, 'Get gone, thou knight, and Devil go with thou; or by He Who me create... me kill thee now so sure as me be Biscayan,'" and when the knight called him an "inconsiderable mortal," and said that if he were a gentleman he would chastise him: "'What! me no gentleman?' replied the Biscayan. 'I swear thou be liar as me be Christian.... Me will show thee me be Biscayan, and gentleman by land, gentleman by sea, gentleman in spite of Devil; and thou lie if thou say the contrary.'"

It is a scene which will have lived in the memory of every reader, and I recurred to it hopefully but vainly in San Sebastian, where this fiery threefold gentleman might have lived in his time. It would be interesting to know how far the Basques speak broken Spanish in a fashion of their own, which Cervantes tried to represent in the talk of his Biscayan. Like the Welsh again they strenuously keep their immemorial language against the inroads of the neighboring speech. How much they fix it in a modern literature it would be easier to ask than to say. I suppose there must be Basque newspapers; perhaps there are Basque novelists, there are notoriously Basque bards who recite their verses to the peasants, and doubtless there are poets who print their rhymes: and I blame myself for not inquiring further concerning them of that kindly Basque banker who wished so much to do something for me in compensation for the loss of my worthless letter. I knew, too cheaply, that the Basques have their poetical contests, as the Welsh have their musical competitions in the Eisteddfod, and they are once more like the Welsh, their brothers in antiquity, in calling themselves by a national name of their own. They call themselves Euskaldunac, which is as different from the name of Basque given them by the alien races as Cymru is from Welsh.

All this lore I have easily accumulated from the guide-books since leaving San Sebastian, but I was carelessly ignorant of it in driving from the hotel to the station when we came away, and was much concerned in the overtures made us in a mixed Spanish, English, and French by a charming family from Chili, through the brother to one of the ladies and husband to the other. When he perceived from my Spanish that we were not English, he rejoiced that we were Americans of the north, and as joyfully proclaimed that they were Americans of the south. We were at once sensible of a community of spirit in our difference from our different ancestral races. They were Spanish, but with a New World blitheness which we nowhere afterward found in the native Spaniards; and we were English, with a willingness to laugh and to joke which they had not perhaps noted in our ancestral contemporaries. Again and again we met them in the different cities where we feared we had lost them, until we feared no more and counted confidently on seeing them wherever we went. They were always radiantly smiling; and upon this narrow ground I am going to base the conjecture that the most distinctive difference of the Western Hemisphere from the Eastern is its habit of seeing the fun of things. With those dear Chilians we saw the fun of many little hardships of travel which might have been insupportable without the vision. Sometimes we surprised one another in the same hotel; sometimes it was in the street that we encountered, usually to exchange amusing misfortunes. If we could have been constantly with these fellow-hemispherists our progress through Spain would have been an unbroken holiday.

There is a superstition of travelers in Spain, much fostered by innkeepers and porters, that you cannot get seats in the fast trains without buying your tickets the day before, and then perhaps not, and we abandoned ourselves to this fear at San Sebastian so far as to get places some hours in advance. But once established in the ten-foot-wide interior of the first-class compartment which we had to ourselves, every anxiety fell from us; and I do not know a more flattering emotion than that which you experience in sinking into your luxurious seat, and, after a glance at your hand-bags in the racks where they have been put with no strain on your own muscles, giving your eyes altogether to the joy of the novel landscape.

The train was what they call a Rapido in Spain; and though we were supposed to be devouring space with indiscriminate gluttony, I do not think that in our mad rush of twenty-five miles an hour we failed to taste any essential detail of the scenery..But I wish now that I had known the Basques were all nobles, and that the peasants owned many of the little farms we saw declaring the general thrift. In the first two hours of the six to Burgos we ran through lovely valleys held in the embrace of gentle hills, where the fields of Indian corn were varied by groves of chestnut trees, where we could see the burrs gaping on their stems. The blades and tassels of the corn had been stripped away, leaving the ripe ears a-tilt at the top of the stalks, which looked like cranes standing on one leg with their heads slanted in pensive contemplation. There were no vineyards, but orchards aplenty near the farmhouses, and all about there were other trees pollarded to the quick and tufted with mistletoe, not only the stout oaks, but the slim poplars trimmed up into tall plumes like the poplars in southern France. The houses, when they did not stand apart like our own farmhouses, gathered into gray-brown villages around some high-shouldered church with a bell-tower in front or at one corner of the façade. In most of the larger houses an economy of the sun's heat, the only heat recognized in the winter of southern countries, was practised by glassing in the balconies that stretched quite across their fronts and kept the cold from at least one story. It gave them a very cheery look, and must have made them livable at least in the daytime. Now and then the tall chimney of one of those manufactories we had seen on the way from Irun invited belief in the march of industrial prosperity; but whether the Basque who took work in a mill or a foundry forfeited his nobility remained a part of the universal Basque secret. From time to time a mountain stream brawled from under a world-old bridge, and then spread a quiet tide for the women to kneel beside and wash the clothes which they spread to dry on every bush and grassy slope of the banks.

The whole scene changed after we ran out of the Basque country and into the austere landscape of old Castile. The hills retreated and swelled into mountains that were not less than terrible in their savage nakedness. The fields of corn and the orchards ceased, and the green of the pastures changed to the tawny gray of the measureless wheat-lands into which the valleys flattened and widened. There were no longer any factory chimneys; the villages seemed to turn from stone to mud; the human poverty showed itself in the few patched and tattered figures that followed the oxen in the interminable furrows shallowly scraping the surface of the lonely levels. The haggard mountain ranges were of stone that seemed blanched with geologic superannuation, and at one place we ran by a wall of hoary rock that drew its line a mile long against the sky, and then broke and fell, and then staggered up again in a succession of titanic bulks. But stupendous as these mountain masses were, they were not so wonderful as those wheat-lands which in harvest-time must wash their shores like a sea of gold. Where these now rose and sank with the long ground-swell of the plains in our own West, a thin gray stubble covered them from the feeble culture which leaves Spain, for all their extent in both the Castiles, in Estremadura, in Andalusia, still without bread enough to feed herself, and obliges her to import alien wheat. At the lunch which we had so good in the dining-car we kept our talk to the wonder of the scenery, and well away from the interesting Spanish pair at our table. It is never safe in Latin Europe to count upon ignorance of English in educated people, or people who look so; and with these we had the reward of our prudence when the husband asked after dessert if we minded his smoking. His English seemed meant to open the way for talk, and we were willing he should do the talking. He spoke without a trace of accent, and we at once imagined circles in which it was now as *chic* for Spaniards to speak English as it once was to speak French. They are said never to speak French quite well; but nobody could have spoken English better than this gentleman, not even we who were, as he said he supposed, English. Truth and patriotism both obliged us to deny his conjecture; and when He intimated that he would not have known us for Americans because we did not speak with the dreadful American accent, I hazarded my belief that this dreadfulness was personal rather than national. But he would not have it. Boston people, yes; they spoke very well, and he allowed other exceptions to the general rule of our nasal twang, which his wife summoned English enough to say was very ugly. They had suffered from it too universally in the Americans they had met during the summer in Germany to believe it was merely personal; and I suppose one may own to strictly American readers that our speech *is* dreadful, that it is very ugly. These amiable Spaniards had no reason and no wish to wound;

and they could never know what sweet and noble natures had been producing their voices through their noses there in Germany. I for my part could not insist; who, indeed, can defend the American accent, which is not so much an accent as a whiffle, a snuffle, a twang? It was mortifying, all the same, to have it openly abhorred by a foreigner, and I willingly got away from the question to that of the weather. We agreed admirably about the heat in England where this gentleman went every summer, and had never found it so hot before. It was hot even in Denmark; but he warned me not to expect any warmth in Spain now that the autumn rains had begun.

If this couple represented a cosmopolitan and modern Spain, it was interesting to escape to something entirely native in the three young girls who got in at the next station and shared our compartment with us as far as we went. They were tenderly kissed by their father in putting them on board, and held in lingering farewells at the window till the train started. The eldest of the three then helped in arranging their baskets in the rack, but the middle sister took motherly charge of the youngest, whom she at once explained to us as *enferma*. She was the prettiest girl of the conventional Spanish type we had yet seen: dark-eyed and dark-haired, regular, but a little overfull of the chin which she would presently have double. She was very, very pale of face, with a pallor in which she had assisted nature with powder, as all Spanish women, old and young, seem to do. But there was no red underglow in the pallor, such as gives many lovely faces among them the complexion of whitewash over pink on a stucco surface. She wrapped up the youngest sister, who would by and by be beautiful, and now being sick had only the flush of fever in her cheeks, and propped her in the coziest corner of the car, where she tried to make her keep still, but could not make her keep silent. In fact, they all babbled together, over the basket of luncheon which the middle sister opened after springing up the little table-leaf of the window, and spread with a substantial variety including fowl and sausage and fruit, such as might tempt any sick appetite, or a well one, even. As she brought out each of these victuals, together with a bottle of wine and a large bottle of milk, she first offered it to us, and when it was duly refused with thanks, she made the invalid eat and drink, especially the milk which she made a wry face at. When she had finished they all began to question whether her fever was rising for the day; the good sister felt the girl's pulse, and got out a thermometer, which together they arranged under her arm, and then duly inspected. It seemed that the fever *was* rising, as it might very well be, but the middle sister was not moved from her notable calm, and the eldest did not fear.

At a place where a class of young men was to be seen before an ecclesiastical college the girls looked out together, and joyfully decided that the brother (or possibly a cousin) whom they expected to see, was really there among them. When we reached Burgos we felt that we had assisted at a drama of family medicine and affection which was so sweet that if the fever was not very wisely it was very winningly treated. It was not perhaps a very serious case, and it meant a good deal of pleasant excitement for all concerned.

# III. BURGOS AND THE BITTER COLD OF BURGOS

It appears to be the use in most minor cities of Spain for the best hotel to send the worst omnibus to the station, as who should say, "Good wine needs no bush." At Burgos we were almost alarmed by the shabbiness of the omnibus for the hotel we had chosen through a consensus of praise in the guide-books, and thought we must have got the wrong one. It was indeed the wrong one, but because there is no right hotel in Burgos when you arrive there on an afternoon of early October, and feel the prophetic chill of that nine months of winter which is said to contrast there with three months of hell.

I

The air of Burgos when it is not the breath of a furnace is so heavy and clammy through the testimony of all comers that Burgos herself no longer attempts to deny it from her high perch on the uplands of Old Castile. Just when she ceased to deny it, I do not know, but probably when she ceased to be the sole capital and metropolis of Christian Spain and shared her primacy with Toledo sometime in the fourteenth century. Now, in the twentieth, we asked nothing of her but two rooms in which we could have fire, but the best hotel in Burgos openly declared that it had not a fireplace in its whole extent, though there must have been one in the kitchen. The landlord pointed out that it was completely equipped with steam-heating apparatus, but when I made him observe that there was no steam in the shining radiators, he owned with a shrug that there was truth in what I said. He showed us large, pleasant rooms to the south which would have been warm from the sun if the sun which we left playing in San Sebastian had been working that day at Burgos; he showed us his beautiful new dining-room, cold, with the same sunny exposure. I rashly declared that all would not do, and that I would look elsewhere for rooms with fireplaces. I had first to find a cab in order to find the other hotels, but I found instead that in a city of thirty-eight thousand inhabitants there was not one cab standing for hire in the streets. I tried to enlist the sympathies of some private carriages, but they remained indifferent, and I went back foiled, but not crushed, to our hotel. There it seemed that the only vehicle to be had was the omnibus which had brought us from the station. The landlord calmly (I did not then perceive the irony of his calm) had the horses put to and our baggage put on, and we drove away. But first we met our dear Chilians coming to our hotel from the hotel they had chosen, and from a search for hearthstones in others; and we drove to the only hotel they had left unvisited. There at our demand for fires the landlord all but laughed us to scorn; he laid his hand on the cold radiator in the hotel as if to ask what better we could wish than that. We drove back, humbled, to our own hotel, where the landlord met us with the Castilian cairn he had kept at our departure. Then there was nothing for me but to declare myself the Prodigal Son returned to take the rooms he had offered us. We were so perfectly in his power that he could magnanimously afford to offer us other rooms equally cold, but we did not care to move. The Chilians had retired baffled to their own hotel, and there was nothing for us but to accept the long evening of gelid torpor which we foresaw must follow the effort of the soup and wine to warm us at dinner. That night we heard through our closed doors agonized voices which we knew to be the voices of despairing American women wailing through the freezing corridors, "Can't she understand that I want *boiling* water?" and, "Can't' we go down-stairs to a fire somewhere?" We knew the one meant the chambermaid and the other the kitchen, but apparently neither prayer was answered.

II

As soon as we had accepted our fate, while as yet the sun had not set behind the clouds which had kept it out of our rooms all day, we hurried out not only to escape the rigors of our hotel, but to see as soon as we could, as much as we could of the famous city. We had got an excellent cup of tea in the glass-roofed pavilion of our beautiful cold dining-room, and now our spirits rose level with the opportunities of the entrancing walk we took along the course of the Arlanson. I say course, because that is the right word to use of a river, but really there was no course in the Arlanzon. Between the fine, wide Embankments and under the noble bridges there were smooth expanses of water (naturally with women washing at them), which reflected like an afterglow of the evening sky the splendid masses of yarn hung red from the dyer's vats on the bank. The expanses of water were bordered by wider spaces of grass which had grown during the rainless summer, but which were no doubt soon to be submerged under the autumnal torrent the river would become. The street which shaped itself to the stream was a rather modern avenue, leading to a beautiful public garden, with the statues and fountains proper to a public garden, and densely shaded against the three infernal months of the Burgos year. But the houses were glazed all along their fronts with the sun-traps which we had noted in the Basque country, and which do not wait for a certain date in the almanac to do the work of steam-heating. They gave a tempting effect to the house-fronts, but they could not distract our admiration from the successive crowds of small boys playing at bull-fighting in the streets below, and in the walks of the public garden. The population of Burgos is above thirty-seven thousand and of the inhabitants at least thirty-six thousand are small boys, as I was convinced by the computation of the husband and brother of the Chilian ladies which agreed perfectly with my own hasty conjecture; the rest are small girls. In fact large families, and large families chiefly of boys, are the rule in Spain everywhere; and they everywhere know how to play bull-fighting, to flap any-colored old shawl, or breadth of cloth in the face of the bull, to avoid his furious charges, and doubtless to deal him his death-wound, though to this climax I could not bear to follow.

One or two of the bull-fighters offered to leave the national sport and show us the House of Miranda, but it was the cathedral which was dominating our desire, as it everywhere dominates the vision, in Burgos and out of Burgos as far as the city can be seen. The iron-gray bulk, all flattered or fretted by Gothic art, rears itself from the clustering brown walls and roofs of the city, which it seems to gather into its mass below while it towers so far above them. We needed no pointing of the way to it; rather we should have needed instruction for shunning it; but we chose the way which led through the gate of Santa Maria where in an arch once part of the city wall, the great Cid, hero above every other hero of Burgos, sits with half a dozen more or less fabled or storied worthies of the renowned city. Then with a minute's walk up a stony sloping little street we were in the beautiful and reverend presence of one of the most august temples of the Christian faith. The avenue where the old Castilian nobles once dwelt in their now empty palaces climbs along the hillside above the cathedral, which on its lower side seems to elbow off the homes of meaner men, and in front to push them away beyond a plaza not large enough for it. Even this the cathedral had not cleared of the horde of small boys who followed us unbidden to its doors and almost expropriated those authorized blind beggars who own the church doors in Spain. When we declined the further company of these boys they left us with expressions which I am afraid accused our judgment and our personal appearance; but in another moment we were safe from their censure, and hidden as it were in the thick smell of immemorial incense.

It was not the moment for doing the cathedral in the wonted tiresome and vulgar way; that was reserved for the next day; now we simply wandered in the vast twilight spaces; and craned our necks to breaking in trying to pierce the gathered gloom in the vaulting overhead. It was a precious moment, but perhaps too weird, and we were glad to find a sacristan with businesslike activity setting red candlesticks about a bier in the area before the choir, which here, as in the other Spanish cathedrals, is planted frankly in the middle of the edifice, a church by itself, as if to emphasize the incomparable grandeur of the cathedral. The sacristan willingly paused in his task and explained that he was preparing the bier for the funeral of a church dignitary (as we learned later, the dean) which was to take place the next day at noon; and if we would come at that hour we should hear some beautiful music. We knew that he was establishing a claim on our future custom, but we thanked him and provisionally feed him, and left him at his work, at which we might have all but fancied him whistling, so cheerfully and briskly he went about it.

Outside we lingered a moment to give ourselves the solemn joy of the Chapel of the Constable which forms the apse of the cathedral and is its chief glory. It mounted to the hard, gray sky, from which a keen wind was sweeping the narrow street leading to it, and blustering round the corner of the cathedral, so that the marble men holding up the Constable's coat-of-arms in the rear of his chapel might well have ached from the cold which searched the marrow of flesh-and-blood men below. These hurried by in flat caps and corduroy coats and trousers, with sashes at their waists and comforters round their necks; and they were picturesque quite in the measure of their misery. Some whose tatters were the most conspicuous feature of their costume, I am sure would have charmed me if I had been a painter; as a mere word-painter I find myself wishing I could give the color of their wretchedness to my page.

III

In the absence of any specific record in my notebook I do not know just how it was between this first glimpse of the cathedral and dinner, but it must have been on our return to our hotel, that the little interpreter who had met us at the station, and had been intermittently constituting himself our protector ever since, convinced us that we ought to visit the City Hall, and see the outside of the marble tomb containing the bones of the Cid and his wife. Such as the bones were we found they were not to be seen themselves, and I do not know that I should have been the happier for their inspection. In fact, I have no great opinion of the Cid as an historical character or a poetic fiction. His epic, or his long ballad, formed no part of my young study in Spanish, and when four or five years ago a friend gave me a copy of it, beautifully printed in black letter, with the prayer that I should read it sometime within the twelvemonth, I found the time far too short. As a matter of fact I have never read the poem to this day, though. I have often tried, and I doubt if its author ever intended it to be read. He intended it rather to be recited in stirring episodes, with spaces for refreshing slumber in the connecting narrative. As for the Cid in real life under his proper name of Rodrigo de Vivas, though he made his king publicly swear that he had had no part in the murder of his royal brother, and though he was the stoutest and bravest knight in Castile, I cannot find it altogether admirable in him that when his king banished him he should resolve to fight thereafter for any master who paid him best. That appears to me the part of a road-agent rather than a reformer, and it seems to me no amend for his service under Moorish princes that he should make war against them on his personal behalf or afterward under his own ungrateful king. He is friends now with the Arabian King of Saragossa, and now he defeats the Aragonese under the Castilian sovereign, and again he sends an insulting message by the Moslems to the Christian Count of Barcelona, whom he takes prisoner with his followers, but releases without ransom after a contemptuous audience. Is it well, I ask, that he helps one Moor against another, always for what there is in it, and when he takes Valencia from the infidels, keeps none of his promises to them, but having tortured the governor to make him give up his treasure, buries him to his waist and then burns him alive? After that, to be sure, he enjoys his declining years by making forays in the neighboring country, and dies "satisfied with having done his duty toward his God."

Our interpreter, who would not let us rest till he had shown us the box holding the Cid's bones, had himself had a varied career. If you believed him he was born in Madrid and had passed, when three years old, to New York, where he grew up to become a citizen and be the driver of a delivery wagon for a large department-store. He duly married an American woman who could speak not only French, German, and Italian, but also Chinese, and was now living with him in Burgos. His own English had somewhat fallen by the way, but what was left he used with great courage; and he was one of those government interpreters whom you find at every large station throughout Spain in the number of the principal hotels of the place. They pay the government a certain tax for their license, though it was our friend's expressed belief that the government, on the contrary, paid him a salary of two dollars a day; but perhaps this was no better founded than his belief in a German princess who, when he went as her courier, paid him ten dollars a day and all his expenses. She wished him to come and live near her in Germany, so as to be ready to go with her to South America, but he had not yet made up his mind to leave Burgos, though his poor eyes watered with such a cold as only Burgos can give a man in the early autumn; when I urged him to look to the bad cough he had, he pleaded that it was a very old cough. He had a fascination of his own, which probably came from his imaginative habit of mind, so that I could have wished more adoptive fellow-citizens were like him. He sympathized strongly with us in our grief with the cold of the hotel, and when we said that a small oil-heater would take the chill off a large room, he said that he had advised that very thing, but that our host had replied, with proud finality, "I am the landlord." Whether this really happened or not, I cannot say, but I have no doubt that our little guide had some faith in it as a real incident. He apparently had faith in the landlord's boast that he was going to have a stately marble staircase to the public entrance to his hotel, which was presently of common stone, rather tipsy in its treads, and much in need of scrubbing.

There is as little question in my mind that he believed the carriage we had engaged to take us next morning to the Cartuja de Miraflores would be ready at a quarter before nine, and that he may have been disappointed when it was not ready until a quarter after. But it was worth waiting for if to have a team composed of a brown mule on the right hand and a gray horse on the left was to be desired. These animals which nature had so differenced were equalized by art through the lavish provision of sleigh-bells, without some strands of which no team in Spain is properly equipped. Besides, as to his size the mule was quite as large as the horse, and as to his tail he was much more decorative. About two inches after this member left his body it was closely shaved for some six inches or more, and for that space it presented the effect of a rather large size of garden-hose; below, it swept his thighs in a lordly switch. If anything could have added distinction to our turnout it would have been the stiff side-whiskers of our driver: the only pair I saw in real life after seeing them so long in pictures on boxes of raisins and cigars. There they were associated with the look and dress of a *torrero*, and our coachman, though an old Castilian of the austerest and most taciturn pattern, may have been in his gay youth an Andalusian bull-fighter.

IV

Our pride in our equipage soon gave way to our interest in the market for sheep, cattle, horses, and donkeys which we passed through just outside the city. The market folk were feeling the morning's cold; shepherds folded in their heavy shawls leaned motionless on their long staves, as if hating to stir; one ingenious boy wore a live lamb round his neck which he held close by the legs for the greater comfort of it; under the trees by the roadside some of the peasants were cooking their breakfasts and warming themselves at the fires. The sun was on duty in a cloudless sky; but all along the road to the Cartuja we drove between rows of trees so thickly planted against his summer rage that no ray of his friendly heat could now reach us. At times it seemed as if from this remorselessly shaded avenue we should escape into the open; the trees gave way and we caught glimpses of wide plains and distant hills; then they closed upon us again, and in their chill shadow it was no comfort to know that in summer, when the townspeople got through their work, they came out to these groves, men, women, and children, and had supper under their hospitable boughs.

One comes to almost any Cartuja at last, and we found ours on a sunny top just when the cold had pinched us almost beyond endurance, and joined a sparse group before the closed gate of the convent. The group was composed of poor people who had come for the dole of food daily distributed from the convent, and better-to-do country-folk who had brought things to sell to the monks, or were there on affairs not openly declared. But it seemed that it was a saint's day; the monks were having service in the church solely for their own edification, and they had shut us sinners out not only by locking the gate, but by taking away the wire for ringing the bell, and leaving nothing but a knocker of feeble note with which different members of our indignation meeting vainly hammered. Our guide assumed the virtue of the greatest indignation, though he ought to have known that we could not get in on that saint's day; but it did not avail, and the little group dispersed, led off by the brown peasant who was willing to share my pleasure in our excursion as a good joke on us, and smiled with a show of teeth as white as the eggs in his basket. After all, it was not wholly a hardship; we could walk about in the sunny if somewhat muddy open, and warm ourselves against the icily shaded drive back to town; besides, there was a little girl crouching at the foot of a tree, and playing at a phase of the housekeeping which is the game of little girls the world over. Her sad, still-faced mother standing near, with an interest in her apparently renewed by my own, said that she was four years old, and joined me in watching her as she built a pile of little sticks and boiled an imaginary little kettle over them. I was so glad even of a make-believe fire that I dropped a copper coin beside it, and the mother smiled pensively as if grateful but not very hopeful from this beneficence, though after reflection I had made my gift a "big dog" instead of a "small dog," as the Spanish call a ten and a five centimo piece. The child bent her pretty head shyly on one side, and went on putting more sticks under her supposititious pot.

I found the little spectacle reward enough in itself and in a sort compensation for our failure to see the exquisite alabaster tomb of Juan II. and his wife Isabel which makes the Cartuja Church so famous. There are a great many beautiful tombs in Burgos, but none so beautiful there (or in the whole world if the books say true) as this; though we made what we could of some in the museum, where we saw for the first time in the recumbent effigies of a husband and wife, with features worn away by time and incapable of expressing the disappointment, the surprise they may have felt in the vain effort to warm their feet on the backs of the little marble angels put there to support them. We made what we could, too, of the noted Casa de Miranda, the most famous of the palaces in which the Castilian nobles have long ceased to live at Burgos. There we satisfied our longing to see a *patio*, that roofless colonnaded court which is the most distinctive feature of Spanish domestic architecture, and more and more distinctively so the farther south you go, till at Seville you see it in constant prevalence. At Burgos it could never have been a great comfort, but in this House of Miranda it must have been a great glory. The spaces between many of the columns have long been bricked in, but there is fine carving on the front and the vaulting of the staircase that climbs up from it in neglected grandeur. So many feet have trodden its steps that they are worn hollow in the middle, and to keep from falling you must go up next the wall. The object in going up at all is to join in the gallery an old melancholy custodian in looking down into the *patio*, with his cat making her toilet beside him, and to give them a fee which they receive with equal calm. Then, when you have come down the age-worn steps without breaking your neck, you have done the House of Miranda, and may lend yourself with what emotion you choose to the fact that this ancient seat of hidalgos has now fallen to the low industry of preparing pigskins to be wine-skins.

I do not think that a company of hidalgos in complete medieval armor could have moved me more strongly than that first sight of these wine-skins, distended with wine, which we had caught in approaching the House of Miranda. We had to stop in the narrow street, and let them pass piled high on a vintner's wagon, and looking like a load of pork: they are trimmed and left to keep the shape of the living pig, which they emulate at its bulkiest, less the head and feet, and seem to roll in fatness. It was joy to realize what they were, to feel how Spanish, how literary, how picturesque, how romantic. There they were such as the wine-skins are that hang from the trees of pleasant groves in many a merry tale, and invite all swains and shepherds and wandering cavaliers to tap their bulk and drain its rich plethora. There they were such as Don Quixote, waking from his dream at the inn, saw them malignant giants and fell enchanters, and slashed them with his sword till he had spilled the room half full of their blood. For me this first sight of them was magic. It brought back my boyhood as nothing else had yet, and I never afterward saw them without a return to those days of my delight in all Spanish things.

Literature and its associations, no matter from how lowly suggestion, must always be first for me, and I still thought of those wine-skins in yielding to the claims of the cathedral on my wonder and reverence when now for the second time we came to it. The funeral ceremony of the dean was still in course, and after listening for a moment to the mighty orchestral music of it—the deep bass of the priests swelling up with the organ notes, and suddenly shot with the shrill, sharp trebles of the choir-boys and pierced with the keen strains of the violins—we left the cathedral to the solemn old ecclesiastics who sat confronting the bier, and once more deferred our more detailed and intimate wonder. We went, in this suspense of emotion, to the famous Convent of Las Huelgas, which invites noble ladies to its cloistered repose a little beyond the town. We entered to the convent church through a sort of slovenly court where a little girl begged severely, almost censoriously, of us, and presently a cold-faced young priest came and opened the church door. Then we found the interior of that rank Spanish baroque which escapes somehow the effeminate effusiveness of the Italian; it does not affect you as decadent, but as something vigorously perfect in its sort, somberly authentic, and ripe from a root and not a graft. In its sort, the high altar, a gigantic triune, with massive twisted columns and swagger statues of saints and heroes in painted wood, is a prodigy of inventive piety, and compositely has a noble exaltation in its powerful lift to the roof.

The nuns came beautifully dressed to hear mass at the grilles giving into the chapel adjoining the church; the tourist may have his glimpse of them there on Sundays, and on week-days he may have his guess of their cloistered life and his wonder how much it continues the tradition of repose which the name of the old garden grounds implies. These lady nuns must be of patrician lineage and of fortune enough to defray their expense in the convent, which is of the courtliest origin, for it was founded eight hundred years ago by Alfonso VIII. "to expiate his sins and to gratify his queen," who probably knew of them. I wish now I had known, while I was there, that the abbess of Las Huelgas had once had the power of life and death in the neighborhood, and could hang people if she liked; I cannot think just what good it would have done me, but one likes to realize such things on the spot. She is still one of the greatest ladies of Spain, though perhaps not still "lady of ax and gibbet," and her nuns are of like dignity. In their chapel are the tombs of Alfonso and his queen, whose figures are among those on the high altar of the church. She was Eleanor Plantagenet, the daughter of our Henry II., and was very fond of Las Huelgas, as if it were truly a rest for her in the far-off land of Spain; I say our Henry II., for in the eleventh century we Americans were still English, under the heel of the Normans, as not the fiercest republican of us now need shame to own.

In a sense of this historical unity, at Las Huelgas we felt as much at home as if we had been English tourists, and we had our feudal pride in the palaces where the Gastilian nobles used to live in Burgos as we returned to the town. Their deserted seats are mostly to be seen after you pass through the Moorish gate overarching the stony, dusty, weedy road hard by the place where the house of the Cid is said to have stood. The arch, so gracefully Saracenic, was the first monument of the Moslem obsession of the country which has left its signs so abundantly in the south; here in the far north the thing seemed almost prehistoric, almost preglacially old, the witness of a world utterly outdated. But perhaps it was not more utterly outdated than the residences of the nobles who had once made the ancient

Castilian capital splendid, but were now as irrevocably merged in Madrid as the Arabs in Africa.

VI

Some of the palaces looked down from the narrow street along the hillside above the cathedral, but only one of them was kept up in the state of other days; and I could not be sure at what point this street had ceased to be the street where our guide said every one kept cows, and the ladies took big pitchers of milk away to sell every morning. But I am sure those ladies could have been of noble descent only in the farthest possible remove, and I do not suppose their cows were even remotely related to the haughty ox-team which blocked the way in front of the palaces and obliged xis to dismount while our carriage was lifted round the cart. Our driver was coldly disgusted, but the driver of the ox-team preserved a calm as perfect as if he had been an hidalgo interested by the incident before his gate. It delayed us till the psychological moment when the funeral of the dean was over, and we could join the formidable party following the sacristan from chapel to chapel in the cathedral.

We came to an agonized consciousness of the misery of this progress in the Chapel of the Constable, where it threatened to be finally stayed by the indecision of certain ladies of our nation in choosing among the postal cards for sale there. By this time we had suffered much from the wonders of the cathedral. The sacristan had not spared us a jewel or a silvered or gilded sacerdotal garment or any precious vessel of ceremonial, so that our jaded wonder was inadequate to the demand of the beautiful tombs of the Constable and his lady upon it. The coffer of the Cid, fastened against the cathedral wall for a monument of his shrewdness in doing the Jews of Burgos, who, with the characteristic simplicity of their race, received it back full of sand and gravel in payment of the gold they had lent him in it, could as little move us. Perhaps if we could have believed that he finally did return the value received, we might have marveled a little at it, but from what we knew of the Cid this was not credible. We did what we could with the painted wood carving of the cloister doors; the life-size head of a man with its open mouth for a key-hole in another portal; a fearful silver-plated chariot given by a rich blind woman for bearing the Host in the procession of Corpus Christi; but it was very little, and I am not going to share my failure with the reader by the vain rehearsal of its details. No literary art has ever reported a sense of picture or architecture or sculpture to me: the despised postal card is better for that; and probably throughout these "trivial fond records" I shall be found shirking as much as I may the details of such sights, seen or unseen, as embitter the heart of travel with unavailing regret for the impossibility of remembering them. I must leave for some visit of the reader's own the large and little facts of the many chapels in the cathedral at Burgos, and I will try to overwhelm him with my sense of the whole mighty interior, the rich gloom, the Gothic exaltation, which I made such shift as I could to feel in the company of those picture-postal amateurs. It was like, say, a somber afternoon, verging to the twilight of a cloudy sunset, so that when I came out of it into the open noon it was like emerging into a clear morrow. Perhaps because I could there shed the harassing human environment the outside of the cathedral seemed to me the best of it, and we lingered there for a moment in glad relief.

## VII

One house in some forgotten square commemorates the state in which the Castilian nobles used to live in Burgos before Toledo, and then Valladolid, contested the primacy of the grim old capital of the northern uplands. We stayed for a moment to glance from our carriage through the open portal into its leafy *patio* shivering in the cold, and then we bade our guide hurry back with us to the hot luncheon which would be the only heat in our hotel. But to reach this we had to pass through another square, which we found full of peasants' ox-carts and mule-teams; and there our guide instantly jumped down and entered into a livelier quarrel with those peaceable men and women than I could afterward have believed possible in Spain. I bade him get back to his seat beside the driver, who was abetting him with an occasional guttural and whom I bade turn round and go another way. I said that I had hired this turnout, and I was master, and I would be obeyed; but it seemed that I was wrong. My proud hirelings never left off their dispute till somehow the ox-carts and mule-teams were jammed together, and a thoroughfare found for us. Then it was explained that those peasants were always blocking that square in that way and that I had, however unwillingly, been discharging the duty of a public-spirited citizen in compelling them to give way. I did not care for that; I prized far more the quiet with which they had taken the whole affair. It was the first exhibition of the national repose of manner which we were to see so often again, south as well as north, and which I find it so beautiful to have seen. In a Europe abounding in volcanic Italians, nervous Germans, and exasperated Frenchmen, it was comforting, it was edifying to see those Castilian peasants so self-respectfully self-possessed in the wrong.

From time to time in the opener spaces we had got into the sun from the chill shadow of the narrow streets, but now it began to be cloudy, and when we re-entered our hotel it was almost as warm indoors as out. We thought our landlord might have so far repented as to put on the steam; but he had sternly adhered to his principle that the radiators were enough of themselves; and after luncheon we had nothing for it but to go away from Burgos, and take with us such scraps of impression as we could. We decided that there was no street of gayer shops than those gloomy ones we had chanced into here and there; I do not remember now anything like a bookseller's or a milliner's or a draper's window. There was no sign of fashion among the ladies of Burgos, so far as we could distinguish them; there was not a glowering or perking hat, and I do not believe there was a hobble-skirt in all the austere old capital except such as some tourist wore; the black lace mantillas and the flowing garments of other periods flitted by through the chill alleys and into the dim doorways. The only cheerfulness in the local color was to be noted in the caparison of the donkeys, which we were to find more and more brilliant southward. Do I say the only cheerfulness? I ought to except also the involuntary hilarity of a certain poor man's suit which was so patched together of myriad scraps that it looked as if cut from the fabric of a crazy-quilt. I owe him this notice the rather because he almost alone did not beg of us in a city which swarmed with beggars in a forecast of that pest of beggary which infests Spain everywhere. I do not say that the thing is without picturesqueness, without real pathos; the little girl who kissed the copper I gave her in the cathedral remains endeared to me by that perhaps conventional touch of poetry.

There was compensation for the want of presence among the ladies of Burgos, in the leading lady of the theatrical company who dined, the night before, at our hotel with the chief actors of her support, before giving a last performance in our ancient city. It happened another time in our Spanish progress that we had the society of strolling players at our hotel, and it was both times told us that the given company was the best dramatic company in Spain; but at Burgos we did not yet know that we were so singularly honored. The leading lady there had luminous black eyes, large like the head-lamps of a motor-car, and a wide crimson mouth which she employed as at a stage banquet throughout the dinner, while she talked and laughed with her fellow-actors, beautiful as bull-fighters, cleanshaven, serious of face and shapely of limb. They were unaffectedly professional, and the lady made no pretense of not being a leading lady. One could see that she was the kindest creature in the world, and that she took a genuine pleasure in her huge, practicable eyes. At the other end of the room a Spanish family— father, mother, and small children, down to some in arms—were dining and the children wailing as Spanish children will, regardless of time and place; and when the nurse brought one of the disconsolate infants to be kissed by the leading lady one's heart went out to her for the amiability and abundance of her caresses. The mere sight of their warmth did something to supply the defect of steam in the steam-heating apparatus, but when one got beyond their radius there was nothing for the shivering traveler except to wrap himself in the down quilt of his bed and spread his steamer-rug over his knees till it was time to creep under both of them between the glacial sheets.

We were sorry we had not got tickets for the leading lady's public performance; it could have been so little more public; but we had not, and there was nothing else in Burgos to invite the foot outdoors after dinner. From my own knowledge I cannot yet say the place was not lighted; but my sense of the tangle of streets lying night long in a rich Gothic gloom shall remain unimpaired by statistics. Very possibly Burgos is brilliantly lighted with electricity; only they have not got the electricity on, as in our steam-heated hotel they had not got the steam on.

## VIII

We had authorized our little interpreter to engage tickets for us by the mail-train the next afternoon for Valladolid; he pretended, of course, that the places could be had only by his special intervention, and by telegraphing for them to the arriving train. We accepted his romantic theory of the case, and paid the bonus due the railroad agent in the hotel for his offices in the matter; we would have given anything, we were so eager to get out of Burgos before we were frozen up there. I do not know that we were either surprised or pained to find that our Chilian friends should have got seats in the same car without anything of our diplomacy, by the simple process of showing their tickets. I think our little interpreter was worth everything he cost, and more. I would not have lost a moment of his company as he stood on the platform with me, adding one artless invention to another for my pleasure, and successively extracting peseta after peseta from me till he had made up the sum which he had doubtless idealized as a just reward for his half-day's service when he first told me that it should be what I pleased. We parted with the affection of fellow-citizens in a strange monarchical country, his English growing less and less as the train delayed, and his eyes watering more and more as with tears of com-patriotic affection. At the moment I could have envied that German princess her ability to make sure of his future companionship at the low cost of fifty pesetas a day; and even now, when my affection has had time to wane, I cannot do less than commend him to any future visitor at Burgos, as in the last degree amiable, and abounding in surprises of intelligence and unexpected feats of reliability.

# IV. THE VARIETY OF VALLADOLID

When you leave Burgos at 3.29 of a passably sunny afternoon you are not at once aware of the moral difference between the terms of your approach and those of your departure. You are not changing your earth or your sky very much, but it is not long before you are sensible of a change of mind which insists more and more. There is the same long ground-swell of wheat-fields, but yesterday you were followed in vision by the loveliness of the frugal and fertile Biscayan farms, and to-day this vision has left you, and you are running farther and farther into the economic and topographic waste of Castile. Yesterday there were more or less agreeable shepherdesses in pleasant plaids scattered over the landscape; to-day there are only shepherds of three days' unshornness; the plaids are ragged, and there is not sufficient compensation in the cavalcades of both men and women riding donkeys in and out of the horizons on the long roads that lose and find themselves there. Flocks of brown and black goats, looking large as cows among the sparse stubble, do little to relieve the scene from desolation; I am not sure but goats, when brown and black, add to the horror of a desolate scene. There are no longer any white farmsteads, or friendly villages gathering about high-shouldered churches, but very far away to the eastward or westward the dun expanse of the wheat-lands is roughed with something which seems a cluster of muddy protuberances, so like the soil at first it is not distinguishable from it, but which as your train passes nearer proves to be a town at the base of tablelands, without a tree or a leaf or any spear of green to endear it to the eye as the abode of living men. You pull yourself together in the effort to visualize the immeasurable fields washing those dreary towns with golden tides of harvest; but it is difficult. What you cannot help seeing is the actual nakedness of the land which with its spindling stubble makes you think of that awful moment of the human head, when utter baldness will be a relief to the spectator.

I

At times and in places, peasants were scratching the dismal surfaces with the sort of plows which Abel must have used, when subsoiling was not yet even a dream; and between the plowmen and their ox-teams it seemed a question as to which should loiter longest in the unfinished furrow. Now and then, the rush of the train gave a motionless goatherd, with his gaunt flock, an effect of comparative celerity to the rearward. The women riding their donkeys over

> *The level waste, the rounding gray*

in the distance were the only women we saw except those who seemed to be keeping the stations, and one very fat one who came to the train at a small town and gabbled volubly to some passenger who made no audible response. She excited herself, but failed to rouse the interest of the other party to the interview, who remained unseen as well as unheard. I could the more have wished to know what it was all about because nothing happened on board the train to distract the mind from the joyless landscape until we drew near Valladolid. It is true that for a while we shared our compartment with a father and his two sons who lunched on slices of the sausage which seems the favorite refection of the Latin as well as the Germanic races in their travels. But this drama was not of intense interest, and we grappled in vain with the question of our companions' social standard. The father, while he munched his bread and sausage, read a newspaper which did not rank him or even define his politics; there was a want of fashion in the cut of the young men's clothes and of freshness in the polish of their tan shoes which defied conjecture. When they left the train without the formalities of leave-taking which had hitherto distinguished our Spanish fellow-travelers, we willingly abandoned them to a sort of middling obscurity; but this may not really have been their origin or their destiny.

That spindling sparseness, worse than utter baldness, of the wheat stubble now disappeared with cinematic suddenness, and our train was running past stretches of vineyard, where, among the green and purple and yellow ranks, the vintagers, with their donkeys and carts, were gathering the grapes in the paling light of the afternoon. Again the scene lacked the charm of woman's presence which the vintage had in southern France. In Spain we nowhere saw the women sharing the outdoor work of the men; and we fancied their absence the effect of the Oriental jealousy lingering from centuries of Moorish domination; though we could not entirely reconcile our theory with the publicity of their washing clothes at every stream. To be sure, that was work which they did not share with men any more than the men shared the labor of the fields with them.

It was still afternoon, well before sunset, when we arrived at Valladolid, where one of the quaintest of our Spanish surprises awaited us. We knew that the omnibus of the hotel we had chosen would be the shabbiest omnibus at the station, and we saw without great alarm our Chilian friends drive off in an indefinitely finer vehicle. But what we were not prepared for was the fact of *octroi* at Valladolid, and for the strange behavior of the local customs officer who stopped us on our way into the town. He looked a very amiable young man as he put his face in at the omnibus door, and he received without explicit question our declaration that we had nothing taxable in our trunks. Then, however, he mounted to the top of the omnibus and thumped our trunks about as if to test them for contraband by the sound. The investigation continued on these strange terms until the officer had satisfied himself of our good faith, when he got down and with a friendly smile at the window bowed us into Valladolid.

In its way nothing could have been more charming; and we rather liked being left by the omnibus about a block from our hotel, on the border of a sort of promenade where no vehicles were allowed. We had been halted near a public fountain, where already the mothers and daughters of the neighborhood were gathered with earthen jars for the night's supply of water. The jars were not so large as to overburden any of them when, after just delay for exchange of gossip, the girls and goodwives put them on their heads and marched erectly away with them, each beautifully picturesque irrespective of her age or looks.

The air was soft, and after Burgos, warm; something southern, unfelt before, began to qualify the whole scene, which as the evening fell grew more dramatic, and made the promenade the theater of emotions permitted such unrestricted play nowhere else in Spain, so far as we were witness. On one side the place was arcaded, and bordered with little shops, not so obtrusively brilliant that the young people who walked up and down before them were in a glare of publicity. A little way off the avenue expanded into a fine oblong place, where some first martyrs of the Inquisition were burned. But the promenades kept well short of this, as they walked up and down, and talked, talked, talked in that inexhaustible interest which youth takes in itself the world over. They were in the standard proportion of two girls to one young man, or, if here and there a girl had an undivided young man to herself, she went before some older maiden or matron whom she left altogether out of the conversation. They mostly wore the skirts and hats of Paris, and if the scene of the fountain was Arabically oriental the promenade was almost Americanly occidental. The promenaders were there by hundreds; they filled the avenue from side to side, and

*The delight of happy laughter*

*The delight of low replies*

that rose from their progress, with the chirp and whisper of their feet cheered the night as long as we watched and listened from the sun balcony of our hotel.

II

There was no more heat in the radiators of the hotel there than at Burgos, but for that evening at least there was none needed. It was the principal hotel of Valladolid, and the unscrubbed and unswept staircase by which we mounted into it was merely a phase of that genial pause, as for second thought, in the march of progress which marks so much of the modern advance in Spain, and was by no means an evidence of arrested development. We had the choice of reaching our rooms either through the dining-room or by a circuitous detour past the pantries; but our rooms had a proud little vestibule of their own, with a balcony over the great square, and if one of them had a belated feather-bed the other had a new hair mattress, and the whole house was brilliantly lighted with electricity. As for the cooking, it was delicious, and the table was of an abundance and variety which might well have made one ashamed of paying so small a rate as two dollars a day for bed and board, wine included, and very fair wine at that.

In Spain you must take the bad with the good, for whether you get the good or not you are sure of the bad, but only very exceptionally are you sure of the bad only. It was a pleasure not easily definable to find our hotel managed by a mother and two daughters, who gave the orders obeyed by the men-servants, and did not rebuke them for joining in the assurance that when we got used to going so abruptly from the dining-room into our bedrooms we would like it. The elder of the daughters had some useful French, and neither of the younger ladies ever stayed for some ultimate details of dishabille in coming to interpret the mother and ourselves to one another when we encountered her alone in the office. They were all thoroughly kind and nice, and they were supported with surpassing intelligence and ability by the *chico*, a radiant boy of ten, who united in himself the functions which the amiable inefficiency of the porters and waiters abandoned to him.

When we came out to dinner after settling ourselves in our almost obtrusively accessible rooms, we were convinced of the wisdom of our choice of a hotel by finding our dear Chilians at one of the tables. We rushed together like two kindred streams of transatlantic gaiety, and in our mingled French, Spanish, and English possessed one another of our doubts and fears in coming to our common conclusion. We had already seen a Spanish gentleman whom we knew as a fellow-sufferer at Burgos, roaming the streets of Valladolid, and in what seemed a disconsolate doubt, interrogating the windows of our hotel; and now we learned from the Chilians that he had been bitterly disappointed in the inn which a patrician omnibus had borne him away to from our envious eyes at the station. We learned that our South American compatriots had found their own chosen hotel impossible, and were now lodged in rapturous satisfaction under our roof. Their happiness penetrated us with a glow of equal content, and confirmed us in the resolution always to take the worst omnibus at a Spanish station as the sure index of the best hotel.

The street-cars, which in Valladolid are poetically propelled through lyre-shaped trolleys instead of our prosaic broomstick appliances, groaned unheeded if not unheard under our windows through the night, and we woke to find the sun on duty in our glazed balcony and the promenade below already astir with life: not the exuberant young life of the night before, but still sufficiently awake to be recognizable as life. A crippled newsboy seated under one of the arcades was crying his papers; an Englishman was looking at a plan of Valladolid in a shop window; a splendid cavalry officer went by in braided uniform, and did not stare so hard as they might have expected at some ladies passing in mantillas to mass or market. In the late afternoon as well as the early morning we saw a good deal of the military in Valladolid, where an army corps is stationed. From time to time a company of infantry marched through the streets to gay music, and toward evening slim young officers began to frequent the arcades and glass themselves in the windows of the shops, their spurs clinking on the pavement as they lounged by or stopped and took distinguished attitudes. We speculated in vain as to their social quality, and to this day I do not know whether "the career is open to the talents" in the Spanish army, or whether military rank is merely the just reward of civil rank. Those beautiful young swells in riding-breeches and tight gray jackets approached an Italian type of cavalry officer; they did not look very vigorous, and the common soldiers we saw marching through the streets, largely followed by the populace, were not of formidable stature or figure, though neat and agreeable enough to the eye.

While I indulge the record of these trivialities, which I am by no means sure the reader will care for so much, I feel that it would be wrong to let him remain as ignorant of the history of Valladolid as I was while there. My ignorance was not altogether my fault; I had fancied easily finding at some bookseller's under the arcade a little sketch of the local history such as you are sure of finding in any Italian town, done by a local antiquary of those always mousing in the city's archives. But the bookseller's boy and then the boy's mother could not at first imagine my wish, and when they did they could only supply me with a sort of business directory, full of addresses and advertisements. So instead of overflowing with information when we set out on our morning ramble, we meagerly knew from the guide-books that Valladolid had once been the capital of Castile, arid after many generations of depression following the removal of the court, had in these latest days renewed its strength in mercantile and industrial prosperity. There are ugly evidences of the prosperity in the windy, dusty avenues and streets of the more modern town; but there are lanes and alleys enough, groping for the churches and monuments in suddenly opening squares, to console the sentimental tourist for the havoc which enterprise has made. The mind readily goes back through these to the palmy prehistoric times from which the town emerged to mention in Ptolemy, and then begins to work forward past Iberian and Roman and Goth and Moor to the Castilian kings who made it their residence in the eleventh century. The capital won its first great distinction when Ferdinand of Aragon and Isabella of Castile were married there in 1469. Thirty-five years later these Catholic Kings, as one had better learn at once to call them in Spain, let Columbus die neglected if not forgotten in the house recently pulled down, where he had come to dwell in their cold shadow; they were much occupied with other things and they could not realize that his discovery of America was the great glory of their reign; probably they thought the conquest of Granada was. Later yet, by twenty years, the dreadful Philip II. was born in Valladolid, and in 1559 a very famous *auto da fe* wag celebrated in the Plaza Mayor. Fourteen Lutherans were burned alive for their heresy, and the body of a woman suspected of imperfect orthodoxy after her death was exhumed and burned with them. In spite of such precautions as these, and of all the pious diligence of the Holy Office, the reader will hardly believe that there is now a Spanish Protestant church in Valladolid; but such is the fact, though whether it derives from the times of the Inquisition, or is a modern missionary church I do not know. That *auto da fe* was of the greatest possible distinction; the Infanta Juana presided, and the universal interest was so great that people paid a dollar and twenty-five cents a seat; money then worth five or six times as much as now. Philip himself came to another *auto* when thirteen persons were burned in the same place, and he always liked Valladolid; it must have pleased him in a different way from Escorial, lying flat as it does on a bare plain swept, but never thoroughly dusted, by winds that blow pretty constantly over it.

While the Inquisition was purging the city of error its great university was renowning it not only throughout Spain, but in France and Italy; students frequented it from those countries, and artists came from many parts of Europe. Literature also came in the person of Cervantes, who seems to have followed the Spanish court in its migrations from Valladolid to Toledo and then to Madrid. Here also came one of the greatest characters in fiction, for it was in Valladolid that Gil Blas learned to practise the art of medicine tinder the instruction of the famous Dr. Sangrado.

# IV

I put these facts at the service of the reader for what use he will while he goes with us to visit the cathedral in Valladolid, a cathedral as unlike that of Burgos as the severest mood of Spanish renaissance can render it. In fact, it is the work of Herrera, the architect who made the Escorial so grim, and is the expression in large measure of his austere mastery. If it had ever been finished it might have been quite as dispiriting as the Escorial, but as it has only one of the four ponderous towers it was meant to have, it is not without its alleviations, especially as the actual tower was rebuilt after the fall of the original seventy years ago. The grass springs cheerfully up in the crevices of the flagging from which the broken steps falter to the portal, but within all is firm and solid. The interior is vast, and nowhere softened by decoration, but the space is reduced by the huge bulk of the choir in the center of it; as we entered a fine echo mounted to the cathedral roof from the chanting and intoning within. When the service ended a tall figure in scarlet crossed rapidly toward the sacristy. It was of such imposing presence that we resolved at once it must be the figure of a cardinal, or of an archbishop at the least. But it proved to be one of the sacristans, and when we followed him to the sacristy with half a dozen other sightseers, he showed us a silver monstrance weighing a hundred and fifty pounds and decked with statites of our first parents as they appeared before the Fall. Besides this we saw, much against our will, a great many ecclesiastical vestments of silk and damask richly wrought in gold and silver. But if we were reluctant there was a little fat priest there who must have seen them hundreds of times and had still a childish delight in seeing them again because he had seen them so often; he dimpled and smiled, and for his sake we pretended a joy in them which it would have been cruel to deny him. I suppose we were then led to the sacrifice at the several side altars, but I have no specific recollection of them; I know there was a pale, sick-looking young girl in white who went about with her father, and moved compassion by her gentle sorrowfulness.

Of the University, which we visited next, I recall only the baroque facade; the interior was in reparation and I do not know whether it would have indemnified us for not visiting the University of Salamanca. That was in our list, but the perversity of the time-table forbade. You could go to Salamanca, yes, but you could not come back except at two o'clock in the morning; you could indeed continue on to Lisbon, but perhaps you did not wish to see Lisbon. A like perversity of the time-table, once universal in Spain, but now much reformed, also kept us away from Segovia, which was on our list. But our knowledge of it enabled us to tell a fellow-countrywoman whom we presently met in the museum of the University, how she could best, or worst, get to that city. Our speech gave us away to her, and she turned to us from the other objects of interest to explain first that she was in a hotel where she paid only six pesetas a day, but where she could get no English explanation of the time-table for any money. She had come to Valladolid with a friend who was going next day to Salamanca, but next day was Sunday and she did not like to travel on Sunday, and Segovia seemed the only alternative. We could not make out why, or if it came to that why she should be traveling alone through Spain with such a slender equipment of motive or object, but we perceived she was one of the most estimable souls in the world, and if she cared more for getting to Segovia that afternoon than for looking at the wonders of the place where we were, we could not blame her. We had to leave her when we left the museum in the charge of two custodians who led her, involuntary but unresisting, to an upper chamber where there were some pictures which she could care no more for than for the wood carvings below. We ourselves cared so little for those pictures that we would not go to see them. Pictures you can see anywhere, but not statuary of such singular interest, such transcendant powerfulness as those carvings of Berruguete and other masters less known, which held us fascinated in the lower rooms of the museum. They are the spoil of convents in the region about, suppressed by the government at different times, and collected here with little relevancy to their original appeal. Some are Scriptural subjects and some are figures of the dancers who take part in certain ceremonials of the Spanish churches (notably the cathedral at Seville), which have a quaint reality, an intense personal character. They are of a fascination which I can hope to convey by no phrase of mine; but far beyond this is the motionless force, the tremendous repose of the figures of the Roman soldiers taken in the part of sleeping at the Tomb. These sculptures are in wood, life-size, and painted in the colors of flesh and costume, with every detail and of a strong mass in which the detail is lost and must be found again by the wondering eye. Beyond all other Spanish sculptures they seemed to me expressive of the national temperament; I thought no other race could have produced them, and that in their return to the Greek ideal of color in statuary they were ingenuously frank and unsurpassably bold.

It might have been the exhaustion experienced from the encounter with their strenuousness that suddenly fatigued us past even the thought of doing any more of Valladolid on foot. At any rate, when we came out of the museum we took refuge in a corner grocery (it seems the nature of groceries to seek corners the world over) and asked the grocer where we could find a cab.

The grocer was young and kind, and not so busy but he could give willing attention to our case. He said he would send for a cab, and he called up from his hands and knees a beautiful blond half-grown boy who was scrubbing the floor, and despatched him on this errand, first making him wipe the suds off his hands. The boy was back wonderfully soon to say the cab would come for us in ten minutes, and to receive with self-respectful appreciation the peseta which rewarded his promptness. In the mean time we feigned a small need which we satisfied by a purchase, and then the grocer put us chairs in front of his counter and made us his guests while his other customers came and went. They came oftener than they went, for our interest in them did not surpass their interest in us. We felt that through this we reflected credit upon our amiable host; rumors of the mysterious strangers apparently spread through the neighborhood and the room was soon filled with people who did not all come to buy; but those who did buy were the most, interesting. An elderly man with his wife bought a large bottle which the grocer put into one scale of his balance, and poured its weight in chick-peas into the other. Then he filled the bottle with oil and weighed it, and then he gave the peas along with it to his customers. It seemed a pretty convention, though we could not quite make out its meaning, unless the peas were bestowed as a sort of bonus; but the next convention was clearer to us. An old man in black corduroy with a clean-shaven face and a rather fierce, retired bull-fighter air, bought a whole dried stock-fish (which the Spaniards eat instead of salt cod) talking loudly to the grocer and at us while the grocer cut it across in widths of two inches and folded it into a neat pocketful; then a glass of wine was poured from a cask behind the counter, and the customer drank it off in honor of the transaction with the effect also of pledging us with his keen eyes; all the time he talked, and he was joined in conversation by a very fat woman who studied us not unkindly. Other neighbors who had gathered in had no apparent purpose but to verify our outlandish presence and to hear my occasional Spanish, which was worth hearing if for nothing but the effort it cost me. The grocer accepted with dignity the popularity we had won him, and when at last our cab arrived from Mount Ararat with the mire of the subsiding Deluge encrusted upon it he led us out to it through the small boys who swarmed upon us wherever we stopped or started in Valladolid; and whose bulk was now much increased by the coming of that very fat woman from within the grocery. As the morning was bright we proposed having the top opened, but here still another convention of the place intervened. In Valladolid it seems that no self-respecting cabman will open the top of his cab for an hour's drive, and we could not promise to keep ours longer. The grocer waited the result of our parley, and then he opened our carriage door and bowed us away. It was charming; if he had a place on Sixth Avenue I would be his customer as long as I lived in New York; and to this moment I do not understand why I did not bargain with that blond boy to come to America with us and be with us always. But there was no city I visited in Spain where I was not sorry to leave some boy behind with the immense rabble of boys whom I hoped never to see again.

## VI

After this passage of real life it was not easy to sink again to the level of art, but if we must come down it there could have been no descent less jarring than that which left us in the exquisite *patio* of the College of San Gregorio, founded for poor students of theology in the time of the Catholic Kings. The students who now thronged the place inside and out looked neither clerical nor poverty-stricken; but I dare say they were good Christians, and whatever their condition they were rich in the constant vision of beauty which one sight of seemed to us more than we merited. Perhaps the facade of the college and that of the neighboring Church of San Pablo may be elsewhere surpassed in the sort of sumptuous delicacy of that Gothic which gets its name of plateresque from the silversmithing spirit of its designs; but I doubt it. The wonderfulness of it is that it is not mechanical or monotonous like the stucco fretting of the Moorish decoration which people rave over in Spain, but has a strength in its refinement which comes from its expression in the exquisitely carven marble. When this is grayed with age it is indeed of the effect of old silver work; but the plateresque in Valladolid does not suggest fragility or triviality; its grace is perhaps rather feminine than masculine; but at the worst it is only the ultimation of the decorative genius of the Gothic. It is, at any rate, the finest surprise which the local architecture has to offer and it leaves one wishing for more rather than less of it, so that after the facade of San Gregorio one is glad of it again in the walls of the *patio*, whose staircases and galleries, with the painted wooden beams of their ceilings, scarcely tempt the eye from it.

We thought the front of San Pablo deserved a second visit, and we were rewarded by finding it far lovelier than we thought. The church was open, and when we went in we had the advantage of seeing a large silver-gilt car moved from the high altar down the nave to a side altar next the door, probably for use in some public procession. The tongue of the car was pulled by a man with one leg; a half-grown boy under the body of it hoisted it on his back and eased it along; and a monk with his white robe tucked up into his girdle pushed it powerfully from behind. I did not make out why so strange a team should have been employed for the work, but the spectacle of that quaint progress was unique among my experiences at Valladolid and of a value which I wish I could make the reader feel with me. We ourselves were so interested in the event that we took part in it so far as to push aside a bench that blocked the way, and we received a grateful smile from the monk in reward of our zeal.

We were in the mood for simple kindness because of our stiff official reception at the Royal Palace, which we visited in the gratification of our passion for *patios*. It is now used for provincial or municipal offices and guarded by sentries who indeed admitted us to the courtyard, but would not understand our wish (it was not very articulately expressed) to mount to the cloistered galleries which all the guide-books united in pronouncing so noble, with their decorative busts of the Roman Emperors and arms of the Spanish provinces. The sculptures are by the school of Berruguete, for whom we had formed so strong a taste at the museum; but our disappointment was not at the moment further embittered by knowing that Napoleon resided there in 1809. We made what we could of other *patios* in the vicinity, especially of one in the palace across from San Gregorio, to which the liveried porter welcomed us, though the noble family was in residence, and allowed us to mount the red-carpeted staircase to a closed portal in consideration of the peseta which he correctly foresaw. It was not a very characteristic *patio,* bare of flower and fountain as it was, and others more fully appointed did not entirely satisfy us. The fact is the *patio* is to be seen best in Andalusia, its home, where every house is built round it, and in summer cooled and in winter chilled by it. But if we were not willing to wait for Seville, Valladolid did what it could; and if we saw no house with quite the *patio* we expected we did see the house where Philip II. was born, unless the enterprising boy who led us to it was mistaken; in that case we were, Ophelia-like, the more deceived.

VII

Such things do not really matter; the guide-book's object of interest is seldom an object of human interest; you may miss it or ignore it without real personal loss; but if we had failed of that mystic progress of the silver car down the nave of San Pablo we should have been really if not sensibly poorer. So we should if we had failed of the charming experience which awaited us in our hotel at lunch-time. When we went out in the morning we saw a table spread the length of the long dining-room, and now when we returned we found every chair taken. At once we surmised a wedding breakfast, not more from the gaiety than the gravity of the guests; and the head waiter confirmed our impression: it was indeed a *boda*. The party was just breaking up, and as we sat down at our table the wedding guests rose from theirs. I do not know but in any country the women on such an occasion would look more adequate to it than the men; at any rate, there in Spain they looked altogether superior. It was not only that they were handsomer and better dressed, but that they expressed finer social and intellectual quality.

All the faces had the quiet which the Spanish face has in such degree that the quiet seems national more than personal; but the women's faces were oval, though rather heavily based, while the men's were squared, with high cheek-bones, and they seemed more distinctly middle class. Men and women had equally repose of manner, and when the women came to put on their headgear near our corner, it was with a surface calm unbroken by what must have been their inner excitement. They wore hats and mantillas in about the same proportion; but the bride wore a black mantilla and a black dress with sprigs of orange blossoms in her hair and on her breast for the only note of white. Her lovely, gentle face was white, of course, from the universal powder, and so were the faces of the others, who talked in low tones around her, with scarcely more animation than so many masks. The handsomest of them, whom we decided to be her sister, arranged the bride's mantilla, and was then helped on with hers by the others, with soft smiles and glances. Two little girls, imaginably sorry the feast was over, suppressed their regret in the tutelage of the maiden aunts and grandmothers who put up cakes in napkins to carry home; and then the party vanished in unbroken decorum. When they were gone we found that in studying the behavior of the bride and her friends we had not only failed to identify the bridegroom, but had altogether forgotten to try.

## VIII

The terrible Torquemada dwelt for years in Valla-dolid and must there have excogitated some of the methods of the Holy Office in dealing with heresy. As I have noted, Ferdinand and Isabella were married there and Philip II. was born there; but I think the reader will agree with me that the highest honor of the city is that it was long the home of the gallant gentleman who after five years of captivity in Algiers and the loss of his hand in the Battle of Lepanto, wrote there, in his poverty and neglect, the first part of a romance which remains and must always remain one of the first if not the very first of the fictions of the world. I mean that

*Dear son of memory, great heir of fame,*

Michael Cervantes; and I wish I could pay here that devoir to his memory and fame which squalid circumstance forbade me to render under the roof that once sheltered him. One can never say enough in his praise, and even Valladolid seems to have thought so, for the city has put up a tablet to him with his bust above it in the front of his incredible house and done him the homage of a reverent inscription. It is a very little house, as small as Ariosto's in Ferrara, which he said was so apt for him, but it is not in a long, clean street like that; it is in a bad neighborhood which has not yet outlived the evil repute it bore in the days of Cervantes. It was then the scene of nightly brawls and in one of these a gentleman was stabbed near the author's house. The alarm brought Cervantes to the door and being the first to reach the dying man he was promptly arrested, together with his wife, his two sisters, and his niece, who were living with him and who were taken up as accessories before the fact. The whole abomination is matter of judicial record, and it appears from this that suspicion fell upon the gentle family (one sister was a nun) because they were living in that infamous place. The man whose renown has since filled the civilized world fuller even than the name of his contemporary, Shakespeare (they died on the same day), was then so unknown to the authorities of Valladolid that he had great ado to establish the innocence of himself and his household. To be sure, his *Don Quixote* had not yet appeared, though he is said to have finished the first part in that miserable abode in that vile region; but he had written poems and plays, especially his most noble tragedy of "Numancia," and he had held public employs and lived near enough to courts to be at least in their cold shade. It is all very Spanish and very strange, and perhaps the wonder should be that in this most provincial of royal capitals, in a time devoted to the extirpation of ideas, the fact that he was a poet and a scholar did not tell fatally against him. In his declaration before the magistrates he says that his literary reputation procured him the acquaintance of courtiers and scholars, who visited him in that pitiable abode where the ladies of his family cared for themselves and him with the help of one servant maid.

They had an upper floor of the house, which stands at the base of a stone terrace dropping from the wide, dusty, fly-blown street, where I stayed long enough to buy a melon (I was always buying a melon in Spain) and put it into my cab before I descended the terrace to revere the house of Cervantes on its own level. There was no mistaking it; there was the bust and the inscription; but it was well I bought my melon before I ventured upon this act of piety; I should not have had the stomach for it afterward. I was not satisfied with the outside of the house, but when I entered the open doorway, meaning to mount to the upper floor, it was as if I were immediately blown into the street again by the thick and noisome stench which filled the place from some unmentionable if not unimaginable source.

It was like a filthy insult to the great presence whose sacred shrine the house should have been religiously kept. But Cervantes dead was as forgotten in Valladolid as Cervantes living had been. In some paroxysm of civic pride the tablet had been set in the wall and then the house abandoned to whatever might happen. I thought foul shame of Valladolid for her neglect, and though she might have answered that her burden of memories was more than she could bear, that she could not be forever keeping her celebrity sweet, still I could have retorted, But Cervantes, but Cervantes! There was only one Cervantes in the world and there never would be another, and could not she watch over this poor once home of his for his matchless sake? Then if Valladolid had come back at me with the fact that Cervantes had lived pretty well all over Spain, and what had Seville done, Cordova done, Toledo done, Madrid done, for the upkeep of his divers sojourns more than she had done, after placing a tablet in his house wall?— certainly I could have said that this did not excuse her, but I must have owned that she was not alone, though she seemed most to blame.

IX

Now I look back and am glad I had not consciously with me, as we drove away, the boy who once meant to write the life of Cervantes, and who I knew from my recollection of his idolatry of that chief of Spaniards would not have listened to the excuses of Valladolid for a moment. All appeared fair and noble in that Spain of his which shone with such allure far across the snows through which he trudged morning and evening with his father to and from the printing-office, and made his dream of that great work the common theme of their talk. Now the boy is as utterly gone as the father, who was a boy too at heart, but who died a very old man many years ago; and in the place of both is another old man trammeled in his tangled memories of Spain visited and unvisited.

It would be a poor sort of make-believe if this survivor pretended any lasting indignation with Valladolid because of the stench of Cervantes's house. There are a great many very bad smells in Spain everywhere, and it is only fair to own that a psychological change toward Valladolid had been operating itself in me since luncheon which Valladolid was not very specifically to blame for. Up to the time the wedding guests left us we had said Valladolid was the most interesting city we had ever seen, and we would like to stay there a week; then, suddenly, we began to turn against it. One thing: the weather had clouded, and it was colder. But we determined to be just, and after we left the house of Cervantes we drove out to the promenades along the banks of the Pisuerga, in hopes of a better mind, for we had read that they were the favorite resort of the citizens in summer, and we did not know but even in autumn we might have some glimpses of their recreation. Our way took us sorrowfully past hospitals and prisons and barracks; and when we came out on the promenade we found ourselves in the gloom of close set mulberry trees, with the dust thick on the paths under them. The leaves hung leaden gray on the boughs and there could never have been a spear of grass along those disconsolate ways. The river was shrunken in its bed, and where its current crept from pool to pool, women were washing some of the rags which already hung so thick on the bushes that it was wonderful there should be any left to wash. Squalid children abounded, and at one point a crowd of people had gathered and stood looking silently and motionlessly over the bank. We looked too and on a sand-bar near the shore we saw three gendarmes standing with a group of civilians. Between their fixed and absolutely motionless figures lay the body of a drowned man on the sand, poorly clothed in a workman's dress, and with his poor, dead clay-white hands stretched out from him on the sand, and his gray face showing to the sky. Everywhere people were stopping and staring; from one of the crowded windows of the nearest house a woman hung with a rope of her long hair in one hand, and in the other the brush she was passing over it. On the bridge the man who had found the body made a merit of his discovery which he dramatized to a group of spectators without rousing them to a murmur or stirring them from their statuesque fixity. His own excitement in comparison seemed indecent.

X

It was now three o'clock and I thought I might be in time to draw some money on my letter of credit, at the bank which we had found standing in a pleasant garden in the course of our stroll through the town the night before. We had said, How charming it would be to draw money in such an environment; and full of the romantic expectation, I offered my letter at the window, where after a discreet interval I managed to call from their preoccupation some unoccupied persons within. They had not a very financial air, and I thought them the porters they really were, with some fear that I had come after banking-hours. But they joined in reassuring me, and told me that if I would return after five o'clock the proper authorities would be there.

I did not know then what late hours Spain kept in every way; but I concealed my surprise; and I came back at the time suggested, and offered my letter at the window with a request for ten pounds, which I fancied I might need. A clerk took the letter and scrutinized it with a deliberation which I thought it scarcely merited. His self-respect doubtless would not suffer him to betray that he could not read the English of it; and with an air of wishing to consult higher authority he carried it to another clerk at a desk across the room. To this official it seemed to come as something of a blow. Tie made a show of reading it several times over, inside and out, and then from the pigeonhole of his desk he began to accumulate what I supposed corroborative documents, or *pieces justificatives*. When lie had amassed a heap several inches thick, he rose and hurried out through the gate, across the hall where I sat, into a room beyond. He returned without in any wise referring himself to me and sat down at his desk again. The first clerk explained to the anxious face with which I now approached him that the second clerk had taken my letter to the director. I went back to my seat and waited fifteen minutes longer, fifteen having passed already; then I presented my anxious face, now somewhat indignant, to the first clerk again. "What is the director doing with my letter?" The first clerk referred my question to the second clerk, who answered from his place, "He is verifying the signature." "But what signature?" I wondered to myself, reflecting that he had as yet had none of mine. Could it be the signature of my New York banker or my London one? I repaired once more to the window, after another wait, and said in polite but firm Castilian, "Do me the favor to return me my letter." A commotion of protest took place within the barrier, followed by the repeated explanation that the director was verifying the signature. I returned to toy place and considered that the suspicious document which I had presented bore record of moneys drawn in London, in Paris, in Tours, in San Sebastian, which ought to have allayed all suspicion; then for the last time I repaired to the window; more in anger now than in sorrow, and gathered nay severest Spanish together for a final demand: "Do me the favor to give me back my letter *without the pounds sterling.*" The clerks consulted together; one of them decided to go to the director's room, and after a dignified delay he came back with my letter, and dashed it down before me with the only rudeness I experienced in Spain.

I was glad to get it on any terms; it was only too probable that it would have been returned without the money if I had not demanded it; and I did what I could with the fact that this amusing financial transaction, involving a total of fifty dollars, had taken place in the chief banking-house of one of the commercial and industrial centers of the country. Valladolid is among other works the seat of the locomotive works of the northern railway lines, and as these machines average a speed of twenty-five miles an hour with express trains, it seemed strange to me that something like their rapidity should not have governed the action of that bank director in forcing me to ask back my discredited letter of credit.

XI

That evening the young voices and the young feet began to chirp again under our sun balcony. But there had been no sun in it since noon and presently a cold thin rain was falling and driving the promenaders under the arcades, where they were perhaps not unhappier for being closely massed. We missed the prettiness of the spectacle, though as yet we did not know that it was the only one of the sort we might hope to see in Spain, where women walk little indoors, and when they go out, drive and increase in the sort of loveliness which may be weighed and measured. Even under the arcades the promenade ceased early and in the adjoining Plaza Mayor, where the *autos da fe* once took place, the rain still earlier made an end of the municipal music, and the dancing of the lower ranks of the people. But we were fortunate in our Chilian friend's representation of the dancing; he came to our table at dinner, and did with charming sympathy a mother waltzing with her babe in arms for a partner.

He came to the omnibus at the end of the promenade, when we were starting for the station next morning, not yet shaven, in his friendly zeal to make sure of seeing us off, and we parted with confident prophecies of meeting each other again in Madrid. We had already bidden adieu with effusion to our landlady-sisters-and-mother, and had wished to keep forever our own the adorable *chico* who, when cautioned against trying to carry a very heavy bag, valiantly jerked it to his shoulder and made off with it to the omnibus, as if it were nothing. I do not believe such a boy breathes out of Spain, where I hope he will grow up to the Oriental calm of so many of his countrymen, and rest from the toils of his nonage. At the last moment after the Chilian had left us, we perceived that one of our trunks had been forgotten, and the *chico* coursed back to the hotel for it and returned with the delinquent porter bearing it, as if to make sure of his bringing it.

When it was put on top of the omnibus, and we were in probably unparalleled readiness for starting to the station, at an hour when scarcely anybody else in Valladolid was up, a mule composing a portion of our team immediately fell down, as if startled too abruptly from a somnambulic dream. I really do not remember how it was got to its feet again; but I remember the anguish of the delay and the fear that we might not be able to escape from Valladolid after all our pains in trying for the Sud-Express at that hour; and I remember that when we reached the station we found that the Sud-Express was forty minutes behind time and that we were a full hour after that before starting for Madrid.

# V. PHASES OF MADRID

I fancied that a kind of Gothic gloom was expressed in the black wine-skins of Old Castile, as contrasted with the fairer color of those which began to prevail even so little south of Burgos as Valladolid. I am not sure that the Old Castilian wine-skins derived their blackness from the complexion of the pigs, or that there are more pale pigs in the south than in the north of Spain; I am sure only of a difference in the color of the skins, which may have come from a difference in the treatment of them. At a venture I should not say that there were more black pigs in Old Castile than in Andalusia, as we observed them from the train, rooting among the unpromising stubble of the wheat-lands. Rather I should say that the prevailing pig of all the Spains was brown, corresponding to the reddish blondness frequent among both the Visigoths and the Moors. The black pig was probably the original, prehistoric Iberian pig, or of an Italian strain imported by the Romans; but I do not offer this as more than a guess. The Visigothic or Arabic pig showed himself an animal of great energy and alertness wherever we saw him, and able to live upon the lean of the land where it was leanest. At his youngest he abounded in the furrows and hollows, matching his russet with the russet of the soil and darting to and fro with the quickness of a hare. He was always of an ingratiating humorousness and endeared himself by an apparent readiness to enter into any joke that was going, especially that of startling the pedestrian by his own sudden apparition from behind a tuft of grass or withered stalk. I will not be sure, but I think we began to see his kind as soon as we got out of Valladolid, when we began running through a country wooded with heavy, low-crowned pines that looked like the stone-pines of Italy, but were probably not the same. After twenty miles of this landscape the brown pig with pigs of other complexions, as much guarded as possible, multiplied among the patches of vineyard. He had there the company of tall black goats and rather unhappy-looking black sheep, all of whom he excelled in the art of foraging among the vines and the stubble of the surrounding wheat-lands. After the vineyards these opened and stretched themselves wearily, from low dull sky to low dull sky, nowise cheered in aspect by the squalid peasants, scratching their tawny expanses with those crooked prehistoric sticks which they use for plows in Spain. It was a dreary landscape, but it was good to be out of Valladolid on any terms, and especially good to be away from the station which we had left emulating the odors of the house of Cervantes.

I

There had been the usual alarm about the lack of places in the Sud-Express which we were to take at Valladolid, but we chanced getting them, and our boldness was rewarded by getting a whole compartment to ourselves, and a large, fat friendly conductor with an eye out for tips in every direction. The lunch in our dining-car was for the first time in Spain not worth the American price asked for it; everywhere else on the Spanish trains I must testify that the meals were excellent and abundant; and the refection may now have felt in some obscure sort the horror of the world in which the Sud-Express seemed to have lost itself. The scene was as alien to any other known aspect of our comfortable planet as if it were the landscape of some star condemned for the sins of its extinct children to wander through space in unimaginable desolation. It seldom happens in Spain that the scenery is the same on both sides of the railroad track, but here it was malignly alike on one hand and on the other, though we seemed to be running along the slope of an upland, so that the left hand was higher and the right lower. It was more as if we were crossing the face of some prodigious rapid, whose surges were the measureless granite boulders tossing everywhere in masses from the size of a man's fist to the size of a house. In a wild chaos they wallowed against one another, the greater bearing on their tops or between them on their shoulders smaller regular or irregular masses of the same gray stone. Everywhere among their awful shallows grew gray live-oaks, and in among the rocks and trees spread tufts of gray shrub. Suddenly, over the frenzy of this mad world, a storm of cold rain broke whirling, and cold gray mists drove, blinding the windows and chilling us where we sat within. From time to time the storm lifted and showed again this vision of nature hoary as if with immemorial eld; if at times we seemed to have run away from it again it closed in upon us and held us captive in its desolation.

With longer and longer intervals of relief it closed upon us for the last time in the neighborhood of the gloomiest pile that ever a man built for his life, his death and his prayer between; but before we came to the palace-tomb of the Escorial, we had clear in the distance the vision of the walls and roofs and towers of the medieval city of Avila. It is said to be the perfectest relic of the Middle Ages after or before Rothenburg, and we who had seen Rothenburg solemnly promised ourselves to come back some day from Madrid and spend it in Avila. But we never came, and Avila remains a vision of walls and roofs and towers tawny gray glimpsed in a rift of the storm that again swept toward the Spanish capital.

II

We were very glad indeed to get to Madrid, though dismayed by apprehensions of the *octroi* which we felt sure awaited us. We recalled the behavior of the amiable officer of Valladolid who bumped our baggage about on the roof of our omnibus, and we thought that in Madrid such an officer could not do less than shatter our boxes and scatter their contents in the streaming street. What was then our surprise, our joy, to find that in Madrid there was no *octroi* at all, and that the amiable *mozos* who took our things hardly knew what we meant when we asked for it. At Madrid they scarcely wanted our tickets at the gate of the station, and we found ourselves in the soft embrace of modernity, so dear after the feudal rigors of Old Castile, when we mounted into a motor-bus and sped away through the spectacular town, so like Paris, so like Rome as to have no personality of its own except in this similarity, and never stopped till the liveried service swarmed upon us at the door of the Hotel Ritz.

Here the modernity which had so winningly greeted us at the station welcomed us more and consolingly. There was not only steam-heating, but the steam was on! It wanted but a turn of the hand at the radiators, and the rooms were warm. The rooms themselves responded to our appeal and looked down into a silent inner court, deaf to the clatter of the streets, and sleep haunted the very air, distracted, if at all, by the instant facility and luxury of the appliances. Was it really in Spain that a metallic tablet at the bed-head invited the wanderer to call with one button for the *camerero*, another for the *camerera*, and another for the *mozo*, who would all instantly come speaking English like so many angels? Were we to have these beautiful chambers for a humble two dollars and forty cents a day; and if it was true, why did we ever leave them and try for something ever so much worse and so very little cheaper? Let me be frank with the reader whom I desire for my friend, and own that we were frightened from the Ritz Hotel by the rumor of Ritz prices. I paid my bill there, which was imagined with scrupulous fullness to the last possible *centimo*, and so I may disinterestedly declare that the Ritz is the only hotel in Madrid where you get the worth of your money, even when the money seems more but scarcely is so. In all Spain I know of only two other hotels which may compare with it, and these are the English hotels, one at Ronda and one at Algeciras. If I add falteringly the hotel where we stayed a night in Toledo and the hotel where we abode a fortnight in Seville, I heap the measure of merit and press it down.

We did not begin at once our insensate search for another hotel in Madrid: but the sky had cleared and we went out into the strange capital so uncharacteristically characteristic, to find tea at a certain cafe we had heard of. It was in the Calle de Alcala (a name which so richly stimulates the imagination), and it looked out across this handsome street, to a club that I never knew the name of, where at a series of open windows was a flare of young men in silk hats leaning out on their elbows and letting no passing fact of the avenue escape them. It was worth their study, and if I had been an idle young Spaniard, or an idle old one, I would have asked nothing better than to spend my Sunday afternoon poring from one of those windows on my well-known world of Madrid as it babbled by. Even in my quality of alien, newly arrived and ignorant of that world, I already felt its fascination.

Sunday in Spain is perhaps different from other days of the week to the Spanish sense, but to the traveler it is too like them to be distinguishable except in that guilty Sabbath consciousness which is probably an effect from original sin in every Protestant soul. The casual eye could not see but that in Madrid every one seemed as much or as little at work as on any other day. My own casual eye noted that the most picturesquely evident thing in the city was the country life which seemed so to pervade it. In the Calle de Alcala, flowing to the Prado out of the Puerta del Sol, there passed a current of farm-carts and farm-wagons more conspicuous than any urban vehicles, as they jingled by, with men and women on their sleigh-belled donkeys, astride or atop the heavily laden panniers. The donkeys bore a part literally leading in all the rustic equipages, and with their superior intellect found a way through the crowds for the string-teams of the three or four large mules that followed them in harness. Whenever we saw a team of mules without this sage guidance we trembled for their safety; as for horses, no team of them attempted the difficult passage, though ox-trains seemed able to dispense with the path-finding donkeys.

To be sure, the horses abounded in the cabs, which were mostly bad, more or less. It is an idiosyncrasy of the cabs in Madrid that only the open victorias have rubber tires; if you go in a coupe you must consent to be ruthlessly bounced over the rough pavements on wheels unsoftened. It "follows as the night the day" that the coupe is not in favor, and that in its conservative disuse it accumulates a smell not to be acquired out of Spain. One such vehicle I had which I thought must have been stabled in the house of Cervantes at Valladolid, and rushed on the Sud-Express for my service at Madrid; the stench in it was such that after a short drive to the house of a friend I was fain to dismiss it at a serious loss in pesetas and take the risk of another which might have been as bad. Fortunately a kind lady intervened with a private carriage and a coachman shaved that very day, whereas my poor old cabman, who was of one and the same smell as his cab, had not been shaved for three days.

III

This seems the place to note the fact that no Spaniard in humble life shaves oftener than once in three days, and that you always see him on the third day just before he has shaved. But all this time I have left myself sitting in the cafe looking out on the club that looks out on the Calle de

Aleala, and keeping the waiter waiting with a jug of hot milk in his hand while I convince him (such a friendly, smiling man he is, and glad of my instruction!) that in tea one always wants the milk cold. To him that does not seem reasonable, since one wants it hot in coffee and chocolate; but he yields to my prejudice, and after that he always says, *"Ah, leche fria!"* and we smile radiantly together in the bond of comradery which cold milk establishes between man and man in Spain. As yet tea is a novelty in that country, though the young English queen, universally loved and honored, has made it the fashion in high life. Still it is hard to overcome such a prepossession as that of hot milk in tea, and in some places you cannot get it cold for love or money.

But again I leave myself waiting in that cafe, where slowly, and at last not very overwhelmingly in number, the beautiful plaster-pale Spanish ladies gather with their husbands and have chocolate. It is a riotous dissipation for them, though it does not sound so; the home is the Spanish ideal of the woman's place, as it is of our anti-suffragists, though there is nothing corresponding to our fireside in it; and the cafe is her husband's place without her. When she walks in the street, where mostly she drives, she walks with her eyes straight before her; to look either to the right or left, especially if a man is on either hand, is a superfluity of naughtiness. The habit of looking straight ahead is formed in youth, and it continues through life; so at least it is said, and if I cannot affirm it I will not deny it. The beautiful black eyes so discreetly directed looked as often from mantillas as hats, even in Madrid, which is the capital, and much infested by French fashions. You must not believe it when any one tells you that the mantilla is going out; it prevails everywhere, and it increases from north to south, and in Seville it is almost universal. Hats are worn there only in driving, but at Madrid there were many hats worn in walking, though whether by Spanish women or by foreigners, of course one could not, though a wayfaring man and an American, stop them to ask.

There are more women in the street at Madrid than in the provincial cities, perhaps because it is the capital and cosmopolitan, and perhaps because the streets are many of them open and pleasant, though there arc enough of them dark and narrow, too. I do not know just why the Puerta del Sol seems so much ampler and gayer than the Calle de Alcala; it is not really wider, but it seems more to concentrate the coming and going, and with its high-hoteled opposition of corners is of a supreme spectacularity. Besides, the name is so fine: what better could any city place ask than to be called Gate of the Sun? Perpetual trams wheeze and whistle through it; large shops face upon it; the sidewalks are thronged with passers, and the many little streets debouching on it pour their streams of traffic and travel into it on the right and left. It is mainly fed by the avenues leaving the royal palace on the west, and its eddying tide empties through the Calle de Alcala into the groves and gardens of the Prado whence it spreads over all the drives and parks east and north and south.

For a capital purposed and planned Madrid is very well indeed. It has not the symmetry which forethought gave the topography of Washington, or the beauty which afterthought has given Paris. But it makes you think a little of Washington, and a great deal of Paris, though a great deal more yet of Rome. It is Renaissance so far as architecture goes, and it is very modern Latin; so that it is of the older and the newer Rome that it makes you think. From, time to time it seemed to me I must be in. Rome, and I recovered myself with a pang to find I was not. Yet, as I say, Madrid was very well indeed, and when I reflected I had to own that I had come there on purpose to be there, and not to be in Rome, where also I should have been so satisfied to be.

IV

I do not know but we chose our hotel when we left the Ritz because it was so Italian, so Roman. It had a wide grape arbor before it, with a generous spread of trellised roof through which dangled the grape bunches among the leaves of the vine. Around this arbor at top went a balustrade of marble, with fat *putti*, or marble boys, on the corners, who would have watched over the fruit if they had not been preoccupied with looking like so many thousands of *putti* in Italy. They looked like Italian *putti* with a difference, the difference that passes between all the Spanish things and the Italian things they resemble. They were coarser and grosser in figure, and though amiable enough in aspect, they lacked the refinement, the air of pretty appeal which Italian art learns from nature to give the faces of *putti*. Yet they were charming, and it was always a pleasure to look at them posing in pairs at the corners of the balustrade, and I do not know but dozing in the hours of *siesta*. If they had been in wood Spanish art would have known how to make them better, but in stone they had been gathering an acceptable weather stain during the human generations they had been there, and their plump stomachs were weather-beaten white.

I do not know if they had been there long enough to have witnessed the murder of Cromwell's ambassador done in our street by two Jacobite gentlemen who could not abide his coming to honor in the land where they were in exile from England. That must have been sometime about the middle of the century after Philip II., bigot as he was, could not bear the more masterful bigotry of the archbishop of Toledo, and brought his court from that ancient capital, and declared Madrid henceforward the capital forever; which did not prevent Philip III. from taking his court to Valladolid and making that the capital *en titre* when he liked. However, some other Philip or Charles, or whoever, returned with his court to Madrid and it has ever since remained the capital, and has come, with many natural disadvantages, to look its supremacy. For my pleasure I would rather live in Seville, but that would be a luxurious indulgence of the love of beauty, and like a preference of Venice in Italy when there was Rome to live in. Madrid is not Rome, but it makes you think of Rome as I have said, and if it had a better climate it would make you think of Rome still more. Notoriously, however, it has not a good climate and we had not come at the right season to get the best of the bad. The bad season itself was perverse, for the rains do not usually begin in their bitterness at Madrid before November, and now they began early in October. The day would open fair, with only a few little white clouds in the large blue, and if we could trust other's experience we knew it would rain before the day closed; only a morning absolutely clear could warrant the hope of a day fair till sunset. Shortly after noon the little white clouds would drift together and be joined by others till they hid the large blue, and then the drops would begin to fall. By that time the air would have turned raw and chill, and the rain would be of a cold which it kept through the night.

This habit of raining every afternoon was what kept us from seeing rank, riches, and beauty in the Paseo de la Castellana, where they drive only on fine afternoons; they now remained at home even more persistently than we did, for with that love of the fashionable world for which I am always blaming myself I sometimes took a cab and fared desperately forth in pursuit of them. Only once did I seem to catch a glimpse of them, and that once I saw a closed carriage weltering along the drive between the trees and the trams that border it, with the coachman and footman snugly sheltered under umbrellas on the box. This was something, though not a great deal; I could not make out the people inside the carriage; yet it helped to certify to me the fact that the great world does drive in the Paseo de la Castellana and does not drive in the Paseo del Prado; that is quite abandoned, even on the wettest days, to the very poor and perhaps unfashionable people.

# V

It may have been our comparative defeat with fashion in its most distinctive moments of pleasuring (for one thing I wished to see how the dreariness of Madrid gaiety in the Paseo de la Castellana would compare with that of Roman gaiety on the Pincian) which made us the more determined to see a bull-fight in the Spanish capital. We had vowed ourselves in coming to Spain to set the Spaniards an example of civilization by inflexibly refusing to see a bull-fight under any circumstances or for any consideration; but it seemed to us that it was a sort of public duty to go and see the crowd, what it was like, in the time and place where the Spanish crowd is most like itself. We would go and remain in our places till everybody else was placed, and then, when the picadors and banderilleros and matadors were all ranged in the arena, and the gate was lifted, and the bull came rushing madly in, we would rise before he had time to gore anybody, and go inexorably away. This union of self-indulgence and self-denial seemed almost an act of piety when we learned that the bull-fight was to be on Sunday, and we prepared ourselves with tickets quite early in the week. On Saturday afternoon it rained, of course, but the worst was that it rained on Sunday morning, and the clouds did not lift till noon. Then the glowing concierge of our hotel, a man so gaily hopeful, so expansively promising that I could hardly believe he was not an Italian, said that there could not possibly be a bull-fight that day; the rain would have made the arena so slippery that man, horse, and bull would all fall down together in a common ruin, with no hope whatever of hurting one another.

We gave up this bull-fight at once, but we were the more resolved to see a bull-fight because we still owed it to the Spanish people to come away before we had time to look at it, and we said we would certainly go at Cordova where we should spend the next Sabbath. At Cordova we learned that it was the closed season for bull-fighting, but vague hopes of usefulness to the Spanish public were held out to us at Seville, the very metropolis of bull-fighting, where the bulls came bellowing up from their native fields athirst for the blood of the profession and the *aficionados,* who outnumber there the amateurs of the whole rest of Spain. But at Seville we were told that there would be no more bull-feasts, as the Spaniards much more preferably call the bullfights, till April, and now we were only in October. We said, Never mind; we would go to a bull-feast in Granada; but at Granada the season was even more hopelessly closed. In Ronda itself, which is the heart, as Seville is the home of the bull-feast, we could only see the inside of the empty arena; and at Algeciras the outside alone offered itself to our vision. By this time the sense of duty was so strong upon us that if there had been a bull-feast we would have shared in it and stayed through till the last *espada* dropped dead, gored through, at the knees of the last bull transfixed by his unerring sword; and the other *toreros,* the *banderilleros* with their darts and the picadors with their disemboweled horses, lay scattered over the blood-stained arena. Such is the force of a high resolve in strangers bent upon a lesson of civilization to a barbarous people when disappointed of their purpose. But we learned too late that only in Madrid is there any bull-feasting in the winter. In the provincial cities the bulls are dispirited by the cold; but in the capital, for the honor of the nation, they somehow pull themselves together and do their poor best to kill and be killed. Yet in the capital where the zeal of the bulls, and I suppose, of the bull-fighters, is such, it is said that there is a subtle decay in the fashionable, if not popular, esteem of the only sport which remembers in the modern world the gladiatorial shows of imperial Rome. It is said, but I do not know whether it is true, that the young English queen who has gladly renounced her nation and religion for the people who seem so to love her, cannot endure the bloody sights of the bull-feast; and when it comes to the horses dragging their entrails across the ring, or the *espada* despatching the bull, or the bull tossing a *landerillero* in the air she puts up her fan. It is said also that the young Spanish king, who has shown himself such a merciful-minded youth, and seems so eager to make the best of the bad business of being a king at all, sympathizes with her, and shows an obviously abated interest at these supreme moments.

I do not know whether or not it was because we had failed with the bull-feast that we failed to go to any sort of public entertainment in Madrid. It certainly was in my book to go to the theater, and see some of those modern plays which I had read so many of, and which I had translated one of for Lawrence Barrett in the far-off days before the flood of native American dramas now deluging our theater. That play was "Un Drama Nueva," by Estebanez, which between us we called "Yorick's Love" and which my very knightly tragedian made his battle-horse during the latter years of his life. In another version Barrett had seen it fail in New York, but its failure left him with the lasting desire to do it himself. A Spanish friend, now dead but then the gifted and eccentric Consul General at Quebec, got me a copy of the play from Madrid, and I thought there was great reason in a suggestion from another friend that it had failed because it put Shakespeare on the stage as one of its characters; but it seemed to me that the trouble could be got over by making the poet Heywood represent the Shakespearian epoch. I did this and the sole obstacle to its success seemed removed. It went, as the enthusiastic Barrett used to say, "with a shout," though to please him I had hurt it all I could by some additions and adaptations; and though it was a most ridiculously romantic story of the tragical loves of Yorick (whom the Latins like to go on imagining out of Hamlet a much more interesting and important character than Shakespeare ever meant him to be fancied), and ought to have remained the fiasco it began, still it gained Barrett much money and me some little.

I was always proud of this success, and I boasted of it to the bookseller in Madrid, whom I interested in finding me some still moderner plays after quite failing to interest another bookseller. Your Spanish merchant seems seldom concerned in a mercantile transaction; but perhaps it was not so strange in the case of this Spanish bookseller because he was a German and spoke a surprising English in response to my demand whether he spoke any. He was the frowsiest bookseller I ever saw, and he was in the third day of his unshavenness with a shirt-front and coat-collar plentifully bedandruffed from his shaggy hair; but he entered into the spirit of my affair and said if that Spanish play had succeeded so wonderfully, then I ought to pay fifty per cent, more than the current price for the other Spanish plays which I wanted him to get me. I laughed with him at the joke which I found simple earnest when our glowing concierge gave me the books next day, and I perceived that the proposed supplement had really been paid for them on my account. I should not now be grieving for this incident if the plays had proved better reading than they did on experiment. Some of them were from the Catalan, and all of them dealt with the simpler actual life of Spain; but they did not deal impressively with it, though they seemed to me more hopeful in conception than certain psychological plays of ten or fifteen years ago, which the Spanish authors had too clearly studied from Ibsen.

They might have had their effect in the theater, but the rainy weather had not only spoiled my sole chance of the bull-feast; the effect of it in a stubborn cold forbade me the night air and kept me from testing any of the new dramas on the stage, which is always giving new dramas in Madrid. The stage, or rather the theater, is said to be truly a passion with the Madrilenos, who go every night to see the whole or the part of a play and do not mind seeing the same play constantly, as if it were opera. They may not care to see the play so much as to be seen at it; that happens in every country; but no doubt the plays have a charm which did not impart itself from the printed page. The companies are reported very good: but the reader must take this from me at second hand, as he must take the general society fact. I only know that people ask you to dinner at nine, and if they go to the theater afterward they cannot well come away till toward one o'clock. It is after this hour that the *tertulia*, that peculiarly Spanish function, begins, but how long it lasts or just what it is I do not know. I am able to report confidently, however, that it is a species of *salon* and that it is said to be called a *tertulia* because of the former habit in the guests, and no doubt the hostess, of quoting the poet Tertullian. It is of various constituents, according as it is a fashionable, a literary, or an artistic *tertulia*, or all three with an infusion of science. Oftenest, I believe, it is a domestic affair and all degrees of cousinship resort to it with brothers and sisters and uncles, who meet with the pleasant Latin liking of frequent meetings among kindred. In some cases no doubt it is a brilliant reunion where lively things are said; in others it may be dull; in far the most cases it seems to be held late at night or early in the morning.

VI

It was hard, after being shut up several days, that one must not go out after nightfall, and if one went out by day, one must go with closed lips and avoid all talking in the street under penalty of incurring the dreaded pneumonia of Madrid. Except for that dreaded pneumonia, I believe the air of Madrid is not so pestilential as it has been reported. Public opinion is beginning to veer in favor of it, just as the criticism which has pronounced Madrid commonplace and unpicturesque because it is not obviously old, is now finding a charm in it peculiar to the place. Its very modernity embodies and imparts the charm, which will grow as the city grows in wideness and straightness. It is in the newer quarter that it recalls Rome or the newer quarters of Rome; but there is an old part of it that recalls the older part of Naples, though the streets are not quite so narrow nor the houses so high. There is like bargaining at the open stands with the buyers and sellers chaffering over them; there is a likeness in the people's looks, too, but when it comes to the most characteristic thing of Naples, Madrid is not in it for a moment. I mean the bursts of song which all day long and all night long you hear in Naples; and this seems as good a place as any to say that to my experience Spain is a songless land. We had read much of the song and dance there, but though the dance might be hired the song was never offered for love or money. To be sure, in Toledo, once, a woman came to her door across the way under otir hotel window and sang over the slops she emptied into the street, but then she shut the door and we heard her no more. In Cordova there was as brief a peal of music from a house which we passed, and in Algeciras we heard one short sweet strain from a girl whom we could not see behind her lattice. Besides these chance notes we heard no other by any chance. But this is by no means saying that there is not abundant song in Spain, only it was kept quiet; I suppose that if we had been there in the spring instead of the fall we should at least have heard the birds singing. In Madrid there were not even many street cries; a few in the Puerta del Sol, yes; but the peasants who drove their mule-teams through the streets scarcely lifted their voices in reproach or invitation; they could trust the wise donkeys that led them to get them safely through the difficult places. There was no audible quarreling among the cabmen, and when you called a cab it was useless to cry "Heigh!" or shake your umbrella; you made play with your thumb and finger in the air and sibilantly whispered; otherwise the cabman ignored you and went on reading his newspaper. The cabmen of Madrid are great readers, much greater, I am sorry to say, than I was, for whenever I bought a Spanish paper I found it extremely well written. Now and then I expressed my political preferences in buying *El Liberal* which I thought very able; even *El Imparcial* I thought able, though it is less radical than *El Liberal*, a paper which is published simultaneously in Madrid, with local editions in several provincial cities.

For all the street silence there seemed to be a great deal of noise, which I suppose came from the click of boots on the sidewalks and of hoofs in roadways and the grind and squeal of the trams, with the harsh smiting of the unrubbered tires of the closed cabs on the rough granite blocks of the streets. But there are asphalted streets in Madrid where the sound of the hoofs and wheels is subdued, and the streets rough and smooth are kept of a cleanliness which would put the streets of New York to shame if anything could. Ordinarily you could get cabs anywhere, but if you wanted one very badly, when remote from a stand, there was more than one chance that a cab marked *Libre* would pass you with lordly indifference. As for motor taxi-cabs there are none in the city, and at Cook's they would not take the responsibility of recommending any automobiles for country excursions.

VII

I linger over these sordid details because I must needs shrink before the mention of that incomparable gallery, the Museo del Prado. I am careful not to call it the greatest gallery in the world, for I think of what the Louvre, the Pitti, and the National Gallery are, and what our own Metropolitan is going to be; but surely the Museo del Prado is incomparable for its peculiar riches. It is part of the autobiographical associations with my Spanish travel that when John Hay, who was not yet, by thirty or forty years, the great statesman he became, but only the breeziest of young Secretaries of Legation, just two weeks from his post in Madrid, blew surprisingly into my little carpenter's box in Cambridge one day, he boasted almost the first thing that the best Titians in the world were in the Prado galleries. I was too lately from Venice in 1867 not to have my inward question whether there could be anywhere a better Titian than the "Assumption," but I loved Hay too much to deny him openly. I said that I had no doubt of it, and when the other day I went to the Prado it was with the wish of finding him perfectly right, triumphantly right. I had been from the first a strong partisan of Titian, and in many a heated argument with Ruskin, unaware of our controversy, I had it out with that most prejudiced partisan of Tintoretto. I always got the better of him, as one does in such dramatizations, where one frames one's opponent's feeble replies for him; but now in the Prado, sadly and strangely enough, I began to wonder if Ruskin might not have tacitly had the better of me all the time. If Hay was right in holding that the best Titians in the world were in the Prado, then I was wrong in having argued for Titian against Tintoretto with Ruskin. I could only wish that I had the "Assumption" there, or some of those senators whose portraits I remembered in the Academy at Venice. The truth is that to my eye he seemed to weaken before the Spanish masters, though I say this, who must confess that I failed to see the room of his great portraits. The Italians who hold their own with the Spaniards are Tintoretto and Veronese; even Murillo was more than a match for Titian in such pictures of his as I saw (I must own that I did not see the best, or nearly all), though properly speaking Murillo is to be known at his greatest only in Seville.

But Velasquez, but Velasquez! In the Prado there is no one else present when he is by, with his Philips and Charleses, and their "villainous hanging of the nether lip," with his hideous court dwarfs and his pretty princes and princesses, his grandees and jesters, his allegories and battles, his pastorals and chases, which fitly have a vast salon to themselves, not only that the spectator may realize at once the rich variety and abundance of the master, but that such lesser lights as Rubens, Titian, Correggio, Giorgione, Tintoretto, Veronese, Rembrandt, Zurbaran, El Greco, Murillo, may not be needlessly dimmed by his surpassing splendor. I leave to those who know painting from the painter's art to appreciate the technical perfection of Velasquez; I take my stand outside of that, and acclaim its supremacy in virtue of that reality which all Spanish art has seemed always to strive for and which in Velasquez it incomparably attains. This is the literary quality which the most untechnical may feel, and which is not clearer to the connoisseur than to the least unlearned.

After Velasquez in the Prado we wanted Goya, and more and more Goya, who is as Spanish and as unlike Velasquez as can very well be. There was not enough Goya abovestairs to satisfy us, but in the Goya room in the basement there was a series of scenes from Spanish life, mostly frolic campestral things, which he did as patterns for tapestries and which came near being enough in their way: the way of that reality which is so far from the reality of Velasquez. There, striving with their strangeness, we found a young American husband and wife who said they were going to Egypt, and seemed so anxious to get out of Spain that they all but asked us which turning to take. They had a Baedeker of 1901. which they had been deceived in at New York as the latest edition, and they were apparently making nothing of the Goyas and were as if lost down there in the basement. They were in doubt about going further in a country which had inveigled them from Gibraltar as far as its capital. They advised with us about Burgos, of all places, and when we said the hotels in Burgos were very cold, they answered, Well they had thought so; and the husband asked, Spain was a pretty good place to cut out, wasn't it? The wife expected that they would find some one in Egypt who spoke English; she had expected they would speak French in Spain, but had been disappointed. They had left their warm things at Gibraltar and were almost frozen already. They were as good and sweet and nice as they could be, and we were truly sorry to part with them and leave them to what seemed to be a mistake which they were not to blame for.

I wish that all Europeans and all Europeanized Americans knew how to value such incorruptible con-nationals, who would, I was sure, carry into the deepest dark of Egypt and over the whole earth undimmed the light of our American single-heartedness. I would have given something to know from just which kind country town and companionable commonwealth of our Union they had come, but I would not have given much, for I knew that they could have come from almost any. In their modest satisfaction with our own order of things, our language, our climate, our weather, they would not rashly condemn those of other lands, but would give them a fair chance; and, if when they got home again, they would have to report unfavorably of the Old World to the Board of Trade or the Woman's Club, it would not be without intelligent reservations, even generous reservations. They would know much more than they knew before they came abroad, and if they had not seen Europe distinctly, but in a glass darkly, still they would have seen it and would be the wiser and none the worse for it. They would still be of their shrewd, pure American ideals, and would judge their recollections as they judged their experiences by them; and I wish we were all as confirmed in our fealty to those ideals.

They were not, clearly enough, of that yet older fashion of Americans who used to go through European galleries buying copies of the masterpieces which the local painters were everywhere making. With this pair the various postal-card reproductions must have long superseded the desire or the knowledge of copies, and I doubt if many Americans of any sort now support that honored tradition. Who, then, does support it? The galleries of the Prado seem as full of copyists as they could have been fifty years ago, and many of them were making very good copies. *I* wish I could say they were working as diligently as copyists used to work, but copyists are now subject to frequent interruptions, not from the tourists but from one another. They used to be all men, mostly grown gray in their pursuit, but now they are both men and women, and younger and the women are sometimes very pretty. In the Prado one saw several pairs of such youth conversing together, forgetful of everything around them, and on terms so very like flirtatious that they could not well be distinguished from them. They were terms that other Spanish girls could enjoy only with a wooden lattice and an iron grille between them and the *novios* outside their windows; and no tourist of the least heart could help rejoicing with them. In the case of one who stood with her little figure slanted and her little head tilted, looking up into the charmed eyes of a tall *rubio*, the tourist could not help rejoicing with the young man too.

The day after our day in the Prado we found ourselves in the Museum of Modern Art through the kind offices of our mistaken cabman when we were looking for the Archaeological Museum. But we were not sorry, for some of the new or newer pictures and sculptures were well worth seeing, though we should never have tried for them. The force of the masters which the ideals of the past held in restraint here raged in unbridled excess: but if I like that force so much, why do I say excess? The new or newer Spanish art likes an immense canvas, say as large as the side of a barn, and it chooses mostly a tragical Spanish history in which it riots with a young sense of power brave to see. There were a dozen of those mighty dramas which I would have liked to bring away with me if I had only had a town hall big enough to put them into after I got them home. There were sculptures as masterful and as mighty as the pictures, but among the paintings there was one that seemed to subdue all the infuriate actions to the calm of its awful repose. This was Gisbert's "Execution of Torrejos and his Companions," who were shot at Malaga in 1830 for a rising in favor of constitutional government. One does not, if one is as wise as I, attempt to depict pictures, and I leave this most heroic, most pathetic, most heart-breaking, most consoling masterpiece for my reader to go and see for himself; it is almost worth going as far as Madrid to see. Never in any picture do I remember the like of those sad, brave, severe faces of the men standing up there to be shot, where already their friends lay dead at their feet. A tumbled top-hat in the foreground had an effect awfuller than a tumbled head would have had.

## VIII

Besides this and those other histories there were energetic portraits and vigorous landscapes in the Modern Museum, where if we had not been bent so on visiting the Archaeological Museum, we would willingly have spent the whole morning. But we were determined to see the Peruvian and Mexican antiquities which we believed must be treasured up in it; and that we might not fail of finding it, I gave one of the custodians a special peseta to take us out on the balcony and show us exactly how to get to it. He was so precise and so full in his directions that we spent the next half-hour in wandering fatuously round the whole region before we stumbled, almost violently, upon it immediately back of the Modern Museum. Will, it be credited that it was then hardly worth seeing for the things we meant to see? The Peruvian and Mexican antiquities were so disappointing that we would hardly look at the Etruscan, Greek, and Roman things which it was so much richer in. To be sure, we had seen and overseen the like of these long before in Italy; but they were admirably arranged in this museum, so that without the eager help of the custodians (which two cents would buy at any turn) we could have found pleasure in them, whereas the Aztec antiquities were mostly copies in plaster and the Inca jewelry not striking.

Before finding the place we had had the help of two policemen and one newsboy and a postman in losing ourselves in the Prado where we mostly sought for it, and with difficulty kept ourselves from being thrust into the gallery there. In Spain a man, or even a boy, does not like to say he does not know where a place is; he is either too proud or too polite to do it, and he will misdirect you without mercy. But the morning was bright, and almost warm, and we should have looked forward to weeks of sunny weather if our experience had not taught us that it would rain in the afternoon, and if greater experience than ours had not instructed us that there would be many days of thick fog now before the climate of Madrid settled itself to the usual brightness of February. We had time to note again in the Paseo Castellana, which is the fashionable drive, that it consists of four rows of acacias and tamarisks and a stretch of lawn, with seats beside it; the rest is bare grasslessness, with a bridle-path on one side and a tram-line on the other. If it had been late afternoon the Paseo would have been filled with the gay world, but being the late forenoon we had to leave it well-nigh unpeopled and go back to our hotel, where the excellent midday breakfast merited the best appetite one could bring to it.

In fact, all the meals of our hotel were good, and of course they were only too superabundant. They were pretty much what they were everywhere in Spain, and they were better everywhere than they were in Granada where we paid most for them. They were appetizing, and not of the cooking which the popular superstition attributes to Spain, where the hotel cooking is not rank with garlic or fiery with pepper, as the untraveled believe. At luncheon in our Madrid hotel we had a liberal choice of eggs in any form, the delicious *arroz a la Valencia,* a kind of risotto, with saffron to savor and color it; veal cutlets or beefsteak, salad, cheese, grapes, pears, and peaches, and often melon; the ever-admirable melon of Spain, which I had learned to like in England. At dinner there were soup, fish, entree, roast beef, lamb, or poultry, vegetables, salad, sweet, cheese, and fruit; and there was pretty poor wine *ad libitum* at both meals. For breakfast there was good and true (or true enough) coffee with rich milk, which if we sometimes doubted it to be goat's milk we were none the worse if none the wiser for, as at dinner we were not either if we unwittingly ate kid for lamb.

There were not many people in the hotel, but the dining-room was filled by citizens who came in with the air of frequenters. They were not people of fashion, as we readily perceived, but kindly-looking mercantile folk, and ladies painted as white as newly calcimined house walls; and all gravely polite. There was one gentleman as large round as a hogshead, with a triple arrangement of fat at the back of his neck which was fascinating. He always bowed when we met (necessarily with his whole back) and he ate with an appetite proportioned to his girth. I could wish still to know who and what he was, for he was a person very much to my mind. So was the head waiter, dark, silent, clean-shaven, who let me use my deplorable Spanish with him, till in the last days he came out with some very fair English which he had been courteously concealing from me. He looked own brother to the room-waiter in our corridor, whose companionship I could desire always to have. One could not be so confident of the sincerity of the little *camarera* who slipped out of the room with a soft, sidelong *"De nada"* at one's thanks for the hot water in the morning; but one could stake one's life on the goodness of this *camarero*. He was not so tall as his leanness made him look; he was of a national darkness of eyes and hair which as imparted to his tertian clean-shavenness was a deep blue. He spoke, with a certain hesitation, a beautiful Castilian, delicately lisping the sibilants and strongly throating the gutturals; and what he said you could believe. He never was out of the way when wanted; he darkled with your boots and shoes in a little closet next your door, and came from it with the morning coffee and rolls. In a stress of frequentation he appeared in evening dress in the dining-room at night, and did honor to the place; but otherwise he was to be seen only in our corridor, or in the cold, dark chamber at the stair head where the *camareras* sat sewing, kept in check by his decorum. Without being explicitly advised of the fact, I am sure he was the best of Catholics, and that he would have burnt me for a heretic if necessary; but he would have done it from his conscience and for my soul's good after I had recanted. He seldom smiled, but when he did you could see it was from his heart.

His contrast, his very antithesis, the joyous concierge, was always smiling, and was every way more like an Italian than a Spaniard. He followed us into the wettest Madrid weather with the sunny rays of his temperament, and welcomed our returning cab with an effulgence that performed the effect of an umbrella in the longish walk from the curbstone to the hotel door, past the grape arbor whose fruit ripened for us only in a single bunch, though he had so confidently prophesied our daily pleasure in it. He seemed at first to be the landlord, and without reference to higher authority he gave us beautiful rooms overlooking the bacchanal vine which would have been filled with sunshine if the weather had permitted. When he lapsed into the concierge, he got us, for five pesetas, so deep and wide a wood-box, covered with crimson cloth, that he was borne out by the fact in declaring that the wood in it would last us as long as we stayed; it was oak wood, hard as iron, and with the bellows that accompanied it we blew the last billet of it into a solid coal by which we drank our last coffee in that hotel. His spirit, his genial hopefulness, reconciled us to the infirmities of the house during the period of transition beginning for it and covering our stay. It was to be rebuilt on a scale out-Ritzing the Ritz; but in the mean while it was not quite the Ritz. There was a time when the elevator-shaft seemed to have tapped the awful sources of the smell in the house of Cervantes at Valladolid, but I do not remember what blameless origin the concierge assigned to the odor, or whether it had anything to do with the horses and the hens which a chance-opened back door showed us stabled in the rear of the hotel's grandiose entrance.

Our tourist clientele, thanks I think to the allure of our concierge for all comers, was most respectable, though there was no public place for people to sit but a small reading-room colder than the baths of Apollo. But when he entered the place it was as if a fire were kindled in the minute stove never otherwise heated, and the old English and French newspapers freshened themselves up to the actual date as nearly as they could. We were mostly, perhaps, Spanish families come from our several provinces for a bit of the season which all Spanish families of civil condition desire more or less of: lean, dark fathers, slender, white-stuccoed daughters, and fat, white-stuccoed mothers; very still-faced, and grave-mannered. We were also a few English, and from time to time a few Americans, but I believe we were not, however worthy, very great-world. The concierge who had so skilfully got us together was instant in our errands and commissions, and when it came to two of us being shut up with colds brought from Burgos it vas he who supplemented the promptness of the apothecaries in sending our medicines and coming himself at times to ask after our welfare.

## IX

In a strange country all the details of life are interesting, and we noticed with peculiar interest that Spain was a country where the prescriptions were written in the vulgar tongue instead of the little Latin in which prescriptions are addressed to the apothecaries of other lands. We were disposed to praise the faculty if not the art for this, but our doctor forbade. He said it was because the Spanish apothecaries were so unlearned that they could not read even so little Latin as the shortest prescription contained. Still I could not think the custom a bad one, though founded on ignorance, and I do not see why it should not have made for the greater safety of those who took the medicine if those who put it up should follow a formula in their native tongue. I know that at any rate we found the Spanish medicines beneficial and were presently suffered to go out-of-doors, but with those severe injunctions against going out after nightfall or opening our lips when we went out by day. It was rather a bother, but it was fine to feel one's self in the classic Madrid tradition of danger from pneumonia and to be of the dignified company of the Spanish gentlemen whom we met with the border of their cloaks over their mouths; like being a character in a *capa y espada* drama.

There was almost as little acted as spoken drama in the streets. I have given my impression of the songlessness of Spain in Madrid as elsewhere, but if there was no street singing there was often street playing by pathetic bands of blind minstrels with guitars and mandolins. The blind abound everywhere in Spain in that profession of street beggary which I always encouraged, believing as I do that comfort in this unbalanced world cannot be too constantly reminded of misery. As the hunchbacks are in Italy, or the wooden peg-legged in England, so the blind are in Spain for number. I could not say how touching the sight of their sightlessness was, or how the remembrance of it makes me wish that I had carried more coppers with me when I set out. I would gladly authorize the reader when he goes to Madrid to do the charity I often neglected; he will be the better man, or even woman, for it; and he need not mind if his beneficiary is occasionally unworthy; he may be unworthy himself; I am sure I was.

But the Spanish street is rarely the theatrical spectacle that the Italian street nearly always is. Now and then there was a bit in Madrid which one would be sorry to have missed, such as the funeral of a civil magistrate, otherwise unknown to me, which I saw pass my cafe window: a most architectural black hearse, under a black roof, drawn by eight black horses, sable-plumed. The hearse was open at the sides, with the coffin fully showing, and a gold-laced *chapeau bras* lying on it. Behind came twenty or twenty-five gentlemen on foot in the modern ineffectiveness of frock-coats and top-hats, and after them eight or ten closed carriages. The procession passed without the least notice from the crowd, which I saw at other times stirred to a flutter of emulation in its small boys by companies of infantry marching to the music of sharply blown bugles. The men were handsomer than Italian soldiers, but not so handsome as the English, and in figure they were not quite the deplorable pigmies one often sees in France. Their bugles, with the rhythmical note which the tram-cars sound, and the guitars and mandolins of the blind minstrels, made the only street music I remember in Madrid.

Between the daily rains, which came in the afternoon, the sun was sometimes very hot, but it was always cool enough indoors. The indoors interests were not the art or story of the churches. The intensest Catholic capital in Christendom is in fact conspicuous in nothing more than the reputed uninterestingness of its churches. I went into one of them, however, with a Spanish friend, and I found it beautiful, most original, and most impressive for its architecture and painting, but I forget which church it was. We were going rather a desultory drive through those less frequented parts of the city which I have mentioned as like a sort of muted Naples: poor folk living much out-of-doors, buying and selling at hucksters' stands and booths, and swarming about the chief market, where the guilty were formerly put to death, but the innocent are now provisioned. Outside the market was not attractive, and what it was within we did not look to see. We went rather to satisfy my wish to see whether the Manzanares is as groveling a stream as the guide-books pretend in their effort to give a just idea of the natural disadvantages of Madrid, as the only great capital without an adequate river. But whether abetted by the arts of my friend or not, the Manzanares managed to conceal itself from me; when we left our carriage and went to look for it, I saw only some pretty rills and falls which it possibly fed and which lent their beauty to the charming up and down hill walks, now a public pleasaunce, but formerly the groves and gardens of the royal palace. Our talk in Spanish from him and Italian from me was of Tolstoy and several esthetic and spiritual interests, and when we remounted and drove back to the city, whom should I see, hard by the King's palace, but those dear Chilians of my heart whom we had left at Valladolid—husband, wife, sister, with the addition of a Spanish lady of very acceptable comeliness, in white gloves, and as blithe as they. In honor of the capital the other ladies wore white gloves too, but the husband and brother still kept the straw hat which I had first known him in at San Sebastian, and which I hope yet to know him by in New York. It was a glad clash of greetings which none of us tried to make coherent or intelligible, and could not if we had tried. They acclaimed their hotel, and I ours; but on both sides I dare say we had our reserves; and then we parted, secure that the kind chances of travel would bring us together again somewhere.

I did not visit the palace, but the Royal Armory I had seen two days before on a gay morning that had not yet sorrowed to the afternoon's rain. At the gate of the palace I fell into the keeping of one of the authorized guides whom I wish I could identify so that I could send the reader to pay him the tip I came short in. It is a pang to think of the repressed disappointment in his face when in a moment of insensate sparing I gave him the bare peseta to which he was officially entitled, instead of the two or three due his zeal and intelligence; and I strongly urge my readers to be on their guard against a mistaken meanness like mine. I can never repair that, for if I went back to the Royal Armory I should not know him by sight, and if I sought among the guides saying I was the stranger who had behaved in that shabby sort, how would that identify me among so many other shabby strangers? He had the intelligence to leave me and the constant companion of these travels to ourselves as we went about that treasury of wonders, but before we got to the armory he stayed us with a delicate gesture outside the court of the palace till a troop for the guard-mounting had gone in. Then he led us across the fine, beautiful quadrangle to the door of the museum, and waited for us there till we came out. By this time the space was brilliant with the confronted bodies of troops, those about to be relieved of guard duty, and those come to relieve them, and our guide got us excellent places where we could see everything and yet be out of the wind which was beginning to blow cuttingly through the gates and colonnades. There were all arms of the service—horse, foot, and artillery; and the ceremony, with its pantomime and parley, was much more impressive than the changing of the colors which I had once seen at Buckingham Palace. The Spanish privates took the business not less seriously than the British, and however they felt the Spanish officers did not allow themselves to look bored. The marching and countermarching was of a refined stateliness, as if the pace were not a goose step but a peacock step; and the music was of an exquisitely plaintive and tender note, which seemed to grieve rather than exult; I believe it was the royal march which they were playing, but I am not versed in *such* matters. Nothing could have been fitter than the quiet beauty of the spectacle, opening through the westward colonnade to the hills and woods of the royal demesne, with yellowing and embrowning trees that billowed from distance to distance. Some day these groves and forests must be for the people's pleasure, as all royal belongings seem finally to be; and in the mean time I did not grudge the landscape to the young king and queen who probably would not have grudged it to me. Our guide valued himself upon our admiration of it; without our special admiration he valued himself upon the impressive buildings of the railway station in the middle distance. I forget whether he followed us out of the quadrangle into the roadway where we had the advantage of some picturesque army wagons, and some wagoners in red-faced jackets and red trousers, and top-boots with heavy fringes of leathern strings. Yet it must have been he who made us aware of a high-walled inclosure where soldiers found worthy of death by court martial could be conveniently shot; though I think we discovered for ourselves the old woman curled up out of the wind in a sentry-box, and sweetly asleep there while the boys were playing marbles on the smooth ground before it. I must not omit the peanut-boaster in front of the palace; it was in the figure of an ocean steamer, nearly as large as the *Lusitania*, and had smoke coming out of the funnel, with rudder and screw complete and doll sailors climbing over the rigging.

But it is impossible to speak adequately of the things in that wonderful armory. If the reader has any pleasure in the harnesses of Spanish kings and captains, from the great Charles the Fifth down through all the Philips and the Charleses, he can glut it there. Their suits begin almost with their steel baby clothes, and adapt themselves almost to their senile decrepitude. There is the horse-litter in which the great emperor was borne to battle, and there is the sword which Isabella the great queen wore; and I liked looking at the lanterns and the flags of the Turkish galleys from the mighty sea-fight cf Lepanto, and the many other trophies won from the Turks. The pavilion of Francis I. taken at Pavia was of no secondary interest, and everywhere was personal and national history told in the weapons and the armor of those who made the history. Perhaps some time the peoples will gather into museums the pens and pencils and chisels of authors and artists, and the old caps and gowns they wore, or the chairs they sat in at their work, or the pianos and violoncellos of famous musicians, or the planes of surpassing carpenters, or the hammers of eminent ironworkers; but these things will never be so picturesque as the equipments with which the military heroes saved their own lives or took others'. We who have never done either must not be unreasonable or impatient. It will be many a long century yet before we are appreciated at the value we now set upon ourselves. In the mean while we do not have such a bad time, and we are not so easily forgotten as some of those princes and warriors.

XI

One of the first errors of our search for the Archaeological Museum, promoted by the mistaken kindness of people we asked the way, found us in the Academy of Fine Arts, where in the company of a fat and flabby Rubens (Susanna, of course, and those filthy Elders) we chanced on a portrait of Goya by himself: a fine head most takingly shrewd. But there was another portrait by him, of the ridiculous Godoy, Prince of the Peace, a sort of handsome, foolish fleshy George Fourthish person looking his character and history: one of the most incredible parasites who ever fattened on a nation. This impossible creature, hated more than feared, and despised more than hated, who misruled a generous people for twenty-five years, throughout the most heroic period of their annals, the low-born paramour of their queen and the beloved friend of the king her husband, who honored and trusted him with the most pathetic single-hearted and simple-minded devotion, could not look all that he was and was not; but in this portrait by Goya he suggested his unutterable worthlessness: a worthlessness which you can only begin to realize by successively excluding all the virtues, and contrasting it with the sort of abandon of faith on the part of the king; this in the common imbecility, the triune madness of the strange group, has its sublimity. In the next room are two pieces of Goya's which recall in their absolute realism another passage of Spanish history with unparalleled effect. They represent, one the accused heretics receiving sentence before a tribunal of the Inquisition, and the other the execution of the sentence, where the victims are mocked by a sort of fools' caps inscribed with the terms of their accusal. Their faces are turned on the spectator, who may forget them if he can.

I had the help of a beautiful face there which Goya had also painted: the face of Moratin, the historian of the Spanish drama whose book had been one of the consolations of exile from Spain in my Ohio village. That fine countenance rapt me far from where I stood, to the village, with its long maple-shaded summer afternoons, and its long lamp-lit winter nights when I was trying to find my way through Moratin's history of the Spanish drama, and somehow not altogether failing, so that fragments of the fact still hang about me. I wish now I could find the way back through it, or even to it, but between me and it there are so many forgotten passes that it would be hopeless trying. I can only remember the pride and joy of finding my way alone through it, and emerging from time to time into the light that glimmered before me. I cannot at all remember whether it was before or after exploring this history that I ventured upon the trackless waste of a volume of the dramatists themselves, where I faithfully began with the earliest and came down to those of the great age when Cervantes and Calderon and Lope de Vega were writing the plays. It was either my misfortune that I read Lope and not Calderon, or that I do not recall reading Calderon at all, and know him only by a charming little play of Madrid life given ten or fifteen years ago by the pupils of the Dramatic Academy in New York. My lasting ignorance of this master was not for want of knowing how great he was, especially from Lowell, who never failed to dwell on it when the talk was of Spanish literature. The fact is I did not get much pleasure out of Lope, but I did enjoy the great tragedy of Cervantes, and such of his comedies as I found in that massive volume.

I did not realize, however, till I saw that play of Calderon's, in New York, how much the Spanish drama lias made Madrid its scene; and until one knows modern Spanish fiction one cannot know how essentially the incongruous city is the capital of the Spanish imagination. Of course the action of Gil Bias largely passes there, but Gil Blas in only adoptively a Spanish novel, and the native picaresque story is oftener at home in the provinces; but since Spanish fiction has come to full consciousness in the work of the modern masters it has resorted more and more to Madrid. If I speak only of Galdos and Valdes by name, it is because I know them best as the greatest of their time; but I fancy the allure of the capital has been felt by every other modern more or less; and if I were a Spanish author I should like to put a story there. If I were a Spaniard at all, I should like to live there a part of the year, or to come up for some sojourn, as the real Spaniards do. In such an event I should be able to tell the reader more about Madrid than I now know. I should not be poorly keeping to hotels and galleries and streets and the like surfaces of civilization; but should be saying all sorts of well-informed and surprising things about my fellow-citizens. As it is I have tried somewhat to say how I think they look to a stranger, and if it is not quite as they have looked to other strangers I do not insist upon my own stranger's impression. There is a great choice of good books about Spain, so that I do not feel bound to add to them with anything like finality.

I have tried to give a sense of the grand-opera effect of the street scene, but I have record of only one passage such as one often sees in Italy where moments of the street are always waiting for transfer to the theater. A pair had posed themselves, across the way from our hotel, against the large closed shutter of a shop which made an admirable background. The woman in a black dress, with a red shawl over her shoulders, stood statuesquely immovable, confronting the middle-class man who, while people went and came about them, poured out his mind to her, with many frenzied gestures, but mostly using one hand for emphasis. He seemed to be telling something rather than asserting himself or accusing her; portraying a past fact or defining a situation; and she waited immovably silent till he had finished. Then she began and warmed to her work, but apparently without anger or prejudice. She talked herself out, as he had talked himself out. He waited and then he left her and crossed to the other corner. She called after him as he kept on down the street. She turned away, but stopped, and turned again and called after him till he passed from sight. Then she turned once more and went her own way. Nobody minded, any more than if they had been two unhappy ghosts invisibly and inaudibly quarreling, but I remained, and remain to this day, afflicted because of the mystery of their dispute.

We did not think there were so many boys, proportionately, or boys let loose, in Madrid as in the other towns we had seen, and we remarked to that sort of foreign sojourner who is so often met in strange cities that the children seemed like little men and women. "Yes," he said, "the Spaniards are not children until they are thirty or forty, and then they never grow up." It was perhaps too epigrammatic, but it may have caught at a fact. From another foreign sojourner I heard that the Catholicism of Spain, in spite of all newspaper appearances to the contrary and many bold novels, is still intense and unyieldingly repressive. But how far the severity of the church characterizes manners it would be hard to say. Perhaps these are often the effect of temperament. One heard more than one saw of the indifference of shop-keepers to shoppers in Madrid; in Andalusia, say especially in Seville, one saw nothing of it. But from the testimony of sufferers it appears to be the Madrid shop-keeper's reasonable conception that if a customer comes to buy something it is because he, or more frequently she, wants it and is more concerned than himself in the transaction. He does not put himself about in serving her, and if she intimates that he is rudely indifferent, and that though she has often come to him before she will never come again, he remains tranquil. From experience I cannot say how true this is; but certainly I failed to awaken any lively emotion in the booksellers of whom I tried to buy some modern plays. It seemed to me that I was vexing them in the Oriental calm which they would have preferred to my money, or even my interest in the new Spanish drama. But in a shop where fans were sold, the shopman, taken in an unguarded moment, seemed really to enter into the spirit of our selection for friends at home; he even corrected my wrong accent in the Spanish word for fan, which was certainly going a great way.

## XII

It was not the weather for fans in Madrid, where it rained that cold rain every afternoon, and once the whole of one day, and we could not reasonably expect to see fans in the hands of ladies in real life so much as in the pictures of ladies on the fans themselves. In fact, I suppose that to see the Madrilenas most in character one should see them in summer which in southern countries is the most characteristic season. Theophile Gautier was governed by this belief when he visited Spain in the hottest possible weather, and left for the lasting delight of the world the record of that *Voyage en Espagne* which he made seventy-two years ago. He then thought the men better dressed than the women at Madrid. Their boots are as "varnished, and they are gloved as white as possible. Their coats are correct and their trousers laudable; but the cravat is not of the same purity, and the waistcoat, that only part of modern dress where the fancy may play, is not always of irreproachable taste." As to the women: "What we understand in France as the Spanish type does not exist in Spain... One imagines usually, when one says *mantilla* and *senora,* an oval, rather long and pale, with large dark eyes, surmounted with brows of velvet, a thin nose, a little arched, a mouth red as a pomegranate, and, above all, a tone warm and golden, justifying the verse of romance, *She is yellow like an orange.* This is the Arab or Moorish type and not the Spanish type. The Madrilenas are charming in the full acceptation of the word; out of four three will be pretty; but they do not answer at all to the idea we have of them. They are small, delicate, well formed, the foot narrow and the figure curved, the bust of a rich contour; but their skin is very white, the features delicate and mobile, the mouth heart-shaped and representing perfectly certain portraits of the Regency. Often they have fair hair, and you cannot take three turns in the Prado without meeting eight blonds of all shades, from the ashen blond to the most vehement red, the red of the beard of Charles V. It is a mistake to think there are no blonds in Spain. Blue eyes abound there, but they are not so much liked as the black."

Is this a true picture of the actual Madrilenas? What I say is that seventy-two years have passed since it was painted and the originals have had time to change. What I say is that it was nearly always raining, and I could not be sure. What I say, above all, is that I am not a Frenchman of the high Romantic moment and that what I chiefly noticed was how beautiful the mantilla was whether worn by old or young, how fit, how gentle, how winning. I suppose that the women we saw walking in it were never of the highest class; who would be driving except when we saw them going to church. But they were often of the latest fashion, with their feet hobbled by the narrow skirts, of which they lost the last poignant effect by not having wide or high or slouch or swashbuckler hats on; they were not top-heavy. What seems certain is that the Spanish women are short and slight or short and fat. I find it recorded that when a young English couple came into the Royal Armory the girl looked impossibly tall and fair.

The women of the lower classes are commonly handsome and carry themselves finely; their heads are bare, even of mantillas, and their skirts are ample. When it did not rain they added to the gaiety of the streets, and when it did to their gloom. Wet or dry the streets were always thronged; nobody, apparently, stayed indoors who could go out, and after two days' housing, even with a fire to air and warm our rooms, we did not wonder at the universal preference. As I have said, the noise that we heard in the streets was mainly the clatter of shoes and hoofs, but now and then there were street cries besides those I have noted. There was in particular a half-grown boy in our street who had a flat basket decorated with oysters at his feet, and for long hours of the day and dark he cried them incessantly. I do not know that he ever sold them or cared; his affair was to cry them.

# VI. A NIGHT AND DAY IN TOLEDO

If you choose to make your visit to Toledo an episode of your stay in Madrid, you have still to choose between going at eight in the morning and arriving back at five in the evening, or going at five one evening and coming back at the same hour the next. In either case you will have two hours' jolting each way over the roughest bit of railroad in the world, and if your *mozo*, before you could stop him, has selected for your going a compartment over the wheels, you can never be sure that he has done worse for you than you will have done for yourself when you come back in a compartment between the trucks. However you go or come, you remain in doubt whether you have been jolting over rails jointed at every yard, or getting on without any track over a cobble-stone pavement. Still, if the compartment is wide and well cushioned, as it is in Spain nearly always, with free play for your person between roof and floor and wall and wall; and if you go at five o'clock you have from your windows, as long as the afternoon light lasts, while you bound and rebound, glimpses of far-stretching wheat-fields, with nearer kitchen-gardens rich in beets and cabbages, alternating with purple and yellow patches of vineyard.

I

I find from my ever-faithful note-book that the landscape seemed to grow drearier as we got away from Madrid, but this may have been the effect of the waning day: a day which at its brightest had been dim from recurrent rain and incessant damp. The gloom was not relieved by the long stops at the frequent stations, though the stops were good for getting one's breath, and for trying to plan greater control over one's activities when the train should be going on again. The stations themselves were not so alluring that we were not willing to get away from them; and we were glad to get away from them by train, instead of by mule-team over the rainy levels to the towns that glimmered along the horizon two or three miles off. There had been nothing to lift the heart in the sight of two small boys ready perched on one horse, or of a priest difficultly mounting another in his long robe. At the only station which I can remember having any town about it a large number of our passengers left the train, and I realized that they were commuters like those who might have been leaving it at some soaking suburb of Long Island or New Jersey. In the sense of human brotherhood which the fact inspired I was not so lonely as I might have been, when we resumed our gloomy progress, with all that punctilio which custom demands of a Spanish way-train. First the station-master rings a bell of alarming note hanging on the wall, and the *mozos* run along the train shutting the car doors. After an interval some other official sounds a pocket whistle, and then there is still time for a belated passenger to find his car and scramble aboard. When the ensuing pause prolongs itself until you think the train has decided to remain all day, or all night, and several passengers have left it again, the locomotive rouses itself and utters a peremptory screech. This really means going, but your doubt has not been fully overcome when the wheels begin to bump under your compartment, and you set your teeth and clutch your seat, and otherwise prepare yourself for the renewal of your acrobatic feats. I may not get the order of the signals for departure just right, but I am sure of their number. Perhaps the Sud-Express starts with less, but the Sud-Express is partly French.

It had been raining intermittently all day; now that the weary old day was done the young night took up the work and vigorously devoted itself to a steady downpour which, when we reached our hotel in Toledo, had taken the role of a theatrical tempest, with sudden peals of thunder and long loud bellowing reverberations and blinding flashes of lightning, such as the wildest stage effects of the tempest in the Catskills when Rip Van Winkle is lost would have been nothing to. Foreboding the inner chill of a Spanish hotel on such a day, we had telegraphed for a fire in our rooms, and our eccentricity had been interpreted in spirit as well as in letter. It was not the habitual hotel omnibus which met us at the station, but a luxurious closed carriage commanded by an interpreter who intuitively opened our compartment door, and conveyed us dry and warm to our hotel, in every circumstance of tender regard for our comfort, during the slow, sidelong uphill climb to the city midst details of historic and romantic picturesqueness which the lightning momently flashed in sight. From our carriage we passed as in a dream between the dress-coated head waiter and the skull-capped landlord who silently and motionlessly received us in the Gothic doorway, and mounted by a stately stair from a beautiful glass-roofed *patio*, columned round with airy galleries, to the rooms from which a smoky warmth gushed out to welcome us.

The warmth was from the generous blaze kindled in the fireplace against our coming, and the smoke was from the crevices in a chimneypiece not sufficiently calked with newspapers to keep the smoke going up the flue. The fastidious may think this a defect in our perfect experience, but we would not have had it otherwise, if we could, and probably we could not. We easily assumed that we were in the palace of some haughty hidalgo, adapted to the uses of a modern hotel, with a magical prevision which need not include the accurate jointing of a chimneypiece. The storm bellowed and blazed outside, the rain strummed richly on the *patio* roof which the lightning illumined, and as we descended that stately stair, with its walls ramped and foliaged over with heraldic fauna and flora, I felt as never before the disadvantage of not being still fourteen years old.

But you cannot be of every age at once and it was no bad thing to be presently sitting down in my actual epoch at one of those excellent Spanish dinners which no European hotel can surpass and no American hotel can equal. It may seem a descent from the high horse, the winged steed of dreaming, to have been following those admirable courses with unflagging appetite, as it were on foot, but man born of woman is hungry after such a ride as ours from Madrid; and it was with no appreciable loss to our sense of enchantment that we presently learned from our host, waiting skull-capped in the *patio,* that we were in no real palace of an ancient hidalgo, but were housed as we found ourselves by the fancy of a rich nobleman of Toledo whom the whim had taken to equip his city with a hotel of poetic perfection. I am afraid I have forgotten his name; perhaps I should not have the right to parade it here if I remembered it; but I cannot help saluting him brother in imagination, and thanking him for one of the rarest pleasures that travel, even Spanish travel, has given me.

II

One must recall the effect of such a gentle fantasy as his with some such emotion as one recalls a pleasant tale unexpectedly told when one feared a repetition of stale commonplaces, and I now feel a pang of retroactive self-reproach for not spending the whole evening after dinner in reading up the story of that most storied city where this Spanish castle received us. What better could I have done in the smoky warmth of our hearth-fire than to con, by the light of the electric bulb dangling overhead, its annals in some such voluntarily quaint and unconsciously old-fashioned volume as Irving's *Legends of the Conquest of Spain;* or to read in some such (if there is any such other) imperishably actual and unfadingly brilliant record of impressions as Gautier's *Voyage en Espagne,* the miserably tragic tale of that poor, wicked, over-punished last of the Gothic kings, Don Roderick? It comes to much the same effect in both, and as I knew it already from the notes to Scott's poem of Don Roderick, which I had read sixty years before in the loft of our log cabin (long before the era of my unguided Spanish studies), I found it better to go to bed after a day which had not been without its pains as well as pleasures. I could recall the story well enough for all purposes of the imagination as I found it in the fine print of those notes, and if I could believe the reader did not know it I would tell him now how this wretched Don Roderick betrayed the daughter of Count Julian whom her father had intrusted to him here in his capital of Toledo, when, with the rest of Spain, it had submitted to his rule. That was in the eighth century when the hearts of kings were more easily corrupted by power than perhaps in the twentieth; and it is possible that there was a good deal of politics mixed up with Count Julian's passion for revenge on the king, when he invited the Moors to invade his native land and helped them overrun it. The conquest, let me remind the reader, was also abetted by the Jews who had been flourishing mightily under the Gothic anarchy, but whom Don Roderick had reduced to a choice between exile or slavery when he came to full power. Every one knows how in a few weeks the whole peninsula fell before the invaders. Toledo fell after the battle of Guadalete, where even the Bishop of Seville fought on their side, and Roderick was lastingly numbered among the missing, and was no doubt killed, as nothing has since been heard of him. It was not until nearly three hundred years afterward that the Christians recovered the city. By this time they were no longer Arians, but good Catholics; so good that Philip II. himself, one of the best of Catholics (as I have told), is said to have removed the capital to Madrid because he could not endure the still more scrupulous Catholicity of the Toledan Bishop.

Nobody is obliged to believe this, but I should be sorry if any reader of mine questioned the insurpassable antiquity of Toledo, as attested by a cloud of chroniclers. Theophile Gautier notes that "the most moderate place the epoch of its foundation before the Deluge," and he does not see why they do not put the time "under the pre-Adamite kings, some years before the creation of the world. Some attribute the honor of laying its first stone to Jubal, others to the Greek; some to the Roman consuls Tolmor and Brutus; some to the Jews who entered Spain with Nebuchadnezzar, resting their theory on the etymology of Toledo, which comes from Toledoth, a Hebrew word signifying generations, because the Twelve Tribes had helped to build and people it."

III

Even if the whole of this was not accurate, it offered such an embarrassing abundance to the choice that I am glad I knew little or nothing of the antagonistic origins when I opened my window to the sunny morning which smiled at the notion of the overnight tempest, and lighted all the landscape on that side of the hotel. The outlook was over vast plowed lands red as Virginia or New Jersey fields, stretching and billowing away from the yellow Tagus in the foreground to the mountain-walled horizon, with far stretches of forest in the middle distance. What riches of gray roof, of white wall, of glossy green, or embrowning foliage in the city gardens the prospect included, one should have the brush rather than the pen to suggest; or else one should have an inexhaustible ink-bottle with every color of the chromatic scale in it to pour the right tints. Mostly, however, I should say that the city of Toledo is of a mellow gray, and the country of Toledo a rich orange. Seen from any elevation the gray of the town made me think of Genoa; and if the reader's knowledge does not enable him, to realize it from this association, he had better lose no time in going to Genoa.

I myself should prefer going again to Toledo, where we made only a day's demand upon the city's wealth of beauty when a lifetime would hardly have exhausted it. Yet I would not counsel any one to pass his whole life in Toledo unless he was sure he could bear the fullness of that beauty. Add insurpassable antiquity, add tragedy, add unendurable orthodoxy, add the pathos of hopeless decay, and I think I would rather give a day than a lifetime to Toledo. Or I would like to go back and give another day to it and come every year and give a day. This very moment, instead of writing of it in a high New York flat and looking out on a prospect incomparably sky-scrapered, I would rather be in that glass-roofed *patio* of our histrionic hotel, engaging the services of one of the most admirable guides who ever fell to the lot of mortal Americans, while much advised by our skull-capped landlord to shun the cicerone of another hotel as "an Italian man," with little or no English.

As soon as we appeared outside the beggars of Toledo swarmed upon us; but I hope it was not from them I formed the notion that the beauty of the place was architectural and not personal, though these poor things were as deplorably plain as they were obviously miserable. The inhabitants who did not ask alms were of course in the majority, but neither were these impressive in looks or bearing. Rather, I should say, their average was small and dark, and in color of eyes and hair as well as skin they suggested the African race that held Toledo for four centuries. Neither here nor anywhere else in Spain are there any traces of the Jews who helped bring the Arabs in; once for all, that people have been banished so perfectly that they do not show their noses anywhere. Possibly they exist, but they do not exist openly, any more than the descendants of the Moorish invaders practise their Moslem rites. As for the beggars, to whom I return as they constantly returned to us, it did not avail to do them charity; that by no means dispersed them; the thronging misery and mutilation in the lame, the halt and the blind, was as great at our coming back to our hotel as our going out of it. They were of every age and sex; the very school-children left their sports to chance our charity; and it is still with a pang that I remember the little girl whom we denied a copper when she was really asking for a *florecito* out of the nosegay that one of us carried. But how could we know that it was a little flower and not a "little dog" she wanted?

There was something vividly spectacular in the square, by no means large, which we came into on turning the corner from our hotel. It was a sort of market-place as well as business place, and it looked as if it might be the resort at certain hours of the polite as well as the impolite leisure of a city of leisure not apparently overworked in any of its classes. But at ten o'clock in the morning it was empty enough, and after a small purchase at one of the shops we passed from it without elbowing or being elbowed, and found ourselves at the portal of that ancient *posada* where Cervantes is said to have once sojourned at least long enough to write one of his *Exemplary Novels*. He was of such a ubiquitous habit that if we had visited every city of Spain we should have found some witness of his stay, but I do not believe we could have found any more satisfactory than this. It is verified by a tablet in its outer wall, and within it is convincingly a *posada* of his time. It has a large low-vaulted interior, with the carts and wagons of the muleteers at the right of the entrance, and beyond these the stalls of the mules where they stood chewing their provender, and glancing uninterestedly round at the intruders, for plainly we were not of the guests who frequent the place. Such, for a chamber like those around and behind the stalls, on the same earthen level, pay five cents of our money a day; they supply their own bed and board and pay five cents more for the use of a fire.

Some guests were coming and going in the dim light of the cavernous spaces; others were squatting on the ground before their morning meal. An endearing smoke-browned wooden gallery went round three sides of the *patio* overhead; half-way to this at one side rose an immense earthen water jar, dim red; piles of straw mats, which were perhaps the bedding of the guests, heaped the ground or hung from the gallery; and the guests, among them a most beautiful youth, black as Africa, but of a Greek perfection of profile, regarded us with a friendly indifference that contrasted strikingly with the fixed stare of the bluish-gray hound beside one of the wagons. He had a human effect of having brushed his hair from his strange grave eyes, and of a sad, hopeless puzzle in the effort to make us out. If he was haunted by some inexplicable relation in me to the great author whose dog he undoubtedly had been in a retroactive incarnation, and was thinking to question me of that ever unfulfilled boyish self-promise of writing the life of Cervantes, I could as successfully have challenged him to say how and where in such a place as that an Exemplary Novelist could have written even the story of *The Illustrious Scullion.* But he seemed on reflection not to push the matter with me, and I left him still lost in his puzzle while I came away in mine. Whether Cervantes really wrote one of his tales there or not, it is certain that he could have exactly studied from that *posada* the setting of the scene for the episode of the enchanted castle in *Don Quixote,* where the knight suffered all the demoniacal torments which a jealous and infuriate muleteer knew how to inflict.

IV

Upon the whole I am not sure that I was more edified by the cathedral of Toledo, though I am afraid to own it, and must make haste to say that it is a cathedral surpassing in some things any other cathedral in Spain. Chiefly it surpasses them in the glory of that stupendous *retablo* which fills one whole end of the vast fane, and mounting from floor to roof, tells the Christian story with an ineffable fullness of dramatic detail, up to the tragic climax of the crucifixion, the *Calvario,* at the summit. Every fact of it fixes itself the more ineffaceably in the consciousness because of that cunningly studied increase in the stature of the actors, who always appear life-size in spite of their lift from level to level above the spectator. But what is the use, what *is* the use? Am I to abandon the young and younger wisdom with which I have refrained in so many books from attempting the portrayal of any Italian, any English church, and fall into the folly, now that I am old, of trying to say again in words what one of the greatest of Spanish churches says in form, in color? Let me rather turn from that vainest endeavor to the trivialities of sight-seeing which endear the memory of monuments and make the experience of them endurable. The beautiful choir, with its walls pierced in gigantic filigree, might have been art or not, as one chose, but the three young girls who smiled and whispered with the young man near it were nature, which there could be no two minds about. They were pathetically privileged there to a moment of the free interplay of youthful interests and emotions which the Spanish convention forbids less in the churches than anywhere else.

The Spanish religion is, in fact, kind to the young in many ways, and on our way to the cathedral we had paused at a shrine of the Virgin in appreciation of her friendly offices to poor girls wanting husbands; they have only to drop a pin inside the grating before her and draw a husband, tall for a large pin and short for a little one; or if they can make their offering in coin, their chances of marrying money are good. The Virgin is always ready to befriend her devotees, and in the cathedral near that beautiful choir screen she has a shrine above the stone where she alighted when she brought a chasuble to St. Ildefonso (she owed him something for his maintenance of her Immaculate Conception long before it was imagined a dogma) and left the print of her foot in the pavement. The fact is attested by the very simple yet absolute inscription:

> *Quando la Reina del Cielo*
>
> *Puso los pies en el suelo,*
>
> *En esta piedra los puso,*

or as my English will have it:

> *When the Queen of Heaven put*
>
> *Upon the earth her foot,*
>
> *She put it on this stone*

and left it indelible there, so that now if you thrust your finger through the grille and touch the place you get off three hundred years of purgatory: not much in the count of eternity, but still something.

We saw a woman and a priest touching it as we stood by and going away enviably comforted; but we were there as connoisseurs, not as votaries; and we were trying to be conscious solely of the surpassing grandeur and beauty of the cathedral. Here as elsewhere in Spain the passionate desire of the race to realize a fact in art expresses itself gloriously or grotesquely according to the occasion. The rear of the chorus is one vast riot of rococo sculpture, representing I do not know what mystical event; but down through the midst of the livingly studied performance a mighty angel comes plunging, with his fine legs following his torso through the air, like those of a diver taking a header into the water. Nothing less than the sublime touch of those legs would have satisfied the instinct from which and for which the artist worked; they gave reality to the affair in every part.

I wish I could give reality to every part of that most noble, that most lovably beautiful temple. We had only a poor half-hour for it, and we could not do more than flutter the pages of the epic it was and catch here and there a word, a phrase: a word writ in architecture or sculpture, a phrase richly expressed in gold and silver and precious marble, or painted in the dyes of the dawns and sunsets which used to lend themselves so much more willingly to the arts than they seem to do now. From our note-books I find that this cathedral of Toledo appeared more wonderful to one of us than the cathedral of Burgos; but who knows? It might have been that the day was warmer and brighter and had not yet shivered and saddened to the cold rain it ended in. At any rate the vast church filled itself more and more with the solemn glow in which we left it steeped when we went out and took our dreamway through the narrow, winding, wandering streets that seemed to lure us where they would. One of them climbed with us to the Alcazar, which is no longer any great thing to see in itself, but which opens a hospitable space within its court for a prospect of so much of the world around Toledo, the world of yellow river and red fields and blue mountains, and white-clouded azure sky, that we might well have mistaken it for the whole earth. In itself, as I say, the Alcazar is no great thing for where it is, but if we had here in New York an Alcazar that remembered historically back through French, English, Arabic, Gothic. Roman, and Carthaginian occupations to the inarticulate Iberian past we should come, I suppose, from far and near to visit it. Now, however, after gasping at its outlook, we left it hopelessly, and lost ourselves, except for our kindly guide, in the crooked little stony lanes, with the sun hot on our backs and the shade cool in our faces. There were Moorish bits and suggestions in the white walls and the low flat roofs of the houses, but these were not so jealous of their privacy as such houses were once meant to be. Through the gate of one we were led into a garden of simple flowers belted with a world-old parapet, over which we could look at a stretch of the Gothic wall of King Wamba's time, before the miserable Roderick won and lost his kingdom. A pomegranate tree, red with fruit, overhung us, and from the borders of marigolds and zinnias and German clover the gray garden-wife gathered a nosegay for us. She said she was three *duros* and a half old, as who should say three dollars and a half, and she had a grim amusement in so translating her seventy years.

V

It was hard by her cottage that we saw our first mosque, which had begun by being a Gothic church, but had lost itself in paynim hands for centuries, in spite of the lamp always kept burning in it. Then one day the Cid came riding by, and his horse, at sight of a white stone in the street pavement, knelt down and would not budge till men came and dug through the wall of the mosque and disclosed this indefatigable lamp in the church. We expressed our doubt of the man's knowing so unerringly that the horse meant them to dig through the mosque. "If you can believe the rest I think you can believe that," our guide argued.

He was like so many taciturn Spaniards, not inconversable, and we had a pleasure in his unobtrusive intelligence which I should be sorry to exaggerate. He supplied us with such statistics of his city as we brought away with us, and as I think the reader may join me in trusting, and in regretting that I did not ask more. Still it is something to have learned that in Toledo now each family lives English fashion in a house of its own, while in the other continental cities it mostly dwells in a flat. This is because the population has fallen from two hundred thousand to twenty thousand, and the houses have not shared its decay, but remain habitable for numbers immensely beyond those of the households. In the summer the family inhabits the first floor which the *patio* and the subterranean damp from the rains keep cool; in the winter it retreats to the upper chambers which the sun is supposed to warm, and which are at any rate dry even on cloudy days. The rents would be thought low in New York: three dollars a month get a fair house in Toledo; but wages are low, too; three dollars a month for a manservant and a dollar and a half for a maid. If the Toledans from high to low are extravagant in anything it is dress, but dress for the outside, not the inside, which does not show, as our guide satirically explained. They scrimp themselves in food and they pay the penalty in lessened vitality; there is not so much fever as one might think; but there is a great deal of consumption; and as we could not help seeing everywhere in the streets there were many blind, who seemed oftenest to have suffered from smallpox. The beggars were not so well dressed as the other classes, but I saw no such delirious patchwork as at Burgos. On the other hand, there were no idle people who were fashionably dressed; no men or women who looked great-world.

Perhaps if the afternoon had kept the sunny promise of the forenoon they might have been driving in the Paseo, a promenade which Toledo has like every Spanish city; but it rained and we did not stop at the Paseo which looked so pleasant.

The city, as so many have told and as I hope the reader will imagine, is a network of winding and crooked lanes, which the books say are Moorish, but which are medieval like those of every old city. They nowhere lend themselves to walking for pleasure, and the houses do not open their *patios* to the passer with Andalusian expansiveness; they are in fact of a quite Oriental reserve. I remember no dwellings of the grade, quite, of hovels; but neither do there seem to be many palaces or palatial houses in my hurried impression. Whatever it may be industrially or ecclesiastically, Toledo is now socially provincial and tending to extinction. It is so near Madrid that if I myself were living in Toledo I would want to live in Madrid, and only return for brief sojourns to mourn my want of a serious object in life; at Toledo it must be easy to cherish such an object.

Industrially, of course, one associates it with the manufacture of the famous Toledo blades, which it is said are made as wonderful as ever, and I had a dim idea of getting a large one for decorative use in a New York flat. But the foundry is a mile out of town, and I only got so far as to look at the artists who engrave the smaller sort in shops open to the public eye; and my purpose dwindled to the purchase of a little pair of scissors, much as a high resolve for the famous marchpane of Toledo ended in a piece of that pastry about twice the size of a silver dollar. Not all of the twenty thousand people of Toledo could be engaged in these specialties, and I owe myself to blame for not asking more about the local industries; but it is not too late for the reader, whom I could do no greater favor than sending him there, to repair my deficiency. In self-defense I urge my knowledge of a military school in the Alcazar, where and in the street leading up to it we saw some companies of the comely and kindly-looking cadets. I know also that there are public night schools where those so minded may study the arts and letters, as our guide was doing in certain directions. Now that there are no longer any Jews in Toledo, and the Arabs to whom they betrayed the Gothic capital have all been Christians or exiles for many centuries, we felt that we represented the whole alien element of the place; there seemed to be at least no other visitors of our lineage or language.

## VI

We were going to spend the rest of the day driving out through the city into the country beyond the Tagus, and we drove off in our really splendid turnout through swarms of beggars whose prayers our horses' bells drowned when we left them to their despair at the hotel door. At the moment of course we believe that it was a purely dramatic misery which the wretched creatures represented; but sometimes I have since had moments of remorse in which I wish I had thrown big and little dogs broadcast among them. They could not all have been begging for the profit or pleasure of it; some of them were imaginably out of work and worthily ragged as I saw them, and hungry as I begin to fear them. I am glad now to think that many of them could not see with their poor blind eyes the face which I hardened against them, as we whirled away to the music of our horses' bells.

The bells pretty well covered our horses from their necks to their haunches, a pair of gallant grays urged to their briskest pace by the driver whose short square face and humorous mouth and eyes were a joy whenever we caught a glimpse of them. He was one of those drivers who know everybody; he passed the time of day with all the men we met, and he had a joking compliment for all the women, who gladdened at sight of him from the thresholds where they sat sewing or knitting: such a driver as brings a gay world to home-keeping souls and leaves them with the feeling of having been in it. I would have given much more than I gave the beggars in Toledo to know just in what terms he and his universal acquaintance bantered each other; but the terms might sometimes have been rather rank. Something, at any rate, qualified the air, which I fancied softer than that of Madrid, with a faint recurrent odor, as if in testimony of the driver's derivation from those old rancid Christians, as the Spaniards used to call them, whose lineage had never been crossed with Moorish blood. If it was merely something the carriage had acquired from the stable, still it was to be valued for its distinction in a country of many smells; and I would not have been without it.

When we crossed the Tagus by a bridge which a company of workmen willingly paused from mending to let us by, and remained standing absent-mindedly aside some time after we had passed, we found ourselves in a scene which I do not believe was ever surpassed for spectacularity in any theater. I hope this is not giving the notion of something fictitious in it; I only mean that here Nature was in one of her most dramatic moods. The yellow torrent swept through a deep gorge of red earth, which on the farther side climbed in precipitous banks, cleft by enormous fissures, or chasms rather, to the wide plateau where the gray city stood. The roofs of mellow tiles formed a succession of levels from which the irregular towers and pinnacles of the churches stamped themselves against a sky now filled with clouds, but in an air so clear that their beautiful irregularities and differences showed to one very noble effect. The city still looked the ancient capital of the two hundred thousand souls it once embraced, and in its stony repair there was no hint of decay.

On our right, the road mounted through country wild enough at times, but for the most part comparatively friendly, with moments of being almost homelike. There were slopes which, if massive always, were sometimes mild and were gray with immemorial olives. In certain orchard nooks there were apricot trees, yellowing to the autumn, with red-brown withered grasses tangling under them. Men were gathering the fruit of the abounding cactuses in places, and in one place a peasant was bearing an arm-load of them to a wide stone pen in the midst of which stood a lordly black pig, with head lifted and staring, indifferent to cactuses, toward Toledo. His statuesque pose was of a fine hauteur, and a more imaginative tourist than I might have fancied him lost in a dream of the past, piercing beyond the time of the Iberian autochtons to those prehistoric ages

*When wild in woods the noble savage ran,*

pursuing or pursued by his tusked and bristled ancestor, and then slowly reverting through the different invasions and civilizations to that signal moment when, after three hundred Moslem years, Toledo became Christian again forever, and pork resumed its primacy at the table. Dark, mysterious, fierce, the proud pig stood, a figure made for sculpture; and if he had been a lion, with the lion's royal ideal of eating rather than feeding the human race, the reader would not have thought him unworthy of literature; I have seldom seen a lion that looked worthier of it.

We must have met farmer-folk, men and women, on our way and have seen their white houses farther or nearer. But mostly the landscape was lonely and at times nightmarish, as the Castilian landscape has a trick of being, and remanded us momently to the awful entourage of our run from Valladolid to Madrid. We were glad to get back to the Tagus, which if awful is not grisly, but wherever it rolls its yellow flood lends the landscape such a sublimity that it was no esthetic descent from the high perch of that proud pig to the mighty gorge through which, geologically long ago, the river had torn its way. When we drove back the bridge-menders stood aside for us while we were yet far off, and the women came to their doorways at the sound of our bells for another exchange of jokes with our driver. By the time a protracted file of mules had preceded us over the bridge, a brisk shower had come up, and after urging our grays at their topmost speed toward the famous church of San Juan de los Reyes Catolicos, we still had to run from our carriage door through the rain.

Happily the portal was in the keeping of one of those authorized beggars who guard the gates of heaven everywhere in that kind country, and he welcomed us so eagerly from the wet that I could not do less than give him a big dog at once. In a moment of confusion I turned about, and taking him for another beggar, I gave him another big dog; and when we came out of the church he had put off his cap and arranged so complete a disguise with the red handkerchief bravely tied round his head, that my innocence was again abused, and once more a big dog passed between us. But if the merit of the church might only be partially attributed to him, he was worth the whole three. The merit of the church was incalculable, for it was meant to be the sepulcher of the Catholic Kings, who were eventually more fitly buried in the cathedral at Granada, in the heart of their great conquest; and it is a most beautiful church, of a mingled Saracenic plateresque Gothic, as the guide-books remind me, and extravagantly baroque as I myself found it. I personally recall also a sense of chill obscurity and of an airy gallery wandering far aloof in the upper gloom, which remains overhead with me still, and the yet fainter sense of the balconies crowning like capitals the two pillars fronting the high altar. I am now sorry for our haste, but one has not so much time for enjoying such churches in their presence as for regretting them in their absence. One should live near them, and visit them daily, if one would feel their beauty in its recondite details; to have come three thousand miles for three minutes of them is no way of making that beauty part of one's being, and I will not pretend that I did in this case. What I shall always maintain is that I had a living heartache from the sight of that space on the façade of this church which is overhung with the chains of the Christian captives rescued from slavery among the Moors by the Catholic Kings in their conquest of Granada. They were not only the memorials of the most sorrowful fact, but they represented the misery of a thousand years of warfare in which the prisoners on either side suffered in chains for being Moslems or being Christians. The manacles and the fetters on the church front are merely decorative to the glance, but to the eye that reads deeper, how structural in their tale of man's inhumanity to man! How heavily they had hung on weary limbs! How pitilessly they had eaten through bleeding ulcers to the bone! Yet they were very, very decorative, as the flowers are that bloom on battle-fields.

Even with only a few minutes of a scant quarter-hour to spare, I would not have any one miss seeing the cloister, from which the Catholic Kings used to enter the church by the gallery to those balcony capitals, but which the common American must now see by going outside the church. The cloister is turned to the uses of an industrial school, as we were glad to realize because our guide, whom we liked so much, was a night student there. It remains as beautiful and reverend as if it were of no secular use, full of gentle sculptures, with a garden in the middle, raised above the pavement with a border of thin tiles, and flower-pots standing on their coping, all in the shadow of tall trees, overhanging a deep secret-keeping well. From this place, where you will be partly sheltered from the rain, your next profitable sally through the storm will be to Santa Maria la Blanca, once the synagogue of the richest Jews of Toledo, but now turned church in spite of its high authorization as a place of Hebrew worship. It was permitted them to build it because they declared they were of that tribe of Israel which, when Caiaphas, the High Priest, sent round to the different tribes for their vote whether Jesus should live or die, alone voted that He should live. Their response, as Theophile Gautier reports from the chronicles, is preserved in the Vatican with a Latin version of the Hebrew text. The fable, if it is a fable, has its pathos; and I for one can only lament the religious zeal to which the preaching of a fanatical monk roused the Christian neighborhood in the fifteenth century, to such excess that these kind Jews were afterward forbidden their worship in the place. It is a very clean-looking, cold-looking white monument of the Catholic faith, with a *retablo* attributed to Berruguete, and much plateresque Gothic detail mingled with Byzantine ornament, and Moorish arabesquing and the famous stucco honeycombing which we were destined at Seville and Granada to find almost sickeningly sweet. Where the Rabbis read the law from their pulpit the high altar stands, and the pious populace has for three hundred years pushed the Jews from the surrounding streets, where they had so humbled their dwellings to the lowliest lest they should rouse the jealousy of their sleepless enemies.

VII

When we had visited this church there remained only the house of the painter known as El Greco, for whom we had formed such a distaste, because of the long features of the faces in his pictures, that our guide could hardly persuade us his house was worth seeing. Now I am glad he prevailed with us, for we have since come to find a peculiar charm in these long features and the characteristic coloring of El Greco's pictures. The little house full of memorials and the little garden full of flowers, which ought to have been all forget-me-nots, were entirely delightful. As every one but I knew, and even I now know, he was born a Greek with the name of Theotocopuli, and studied tinder Titian till he found his account in a manner of his own, making long noses and long chins and high narrow foreheads in ashen gray, and at last went mad in the excess of his manner. The house has been restored by the Marquis de la Vega, according to his notion of an old Spanish house, and has the pleasantest small *patio* in the world, looked down into from a carved wooden gallery, with a pavement of red tiles interset with Moorish tiles of divers colors. There are interesting pictures everywhere, and on one wall the certificate of the owner's membership in the Hispanic Society of America, which made me feel at home because it was signed with the name of an American friend of mine, who is repressed by prosperity from being known as a poet and one of the first Spanish scholars of any time.

The whole place is endearingly homelike and so genuinely hospitable that we almost sat down to luncheon in the kitchen with the young Spanish king who had lunched with the Marquis there a few weeks before. There was a veranda outside where we could linger till the rain held up, and look into the garden where the flowers ought to have been forget-me-nots, but were as usual mostly marigolds and zinnias. They crowded round tile-edged pools, and other flowers bloomed in pots on the coping of the garden-seats built up of thin tiles carved on their edges to an inward curve. It is strongly believed that there are several stories under the house, and the Marquis is going some day to dig them up or out to the last one where the original Jewish owner of the house is supposed to have hid his treasure. In the mean time we could look across the low wall that belted the garden in, to a vacant ground a little way off where some boys were playing with a wagon they had made. They had made it out of an oblong box, with wheels so rudely and imperfectly rounded, that they wabbled fearfully and at times gave way under the body; just as they did with the wagons that the boys I knew seventy years ago used to make.

I became so engrossed in the spectacle, so essentially a part of the drama, that I did not make due account of some particulars of the subterranean six stories of El Greco's house. There must have been other things worth seeing in Toledo, thousands of others, and some others we saw, but most we missed, and many I do not remember. It was now coming the hour to leave Toledo, and we drove back to our enchanted castle for our bill, and for the omnibus to the station. I thought for some time that there was no charge for the fire, or even the smoke we had the night before, but my eyes were holden from the item which I found later, by seeing myself addressed as Milor. I had never been addressed as a lord in any bill before, but I reflected that in the proud old metropolis of the Goths I could not be saluted as less, and I gladly paid the bill, which observed a golden mean between cheapness and dearness, and we parted good friends with our host, and better with our guide, who at the last brought out an English book, given him by an English friend, about the English cathedrals. He was fine, and I could not wish any future traveler kinder fortune than to have his guidance in Toledo. Some day I am going back to profit more fully by it, and to repay him the various fees which he disbursed for me to different doorkeepers and custodians and which I forgot at parting and he was too delicate to remind me of.

When all leaves were taken and we were bowed out and away our horses, covered with bells, burst with the omnibus through a solid mass of beggars come to give us a last chance of meriting heaven by charity to them, and dashed down the hill to the station. There we sat a long half-hour in the wet evening air, wondering how we had been spared seeing those wretches trampled under our horses' feet, or how the long train of goats climbing to the city to be milked escaped our wheels. But as we were guiltless of inflicting either disaster, we could watch with a good conscience the quiescent industry of some laborers in the brickyard beyond the track. Slowly and more slowly they worked, wearily, apathetically, fetching, carrying, in their divided skirts of cross-barred stuff of a rich Velasquez dirt color. One was especially worthy of admiration from his wide-brimmed black hat and his thoughtful indifference to his task, which was stacking up a sort of bundles of long grass; but I dare say he knew what it all meant. Throughout I was tormented by question of the precise co-racial quality of some English-speaking folk who had come to share our bone-breaking return to Madrid in the train so deliberately waiting there to begin afflicting us. English English they certainly were not; American English as little. If they were Australian English, why should not it have been a convention of polite travel for them to come up and say so, and save us that torment of curiosity? But perhaps they were not Australians.

# VII. THE GREAT GRIDIRON OF ST. LAWRENCE

It seems a duty every Protestant owes his heresy to go and see how dismally the arch-enemy of heresy housed his true faith in the palace-tomb-and-church of the Escorial. If the more light-minded tourist shirks this act of piety, he makes a mistake which he will repent afterward in vain. The Escorial is, for its plainness, one of the two or three things worthiest seeing among the two or three hundred things worth seeing in Spain. Yet we feigned meaning to miss it after we returned to Madrid from Toledo, saying that everybody went to the Escorial and that it would be a proud distinction not to go. All the time we knew we should go, and we were not surprised when we were chosen by one of our few bright days for the excursion, though we were taken inordinately early, and might well have been started a little later.

I

Nothing was out of the common on the way to the station, and our sense of the ordinary was not relieved when we found ourselves in a car of the American open-saloon pattern, well filled with other Americans bent upon the same errand as ourselves; though I am bound to say that the backs of the transverse seats rose well toward the roof of the car with a certain originality.

When we cleared the city streets and houses, we began running out into the country through suburbs vulgarly gay with small, bright brick villas, so expressive of commuting that the eye required the vision of young husbands and fathers going in at the gates with gardening tools on their shoulders and under their arms. To be sure, the time of day and the time of year were against this; it was now morning and autumn, though there was a vernal brilliancy in the air; and the grass, flattered by the recent rains, was green where we had last seen it gray. Along a pretty stream, which, for all I know may have been the Manzanares, it was so little, files of Lombardy poplars followed away very agreeably golden in foliage; and scattered about were deciduous-looking evergreens which we questioned for live-oaks. We were going northward over the track which had brought us southward to Madrid two weeks before, and by and by the pleasant levels broke into rough hills and hollows, strewn with granite boulders which, as our train mounted, changed into the savage rock masses of New Castile, and as we drew near the village of Escorial gave the scene the look of that very desolate country. But it could not be so gloomy in the kind sunlight as it was when lashed by the savage storm which we had seen it cowering under before; and at the station we lost all feeling of friendlessness in the welcome of the thronging guides and hotel touters.

Our ideal was a carriage which we could keep throughout the day and use for our return to the train in the afternoon; and this was so exactly the ideal of a driver to whom we committed ourselves that we were somewhat surprised to have his vehicle develop into a motor-omnibus, and himself into a conductor.

When we arrived at the palace some miles off, up a winding way, he underwent another change, and became our guide to the Escorial. In the event he proved a very intelligent guide, as guides go, and I really cannot now see how we could have got on without him. He adapted the Spanish names of things to our English understanding by shortening them; a *patio* became a *pat'*, and an old master an old mast'; and an endearing quality was imparted to the grim memory of Philip II. by the diminutive of Philly. We accepted this, but even to have Charles V. brought nearer our hearts as Charley Fif, we could not bear to have our guide exposed to the mockery of less considerate travelers. I instructed him that the emperor's name was Charles, and that only boys and very familiar friends of that name were called Charley among us. He thanked me, and at once spoke again of Charley Fif; which I afterward found was the universally accepted style of the great emperor among the guides of Spain. In vain I tried to persuade them out of it at Cordova, at Seville, at Granada, and wherever else they had to speak of an emperor whose memory really seems to pervade the whole land.

II

The genuine village of Escorial lies mostly to the left of the station, but the artificial town which grew up with the palace is to the right. Both are called after the slag of the iron-smelting works which were and are the vital industry of the first Escorial; but the road to the palace takes you far from the slag, with a much-hoteled and garden-walled dignity, to the plateau, apparently not altogether natural, where the massive triune edifice stands in the keeping of a throng of American women wondering how they are going to see it, and lunch, and get back to their train in time. Many were trying, the day of our visit, to see the place with no help but that of their bewildering Baedekers, and we had constant reason to be glad of our guide as we met or passed them in the measureless courts and endless corridors.

At this distance of time and place we seem to have hurried first to the gorgeous burial vault where the kings and queens of Spain lie, each one shut in a gilded marble sarcophagus in their several niches of the circular chamber, where under the high altar of the church they have the advantage of all the masses said above them. But on the way we must have passed through the church, immense, bare, cold, and sullener far than that sepulcher; and I am sure that we visited last of all the palace, where it is said the present young king comes so seldom and unwillingly, as if shrinking from the shelf appointed for him in that crypt shining with gold and polished marble.

It is of death, not life, that the Escorial preaches, and it was to eternal death, its pride and gloom, and not life everlasting, that the dark piety of Philip voluntarily, or involuntarily, consecrated the edifice. But it would be doing a wrong to one of the greatest achievements of the human will, if one dwelt too much, or too wholly, upon this gloomy ideal. The Escorial has been many times described; I myself forbear with difficulty the attempt to describe it, and I satisfy my longing to set it visibly before the reader by letting an earlier visitor of my name describe it for me. I think he does it larger justice than modern observers, because he escapes the cumulative obligation which time has laid upon them to find the subjective rather than the objective fulfilment of its founder's intention in it. At any rate, in March, 1623, James Howell, waiting as secretary of the romantic mission the bursting of the iridescent love-dream which had brought Charles Stuart, Prince of Wales, from England to woo the sister of the Spanish king in Madrid, had leisure to write one of his most delightful "familiar letters" concerning the Escorial to a friend in London.

"I was yesterday at the Escorial to see the monastery of St. Lawrence, the eighth wonder of the world; and truly considering the site of the place, the state of the thing, the symmetry of the structure, with diverse other rareties, it may be called so; for what I have seen in Italy and other places are but baubles to it. It is built among a company of craggy hills, which makes the air the hungrier and wholesomer; it is all built of freestone and marble, and that with such solidity and moderate height that surely Philip the Second's chief design was to make a sacrifice of it to eternity, and to contest with the meteors and time itself. It cost eight millions; it was twenty-four years abuilding, and the founder himself saw it furnished and enjoyed it twelve years after, and carried his bones himself thither to be buried. The reason that moved King Philip to waste so much treasure was a vow he had made at the battle of St. Quentin, where he was forced to batter a monastery of St. Lawrence friars, and if he had the victory he would erect such a monument to St. Lawrence that the world had not the like; therefore the form of it is like a gridiron, the handle is a huge royal palace, and the body a vast monastery or assembly of quadrangular cloisters, for there are as many as there be months of the year. There be a hundred monks, and every one hath his man and his mule, and a multitude of officers; besides there are three libraries there full of the choicest books for all sciences. It is beyond all expression what grots, gardens, walks, and aqueducts there are there, and what curious fountains in the upper cloisters, for there be two stages of cloisters. In fine, there is nothing that is vulgar there. To take a view of every room in the house one must make account to go ten miles; there is a vault called the Pantheon under the high altar, which is all paved, walled, and arched with marble; there be a number of huge silver candlesticks taller than I am; lamps three yards compass, and diverse chalices and crosses of massive gold; there is one choir made all of burnished brass; pictures and statues like giants; and a world of glorious things that purely ravished me. By this mighty monument it may be inferred that Philip the Second, though he was a little man, yet he had vast gigantic thoughts in him, to leave such a huge pile for posterity to gaze upon and admire in his memory."

III

Perhaps this description is not very exact, but precision of statement is not to be expected of a Welshman; and if Howell preferred to say Philip built the place in fulfilment of that vow at the battle of St. Quentin, doubtless he believed it; many others did; it has only of late been discovered that Philip was not at St. Quentin, and did not "batter a monastery of St. Lawrence friars" there. I like to think the rest is all as Howell says down to the man and mule for every monk. If there are no men and mules left, there are very few monks either, after the many suppressions of convents. The gardens are there of an unquestionable symmetry and beauty, and the "company of craggy hills" abides all round the prodigious edifice, which is at once so prodigious, and grows larger upon you in the retrospect.

Now that I am this good distance away, and cannot bring myself to book by a second experience, I feel it safe to say that I had a feeling of St. Peter's-like immensity in the church of the Escorial, with more than St. Peter's-like bareness. The gray colorlessness of the architecture somberly prevails in memory over the frescoes of the painters invited to relieve it in the roof and the *retablo*, and thought turns from the red-and-yellow jasper of altar and pulpit, and the bronze-gilt effigies of kneeling kings and queens to that niche near the oratory where the little terrible man who imagined and realized it all used to steal in from his palace, and worship next the small chamber where at last he died. It is said he also read despatches and state papers in this nook, but doubtless only in the intervals of devotion.

Every one to his taste, even in matters of religion; Philip reared a temple to the life beyond this, and as if with the splendor of the mausoleum which it enshrines he hoped to overcome the victorious grave; the Caliph who built the mighty mosque at Cordova, which outlasts every other glory of his capital, dedicated it to the joy of this life as against the gloom of whose who would have put it under the feet of death. "Let us build," he said to his people, "the Kaaba of the West upon the site of a Christian temple, which we will destroy, so that we may set forth how the Cross shall fall and become abased before the True Prophet. Allah will never place the world beneath the feet of those who make themselves the slaves of drink and sensuality while they preach penitence and the joys of chastity, and while extolling poverty enrich themselves to the loss of their neighbors. For these the sad and silent cloister; for us, the crystalline fountain and the shady grove; for them, the rude and unsocial life of dungeon-like strongholds; for us, the charm of social life and culture; for them, intolerance and tyranny; for us, a ruler who is our father; for them, the darkness of ignorance; for us, letters and instruction as wide-spread as our creed; for them, the wilderness, celibacy, and the doom of the false martyr; for us, plenty, love, brotherhood, and eternal joy."

In spite of the somewhat vaunting spirit of his appeal, the wager of battle decided against the Arab; it was the Crescent that fell, the Cross that prevailed; in the very heart of Abderrahman's mosque a Christian cathedral rises. Yet in the very heart of Philip's temple to the spirit of the cloister, the desert, the martyrdom, one feels that a great deal could be said on Abderrahman's side. This is a world which will not be renounced, in fact, and even in Christian Spain it has triumphed in the arts and sciences beyond its earlier victories in Moslem Spain. One finds Philip himself, with his despatches in that high nook, rather than among the bronze-gilt royalties at the high altar, though his statue is duly there with those of his three wives. The group does not include that poor Bloody Mary of England, who should have been the fourth there, for surely she suffered enough for his faith and him to be of his domestic circle forever.

IV

It is the distinct merit of the Escorial that it does not, and perhaps cannot take long in doing; otherwise the doer could not bear it. A look round the sumptuous burial chamber of the sovereigns below the high altar of the church; a glance at the lesser sepulchral glories of the infantes and infantas in their chapels and corridors, suffices for the funereal third of the trinity of tomb and temple and palace; and though there are gayer constituents of the last, especially the gallery of the chapter-house, with its surprisingly lively frescoes and its sometimes startling canvases, there is not much that need really keep you from the royal apartments which seem the natural end of your visit. Of these something better can be said than that they are no worse than most other royal apartments; our guide led us to them through many granite courts and corridors where we left groups of unguided Americans still maddening over their Baedekers; and we found them hung with pleasing tapestries, some after such designs of Goya's as one finds in the basement of the Prado. The furniture was in certain rooms cheerily upholstered in crimson and salmon without sense of color, but as if seeking relief from the gray of the church; and there are battle-pieces on the walls, fights between Moors and Christians, which interested me. The dignified consideration of the custodian who showed us through the apartments seemed to have adapted to our station a manner left over from the infrequent presence of royalty; as I have said, the young king of Spain does not like coming to the Escorial.

I do not know why any one comes there, and I search my consciousness in vain for a better reason than the feeling that I must come, or would be sorrier if I did not than if I did. The worthy Howell does not commit himself to any expression of rejoicing or regretting in having done the Escorial. But the good Theophile Gautier, who visited the place more than two hundred years after, owns frankly that he is "excessively embarrassed in giving his opinion" of it. "So many people," he says, "serious and well-conditioned, who, I prefer to think, have never seen it, have spoken of it as a *chef d'oeuvre*, and a supreme effort of the human spirit, so that I should have the air, poor devil of a *facilletoniste errant*, of wishing to play the original and taking pleasure in my contrary-mindedness; but still in my soul and conscience I cannot help finding the Escorial the most tiresome and the most stupid monument that could be imagined, for the mortification of his fellow-beings, by a morose monk and a suspicious tyrant. I know very well that the Escorial had a serious and religious aim; but gravity is not dryness, melancholy is not marasm, meditation is not ennui, and beauty of forms can always be happily wedded to elevation of ideas." This is the Frenchman's language as he goes into the Escorial; he does not cheer up as he passes through the place, and when he comes out he has to say: "I issued from that desert of granite, from that monkish necropolis with an extraordinary feeling of release, of exultation; it seemed to me I was born into life again, that I could be young once more, and rejoice in the creation of the good God, of which I had lost all hope in those funeral vaults. The bland and luminous air wrapt me round like a soft robe of fine wool, and warmed my body frozen in that cadaverous atmosphere; I was saved from that architectural nightmare, which I thought never would end. I advise people who are so fatuous as to pretend that they are ever bored to go and spend three or four days in the Escorial; they will learn what real ennui is and they will enjoy themselves all the rest of their lives in reflecting that they might be in the Escorial and that they are not."

That was well toward a century ago. It is not quite like that now, but it is something like it; the human race has become inured to the Escorial; more tourists have visited the place and imaginably lightened its burden by sharing it among their increasing number. Still there is now and then one who is oppressed, crushed by it, and cannot relieve himself in such ironies as Gautier's, but must cry aloud in suffering like that of the more emotional De Amicis: "You approach a courtyard and say, 'I have seen this already.' No. You are mistaken; it is another.... You ask the guide where the cloister is and he replies, 'This is it,' and you walk on for half an hour. You see the light of another world: you have never seen just such a light; is it the reflection from the stone, or does it come from the moon? No, it is daylight, but sadder than darkness. As you go on from corridor to corridor, from court to court, you look ahead with misgivings, expecting to see suddenly, as you turn a corner, a row of skeleton monks with hoods over their eyes and crosses in their hands; you think of Philip II.... You remember all that you have read about him, of his terrors and the Inquisition; and everything becomes clear to your mind's eye with a sudden light; for the first time you understand it all; the Escorial is Philip II.... He is still there alive and terrible, with the image of his dreadful God... . Even now, after so long a time, on rainy days, when I am feeling sad, I think of the Escorial, and then look at the walls of my room and congratulate myself.... I see again the courtyards of the Escorial. ... I dream of wandering through the corridors alone in the dark, followed by the ghost of an old friar, crying and pounding at all the doors without finding a way of escape."

I am of another race both from the Frenchman and the Italian, and I cannot pretend to their experiences, their inferences, and their conclusions; but I am not going to leave the Escorial to the reader without trying to make him feel that I too was terribly impressed by it. To be sure, I had some light moments in it, because when gloom goes too far it becomes ridiculous; and I did think the convent gardens as I saw them from the chapter-house window were beautiful, and the hills around majestic and serious, with no intention of falling upon my prostrate spirit. Yes, and after a lifelong abhorrence of that bleak king who founded the Escorial, I will own that I am, through pity, beginning to feel an affection for Philip II.; perhaps I was finally wrought upon by hearing him so endearingly called Philly by our guide.

Yet I will not say but I was glad to get out of the Escorial alive; and that I welcomed even the sulkiness of the landlord of the hotel where our guide took us for lunch. To this day I do not know why that landlord should have been so sour; his lunch was bad, but I paid his price without murmuring; and still at parting he could scarcely restrain his rage; the Escorial might have entered into his soul. On the way to his hotel the street was empty, but the house bubbled over with children who gaped giggling at his guests from the kitchen door, and were then apparently silenced with food, behind it. There were a great many flies in the hotel, and if I could remember its name I would warn the public against it.

After lunch our guide lapsed again to our conductor and reappeared with his motor-bus and took us to the station, where he overcame the scruples of the lady in the ticket-office concerning our wish to return to Madrid by the Sud-Express instead of the ordinary train. The trouble was about the supplementary fare which we easily paid on board; in fact, there is never any difficulty in paying a supplementary fare in Spain; the authorities meet you quite half-way. But we were nervous because we had already suffered from the delays of people at the last hotel where our motor-bus stopped to take up passengers; they lingered so long over lunch that we were sure we should miss the Sud-Express, and we did not see how we could live in Escorial till the way-train started; yet for all their delays we reached the station in time and more. The train seemed strangely reduced in the number of its cars, but we confidently started with others to board the nearest of them; there we were waved violently away, and bidden get into the dining-car at the rear of the train. In some dudgeon we obeyed, but we were glad to get away from Escorial on any terms, and the dining-car was not bad, though it had a somewhat disheveled air. We could only suppose that all the places in the two other cars were taken, and we resigned ourselves to choosing the least coffee-stained of the coffee-stained tables and ordered more coffee at it. The waiter brought it as promptly as the conductor collected our supplementary fare; he even made a feint of removing the stains from our table-cloth with a flourish of his napkin, and then he left us to our conjectures and reflections till he came for his pay and his fee just before we ran into Madrid.

VI

The mystery persisted and it was only when our train paused in the station that it was solved. There, as we got out of our car, we perceived that a broad red velvet carpet was laid from the car in front into the station; a red carpet such as is used to keep the feet of distinguished persons from their native earth the world over, but more especially in Europe. Along this carpet were loosely grouped a number of solemnly smiling gentlemen in frock-coats with their top-hats genteelly resting in the hollows of their left arms, and without and beyond the station in the space usually filled by closed and open cabs was a swarm of automobiles. Then while our spirits were keyed to the highest pitch, the Queen of Spain descended from the train, wearing a long black satin cloak and a large black hat, very blond and beautiful beyond the report of her pictures. By each hand she led one of her two pretty boys, Don Jaime, the Prince of Asturias, heir apparent, and his younger brother. She walked swiftly, with glad, kind looks around, and her ladies followed her according to their state; then ushered and followed by the gentlemen assembled to receive them, they mounted to their motors and whirred away like so many persons of a histrionic pageant: not least impressive, the court attendants filled a stage drawn by six mules, and clattered after.

From hearsay and reasonable surmise we learned that we had not come from Escorial in the Sud-Express at all, but in the Queen's special train bringing her and her children from their autumn sojourn at La Granja, and that we had been for an hour a notable feature of the royal party without knowing it, and of course without getting the least good of it. We had indeed ignorantly enjoyed no less of the honor than two other Americans, who came in the dining-car with us, but whether the nice-looking Spanish couple who sat in the corner next us were equally ignorant of their advantage I shall never know. It was but too highly probable that the messed condition of the car was due to royal luncheon in it just before we came aboard; but why we were suffered to come aboard, or why a supplementary fare should have been collected from us remains one of those mysteries which I should once have liked to keep all Spain.

We had to go quite outside of the station grounds to get a cab for our hotel, but from this blow to our dignity I recovered a little later in the day, when the king, attended by as small a troop of cavalry as I suppose a king ever has with him, came driving by in the street where I was walking. As he sat in his open carriage he looked very amiable, and handsomer than most of the pictures make him. He seemed to be gazing at me, and when he bowed I could do no less than return his salutation. As I glanced round to see if people near me were impressed by our exchange of civilities, I perceived an elderly officer next me. He was smiling as I was, and I think he was in the delusion that the king's bow, which I had so promptly returned, was intended for him.

# VIII. CORDOVA AND THE WAY THERE

I should be sorry if I could believe that Cordova experienced the disappointment in us, which I must own we felt in her; but our disappointment was unquestionable, and I will at once offer it to the reader as an inducement for him to go to Cordova with less lively expectations than ours. I would by no means have him stay away; after all, there is only one Cordova in the world which the capital of the Caliphate of the West once filled with her renown; and if the great mosque of Abderrahman is not so beautiful as one has been made to fancy it, still it is wonderful, and could not be missed without loss.

I

Better, I should say, take the *rapido* which leaves Madrid three times a week at nine-thirty in the morning, than the night express which leaves as often at the same hour in the evening. Since there are now such good day trains on the chief Spanish lines, it is flying in the face of Providence not to go by them; they might be suddenly taken off; besides, they have excellent restaurant-cars, and there is, moreover, always the fascinating and often the memorable landscape which they pass through. By no fault of ours that I can remember, our train was rather crowded; that is, four or five out of the eight places in our corridor compartment were taken, and we were afraid at every stop that more people would get in, though I do not know that it was our anxieties kept them out. For the matter of that, I do not know why I employed an interpreter at Madrid to get my ticket stamped at the ticket-office; it required merely the presentation of the ticket at the window; but the interpreter seemed to wish it and it enabled him to practise his English with me, and I realized that he must live. In a peseta's worth of gratitude he followed us to our carriage, and he did not molest the *mozo* in putting our bags into the racks, though he hovered about the door till the train started; and it just now occurs to me that he may have thought a peseta was not a sufficient return for his gratitude; he had rendered us no service.

At Aranjuez the wheat-lands, which began to widen about us as soon as we got beyond the suburbs of Madrid, gave way to the groves and gardens of that really charming pleasaunce, charming quite from the station, with grounds penetrated by placid waters overhung by the English elms which the Castilians are so happy in having naturalized in their treeless waste. Multitudes of nightingales are said to sing among them, but it was not the season for hearing them from the train; and we made what shift we could with the strawberry and asparagus beds which we could see plainly, and the peach trees and cherry trees. One of these had committed the solecism of blossoming in October, instead of April or May, when the nobility came to their villas.

We had often said during our stay in Madrid that we should certainly come for a day at Aranjuez; and here we were, passing it with a five minutes' stop. I am sure it merited much more, not only for its many proud memories, but for its shameful ones, which are apt to be so much more lasting in the case of royal pleasaunces. The great Catholic King Ferdinand inherited the place with the Mastership of the Order of Santiago; Charles V. used to come there for the shooting, and Philip II., Charleses III. and IV., and Ferdinand VII. built and rebuilt its edifices. But it is also memorable because the wretched Godoy fled there with the king, his friend, and the queen, his paramour, and there the pitiable king abdicated in favor of his abominable son Ferdinand VII. It is the careful Murray who reminds me of this fact; Gautier, who apparently fails to get anything to his purpose out of Aranjuez, passes it with the remark that Godoy built there a gallery from his villa to the royal palace, for his easier access to the royal family in which he held a place so anomalous. From Mr. Martin Hume's *Modern Spain* I learn that when the court fled to Aranjuez from Madrid before the advance of Murat, and the mob, civil and military, hunted Godoy's villa through for him, he jumped out of bed and hid himself under a roll of matting, while the king and the queen, to save him, decreed his dismissal from all his offices and honors.

But here just at the most interesting moment the successive bells and whistles are screeching, and the *rapido* is hurrying me away from Aranjuez. We are leaving a railway station, but presently it is as if we had set sail on a gray sea, with a long ground-swell such as we remembered from Old Castile. These innumerable pastures and wheat-fields are in New Castile, and before long more distinctively they are in La Mancha, the country dear to fame as the home of Don Quixote. I must own at once it does not look it, or at least look like the country I had read out of his history in my boyhood. For the matter of that, no country ever looks like the country one reads out of a book, however really it may be that country. The trouble probably is that one carries out of one's reading an image which one had carried into it. When I read *Don Quixote* and read and read it again, I put La Mancha first into the map of southern Ohio, and then into that, after an interval of seven or eight years, of northern Ohio; and the scenes I arranged for his adventures were landscapes composed from those about me in my earlier and later boyhood. There was then always something soft and mild in the *Don Quixote* country, with a blue river and gentle uplands, and woods where one could rest in the shade, and hide one's self if one wished, after easily rescuing the oppressed. Now, instead, a treeless plain unrolled itself from sky to sky, clean, dull, empty; and if some azure tops dimmed the clear line of the western horizon, how could I have got them into my early picture when I had never yet seen a mountain in my life? I could not put the knight and his squire on those naked levels where they should not have got a mile from home without discovery and arrest. I tried to think of them jogging along in talk of the adventures which the knight hoped for; but I could not make it work. I could have done better before we got so far from Aranjuez; there were gardens and orchards and a very suitable river there, and those elm trees overhanging it; but the prospect in La Mancha had only here and there a white-availed white farmhouse to vary its lonely simplicity, its desert fertility; and I could do nothing with the strips and patches of vineyard. It was all strangely African, strangely Mexican, and not at all American, not Ohioan, enough to be anything like the real La Mancha of my invention. To be sure, the doors and windows of the nearer houses were visibly netted against mosquitoes and that was something, but even that did not begin to be noticeable till we were drawing near the Sierra Morena. Then, so long before we reached the mighty chain of mountains which nature has stretched between the gravity of New Castile and the gaiety of Andalusia, as if they could not bear immediate contact, I experienced a moment of perfect reconciliation to the landscape as really wearing the face of that La Mancha familiar to my boyish vision. Late in the forenoon, but early enough to save the face of La Mancha, there appeared certain unquestionable shapes in the nearer and farther distance which I joyously knew for those windmills which Don Quixote had known for giants and spurred at, lance in rest. They were waving their vans in what he had found insolent defiance, but which seemed to us glad welcome, as of windmills waiting that long time for a reader of Cervantes who could enter into their feelings and into the friendly companionship they were offering.

## II

Our train did not pass very near, but the distance was not bad for them; it kept them sixty or sixty-five years back in the past where they belonged, and in its dimness I could the more distinctly see Don Quixote careering against them, and Sancho Panza vainly warning, vainly imploring him, and then in his rage and despair, "giving himself to the devil," as he had so often to do in that master's service; I do not know now that I would have gone nearer them if I could. Sometimes in the desolate plains where the windmills stood so well aloof men were lazily, or at least leisurely, plowing with their prehistoric crooked sticks. Here and there the clean levels were broken by shallow pools of water; and we were at first much tormented by expanses, almost as great as these pools, of a certain purple flower, which no curiosity of ours could prevail with to yield up the secret of its name or nature. It was one of the anomalies of this desert country that it was apparently prosperous, if one might guess from the comfortable-looking farmsteads scattered over it, inclosing house and stables in the courtyard framed by their white walls. The houses stood at no great distances from one another, but were nowhere grouped in villages. There were commonly no towns near the stations, which were not always uncheerful; sometimes there were flower-beds, unless my memory deceives me. Perhaps there would be a passenger or two, and certainly a loafer or two, and always of the sex which in town life does the loafing; in the background or through the windows the other sex could be seen in its domestic activities. Only once did we see three girls of such as stay for the coming and going of trains the world over; they waited arm in arm, and we were obliged to own they were plain, poor things.

Their whitewash saves the distant towns from the effect of sinking into the earth, or irregularly rising from it, as in Old Castile, and the landscape cheered up more and more as we ran farther south. We passed through the country of the Valdepenas wine, which it is said would so willingly be better than it is; there was even a station of that name, which looked much more of a station than most, and had, I think I remember, buildings necessary to the wine industry about it. Murray, indeed, emboldens me in this halting conjecture with the declaration that the neighboring town of Valdepenas is "completely undermined by wine-cellars of very ancient date" where the wine is "kept in caves in huge earthen jars," and when removed is put into goat or pig skins in the right Don Quixote fashion.

The whole region begins to reek of Cervantean memories. Ten miles from the station of Argamasilla is the village where he imagined, and the inhabitants believe, Don Quixote to have been born. Somewhere among these little towns Cervantes himself was thrown into prison for presuming to attempt collecting their rents when the people did not want to pay them. This is what I seem to remember having read, but heaven knows where, or if. What is certain is that almost before I was aware we were leaving the neighborhood of Valdepenas, where we saw men with donkeys gathering grapes and letting the donkeys browse on the vine leaves. Then we were mounting among the foothills of the Sierra Morena, not without much besetting trouble of mind because of those certain circles and squares of stone on the nearer and farther slopes which we have since somehow determined were sheep-folds. They abounded almost to the very scene of those capers which Don Quixote cut on the mountainside to testify his love for Dulcinea del Toboso, to the great scandal of Sancho Panza riding away to give his letter to the lady, but unable to bear the sight of the knight skipping on the rocks in a single garment.

## III

In the forests about befell all those adventures with the mad Cardenio and the wronged Dorothea, both self-banished to the wilderness through the perfidy of the same false friend and faithless lover. The episodes which end so well, and which form, I think, the heart of the wonderful romance, have, from the car windows, the fittest possible setting; but suddenly the scene changes, and you are among aspects of nature as savagely wild as any in that new western land where the countrymen of Cervantes found a New Spain, just as the countrymen of Shakespeare found a New England. Suddenly, or if not suddenly, then startlingly, we were in a pass of the Sierra called (for some reason which I will leave picturesquely unexplained) the Precipice of Dogs, where bare sharp peaks and spears of rock started into the air, and the faces of the cliffs glared down upon us like the faces of Indian warriors painted yellow and orange and crimson, and every other warlike color. With my poor scruples of moderation I cannot give a just notion of the wild aspects; I must leave it to the reader, with the assurance that he cannot exaggerate it, while I employ myself in noting that already on this awful summit we began to feel ourselves in the south, in Andalusia. Along the mountain stream that slipped silverly away in the valley below, there were oleanders in bloom, such as we had left in Bermuda the April before. Already, north of the Sierra the country had been gentling. The upturned soil had warmed from gray to red; elsewhere the fields were green with sprouting wheat; and there were wide spaces of those purple flowers, like crocuses, which women were gathering in large baskets. Probably they were not crocuses; but there could be no doubt of the vineyards increasing in their acreage; and the farmhouses which had been without windows in their outer walls, now sometimes opened as many as two to the passing train. Flocks of black sheep and goats, through the optical illusion frequent in the Spanish air, looked large as cattle in the offing. Only in one place had we seen the tumbled boulders of Old Castile, and there had been really no greater objection to La Mancha than that it was flat, stale, and unprofitable and wholly unimaginable as the scene of even Don Quixote's first adventures.

But now that we had mounted to the station among the summits of the Sierra Morena, my fancy began to feel at home, and rested in a scene which did all the work for it. There was ample time for the fancy to rest in that more than co-operative landscape. Just beyond the first station the engine of a freight-train had opportunely left the track in front of us, and we waited there four hours till it could be got back. It would be inhuman to make the reader suffer through this delay with us after it ceased to be pleasure and began to be pain. Of course, everybody of foreign extraction got out of the train and many even, went forward to look at the engine and see what they could do about it; others went partly forward and asked the bolder spirits on their way back what was the matter. Now and then our locomotive whistled as if to scare the wandering engine back to the rails. At moments the station-master gloomily returned to the station from somewhere and diligently despaired in front of it. Then we backed as if to let our locomotive run up the siding and try to butt the freight-train off the track to keep its engine company.

About this time the restaurant-car bethought itself of some sort of late-afternoon repast, and we went forward and ate it with an interest which we prolonged as much as possible. We returned to our car which was now pervaded by an extremely bad smell. The smell drove us out, and we watched a public-spirited peasant beating the acorns from a live-oak near the station with a long pole. He brought a great many down, and first filled his sash-pocket with them; then he distributed them among the children of the third-class passengers who left the train and flocked about him. But nobody seemed to do anything with the acorns, though they were more than an inch long, narrow, and very sharp-pointed. As soon as he had discharged his self-assumed duty the peasant lay down on the sloping bank under the tree, and with his face in the grass, went to sleep for all our stay, and for what I know the whole night after.

It did not now seem likely that we should ever reach Gordova, though people made repeated expeditions to the front of the train, and came back reporting that in an hour we should start. We interested ourselves as intensely as possible in a family from the next compartment, London-tailored, and speaking either Spanish or English as they fancied, who we somehow understood lived at Barcelona; but nothing came of our interest. Then as the day waned we threw ourselves into the interest taken by a fellow-passenger in a young Spanish girl of thirteen or fourteen who had been in the care of a youngish middle-aged man when our train stopped, and been then abandoned by him for hours, while he seemed to be satisfying a vain curiosity at the head of the train. She owned that the deserter was her father, and while we were still poignantly concerned for her he came back and relieved the anxiety which the girl herself had apparently not shared even under pressure of the whole compartment's sympathy.

IV

The day waned more and more; the sun began to sink, and then it sank with that sudden drop which the sun has at last. The sky flushed crimson, turned mauve, turned gray, and the twilight thickened over the summits billowing softly westward. There had been a good deal of joking, both Spanish and English, among the passengers; I had found particularly cheering the richness of a certain machinist's trousers of bright golden corduroy; but as the shades of night began to embrown the scene our spirits fell; and at the cry of a lonesome bird, far off where the sunset had been, they followed the sun in its sudden drop. Against the horizon a peasant boy leaned on his staff and darkled against the darkening sky.

Nothing lacked now but the opportune recollection that this was the region where the natives had been so wicked in times past that an ingenious statesman, such as have seldom been wanting to Spain, imagined bringing in a colony of German peasants to mix with them and reform them. That is what some of the books say, but others say that the region had remained unpeopled after the first exile of the conquered Moors. All hold that the notion of mixing the colonists and the natives worked the wrong way; the natives were not reformed, but the colonists were depraved and stood in with the local brigands, ultimately, if not immediately. This is the view suggested, if not taken, by that amusing emissary, George Borrow, who seems in his *Bible in Spain* to have been equally employed in distributing the truths of the New Testament and collecting material for the most dramatic study of Spanish civilization known to literature. It is a delightful book, and not least delightful in the moments of misgiving which it imparts to the reader, when he does not know whether to prize more the author's observation or his invention, whichever it may be. Borrow reports a conversation with an innkeeper and his wife of the Colonial German descent, who gave a good enough account of themselves, and then adds the dark intimation of an Italian companion that they could not be honestly keeping a hotel in that unfrequented place. It was not just in that place that our delay had chosen to occur, but it was in the same colonized region, and I am glad now that I had not remembered the incident from my first reading of Borrow. It was sufficiently uncomfortable to have some vague association with the failure of that excellent statesman's plan, blending creepily with the feeling of desolation from the gathering dark, and I now recall the distinct relief given by the unexpected appearance of two such Guardias Civiles as travel with every Spanish train, in the space before our lonely station.

These admirable friends were part of the system which has made travel as safe throughout Spain as it is in Connecticut, where indeed I sometimes wonder that road-agents do not stop my Boston express in the waste expanse of those certain sand barrens just beyond New Haven. The last time I came through that desert I could not help thinking how nice it would be to have two Guardias Civiles in our Pullman car; but of course at the summit of the Sierra Morena, where our *rapido* was stalled in the deepening twilight, it was still nicer to see that soldier pair, pacing up and down, trim, straight, very gentle and polite-looking, but firm, with their rifles lying on their shoulders which they kept exactly together. It is part of the system that they may use those rifles upon any evil-doer whom they discover in a deed of violence, acting at once as police, court of law, and executioners; and satisfying public curiosity by pinning to the offender's coat their official certificate that he was shot by such and such a civil guard for such and such a reason, and then notifying the nearest authorities. It is perhaps too positive, too peremptory, too precise; and the responsibility could not be intrusted to men who had not satisfied the government of their fitness by two years' service in the army without arrest for any offense, or even any question of misbehavior. But these conditions once satisfied, and their temperament and character approved, they are intrusted with what seem plenary powers till they are retired for old age; then their sons may serve after them as Civil Guards with the same prospect of pensions in the end. I suppose they do not always travel first class, but once their silent, soldierly presence honored our compartment between stations; and once an officer of their corps conversed for long with a fellow-passenger in that courteous ease and self-respect which is so Spanish between persons of all ranks.

It was not very long after the guards appeared so reassuringly before the station, when a series of warning bells and whistles sounded, and our locomotive with an impatient scream began to tug at our train. We were really off, starting from Santa Elena at the very time when we ought to have been stopping at Cordova, with a good stretch of four hours still before us. As our fellow-travelers quitted us at one station and another we were finally left alone with the kindly-looking old man who had seemed interested in us from the first, and who now made some advances in broken English. Presently he told us in Spanish, to account for the English accent on which we complimented him, that he had two sons studying some manufacturing business in Manchester, where he had visited them, and acquired so much of our tongue as we had heard. He was very proud and glad to speak of his sons, and he valued us for our English and the strangeness which commends people to one another in travel. When he got out at a station obscured past identification by its flaring lamps, he would not suffer me to help him with his hand-baggage; while he deplored my offered civility, he reassured me by patting my back at parting. Yet I myself had to endure the kindness which he would not when we arrived at Cordova, where two young fellows, who had got in at a suburban station, helped me with our bags and bundles quite as if they had been two young Americans.

V

Somewhere at a junction our train had been divided and our car, left the last of what remained, had bumped and threatened to beat itself to pieces during its remaining run of fifteen miles. This, with our long retard at Santa Elena, and our opportune defense from the depraved descendants of the reforming German colonists by the Guardias Civiles, had given us a day of so much excitement that we were anxious to have it end tranquilly at midnight in the hotel which we had chosen from, our Baedeker. I would not have any reader of mine choose it again from my experience of it, though it was helplessly rather wilfully bad; certainly the fault was not the hotel's that it seemed as far from the station as Cordova was from Madrid. It might, under the circumstances, have, been *a* merit in it to be undergoing a thorough overhauling of the furnishing and decoration of the rooms on the *patio* which had formed our ideal for a quiet night. A conventionally napkined waiter welcomed us from the stony street, and sent us up to our rooms with the young interpreter who met us at the station, but was obscure as to their location. When we refused them because they were over that loud-echoing alley, the interpreter made himself still more our friend and called mandatorially down the speaking-tube that we wished *interiores* and would take nothing else, though he must have known that no such rooms were to be had. He even abetted us in visiting the rooms on the *patio* and satisfying ourselves that they were all dismantled; when the waiter brought up the hot soup which was the only hot thing in the house beside our tempers, he joined with that poor fellow in reconciling us to the inevitable. They declared that the people whom we heard uninterruptedly clattering and chattering by in the street below, and the occasional tempest of wheels and bells and hoofs that clashed up to us would be the very last to pass through there that night, and they gave such good and sufficient reasons for their opinion that we yielded as we needs must. Of course, they were wrong; and perhaps they even knew that they were wrong; but I think we were the only people in that neighborhood who got any sleep that night or the next. We slept the sleep of exhaustion, but I believe those Cordovese preferred waking outdoors to trying to sleep within. It was apparently their custom to walk and talk the night away in the streets, not our street alone, but all the other streets of Cordova; the laughing which I heard may have expressed the popular despair of getting any sleep. The next day we experimented in listening from rooms offered us over another street, and then we remained measurably contented to bear the ills we had. This was after an exhaustive search for a better hotel had partly appeased us; but there remained in the Paseo del Gran Capitan one house unvisited which has ever since grown upon my belief as embracing every comfort and advantage lacking to our hotel. I suppose I am the stronger in this belief because when we came to it we had been so disappointed with the others that we had not the courage to go inside. Smell for smell, the interior of that hotel may have harbored a worse one than the odor of henhouse which pervaded ours, I hope from the materials for calciming the rooms on the *patio*.

By the time we returned we found a guide waiting for us, and we agreed with him for a day's service. He did not differ with other authorities as to the claims of Cordova on the tourist's interest. From being the most brilliant capital of the Western world in the time of the Caliphs it is now allowed by all the guides and guide-books and most of the travelers, to be one of the dullest of provincial towns. It is no longer the center of learning; and though it cannot help doing a large business in olives, with the orchards covering the hills around it, the business does not seem to be a very active one. "The city once the abode of the flower of Andalusian nobility," says the intelligent O'Shea in his *Guide to Spain*, "is inhabited chiefly by administradores of the absentee senorio; their 'solares' are desert and wretched, the streets ill paved though clean, and the whitewashed houses unimportant, low, and denuded of all art and meaning, either past or present." Baedeker gives like reasons for thinking "the traveler whose expectation is on tiptoe as he enters the ancient capital of the Moors will probably be disappointed in all but the cathedral." *Cook's Guide,* latest but not least commendable of the authorities, is of a more divided mind and finds the means of trade and industry and their total want of visible employment at the worst anomalous.

Vacant, narrow streets where the grass does not grow, and there is only an endless going and coming of aimless feet; a market without buyers or sellers to speak of, and a tangle of squat white houses, abounding in lovely *patios,* sweet and bright with flowers and fountains: this seems to be Cordova in the consensus of the manuals, and with me in the retrospect a sort of puzzle is the ultimate suggestion of the dead capital of the Western Caliphs. Gautier thinks, or seventy-two years ago he thought (and there has not been much change since), that "Cordova has a more African look than any other city of Andalusia; its streets, or rather its lanes, whose tumultuous pavement resembles the bed of dry torrents, all littered with straw from the loads of passing donkeys, have nothing that recalls the manners and customs of Europe. The Moors, if they came back, would have no great trouble to reinstate themselves. ... The universal use of lime-wash gives a uniform tint to the monuments, blunts the lines of the architecture, effaces the ornamentation, and forbids you to read their age.... You cannot know the wall of a century ago from the wall of yesterday. Cordova, once the center of Arab civilization, is now a huddle of little white houses with corridors between them where two mules could hardly pass abreast. Life seems to have ebbed from the vast body, once animated by the active circulation of Moorish blood; nothing is left now but the blanched and calcined skeleton.... In spite of its Moslem air, Cordova is very Christian and rests under the special protection of the Archangel Raphael." It is all rather contradictory; but Gautier owns that the great mosque is a "monument unique in the world, and novel even for travelers who have had the fortune to admire the wonders of Moorish architecture at Granada or Seville."

De Amicis, who visited Cordova nearly forty-five years later, and in the heart of spring, brought letters which opened something of the intimate life of that apparently blanched and calcined skeleton. He meets young men and matches Italian verses with their Spanish; spends whole nights sitting in their cafes or walking their plazas, and comes away with his mouth full of the rapturous verses of an Arab poet: "Adieu, Cordova! Would that my life were as long as Noah's, that I might live forever within thy walls! Would that I had the treasures of Pharaoh, to spend them upon wine and the beautiful women of Cordova, with tho gentle eyes that invite kisses!" He allows that the lines may be "a little too tropical for the taste of a European," and it seems to me that there may be a golden mean between scolding and flattering which would give the truth about Cordova. I do not promise to strike it; our hotel still rankles in my heart; but I promise to try for it, though I have to say that the very moment we started for the famous mosque it began to rain, and rained throughout the forenoon, while we weltered from wonder to wonder through the town. We were indeed weltering in a closed carriage, which found its way not so badly through the alleys where two mules could not pass abreast. The lime-wash of the walls did not emit the white heat in which the other tourists have basked or baked; the houses looked wet and chill, and if they had those flowered and fountained *patios* which people talk of they had taken them in out of the rain.

## VI

At the mosque the *patio* was not taken in only because it was so large, but I find by our records that it was much molested by a beggar who followed us when we dismounted at the gate of the Court of Oranges, and all but took our minds off the famous Moorish fountain in the midst. It was not a fountain of the plashing or gushing sort, but a noble great pool in a marble basin. The women who clustered about it were not laughing and chattering, or singing, or even dancing, in the right Andalusian fashion, but stood silent in statuesque poses from which they seemed in no haste to stir for filling their water jars and jugs. The Moorish tradition of irrigation confronting one in all the travels and histories as a supreme agricultural advantage which the Arabs took back to Africa with them, leaving Spain to thirst and fry, lingers here in the circles sunk round the orange trees and fed by little channels. The trees grew about as the fancy took them, and did not mind the incongruous palms towering as irregularly above them. While we wandered toward the mosque a woman robed in white cotton, with a lavender scarf crossing her breast, came in as irrelevantly as the orange trees and stood as stably as the palms; in her night-black hair she alone in Cordova redeemed the pledge of beauty made for all Andalusian women by the reckless poets and romancers, whether in ballads or books of travel.

One enters the court by a gate in a richly yellow tower, with a shrine to St. Michael over the door, and still higher at the lodging of the keeper a bed of bright flowers. Then, however, one is confronted with the first great disappointment in the mosque. Shall it be whispered in awe-stricken undertone that the impression of a bull-ring is what lingers in the memory of the honest sight-seer from his first glance at the edifice? The effect is heightened by the filling of the arcades which encircle it, and which now confront the eye with a rounded wall, where the Saracenic horseshoe remains distinct, but the space of yellow masonry below seems to forbid the outsider stealing knowledge of the spectacle inside. The spectacle is of course no feast of bulls (as the Spanish euphemism has it), but the first amphitheatrical impression is not wholly dispersed by the sight of the interior. In order that the reader at his distance may figure this, he must imagine an indefinite cavernous expanse, with a low roof supported in vaulted arches by some thousand marble pillars, each with a different capital. There used to be perhaps half a thousand more pillars, and Charles V. made the Cordovese his reproaches for destroying the wonder of them when they planted their proud cathedral in the heart of the mosque. He held it a sort of sacrilege, but I think the honest traveler will say that there are still enough of those rather stumpy white marble columns left, and enough of those arches, striped in red and white with their undeniable suggestion of calico awnings. It is like a grotto gaudily but dingily decorated, or a vast circus-tent curtained off in hangings of those colors.

One sees the sanctuary where the great Caliph said his prayers, and the Koran written by Othman and stained with his blood was kept; but I know at least one traveler who saw it without sentiment or any sort of reverent emotion, though he had not the authority of the "old rancid Christianity" of a Castilian for withholding his homage. If people would be as sincere as other people would like them to be, I think no one would profess regret for the Arab civilization in the presence of its monuments. Those Moors were of a religion which revolts all the finer instincts and lifts the soul with no generous hopes; and the records of it have no appeal save to the love of mere beautiful decoration. Even here it mostly fails, to my thinking, and I say that for my part I found nothing so grand in the great mosaue of Cordova as the cathedral which rises in the heart of it. If Abderrahman boasted that he would rear a shrine to the joy of earthly life and the hope of an earthly heaven, in the place of the Christian temple which he would throw down, I should like to overhear what his disembodied spirit would have to say to the saint whose shrine he demolished. I think the saint would have the better of him in any contention for their respective faiths, and could easily convince the impartial witness that his religion then abiding in medieval gloom was of promise for the future which Islam can never be.

Yet it cannot be denied that when Abderraham built his mosque the Arabs of Cordova were a finer and wiser people than the Christians who dwelt in intellectual darkness among them, with an ideal of gloom and self-denial and a zeal for aimless martyrdom which must have been very hard for a gentleman and scholar to bear. Gentlemen and scholars were what the Arabs of the Western Caliphate seem to have become, with a primacy in medicine and mathematics beyond the learning of all other Europe in their day. They were tolerant skeptics in matters of religion; polite agnostics, who disliked extremely the passion of some Christians dwelling among them for getting themselves put to death, as they did, for insulting the popularly accepted Mohammedan creed. Probably people of culture in Cordova were quite of Abderrahman's mind in wishing to substitute the temple of a cheerfuler ideal for the shrine of the medieval Christianity which he destroyed; though they might have had their reserves as to the taste in which his mosque was completed. If they recognized it as a concession to the general preference, they could do so without the discomfort which they must have suffered when some new horde of Berbers, full of faith and fight, came over from Africa to push back the encroaching Spanish frontier, and give the local Christians as much martyrdom as they wanted.

It is all a conjecture based upon material witness no more substantial than that which the Latin domination left long centuries before the Arabs came to possess the land. The mosque from which you drive through the rain to the river is neither newer nor older looking than the beautiful Saracenic bridge over the Guadalquivir which the Arabs themselves say was first built by the Romans in the time of Augustus; the Moorish mill by the thither shore might have ground the first wheat grown in Europe. It is intensely, immemorially African, flat-roofed, white-walled; the mules waiting outside in the wet might have been drooping there ever since the going down of the Flood, from which the river could have got its muddy yellow.

If the reader will be advised by me he will not go to the Archaeological Museum, unless he wishes particularly to contribute to the support of the custodian; the collection will not repay him even for the time in which a whole day of Cordova will seem so superabundant. Any little street will be worthier his study, with its type of passing girls in white and black mantillas, and its shallow shops of all sorts, their fronts thrown open, and their interiors flung, as it were, on the sidewalk. It is said that the streets were the first to be paved in Europe, and they have apparently not been repaved since 850. This indeed will not Hold quite true of that thoroughfare, twenty feet wide at least, which led from our hotel to the Paseo del Gran Capitan. In this were divers shops of the genteeler sort, and some large cafes, standing full of men of leisure, who crowded to their doors and windows, with their hats on and their hands in their pockets, as at a club, and let no fact of the passing world escape their hungry eyes. Their behavior expressed a famine of incident in Cordova which was pathetic.

## VII

The people did not look very healthy as to build or color, and there was a sound of coughing everywhere. To be sure, it was now the season of the first colds, which would no doubt wear off with the coming of next spring; and there was at any rate not nearly so much begging as at Toledo, because there could not be anywhere. I am sorry I can contribute no statistics as to the moral or intellectual condition of Cordova; perhaps they will not be expected or desired of me; I can only say that the general intelligence is such that no one will own he does not know anything you ask him even when he does not; but this is a national rather than a local trait, which causes the stranger to go in many wrong directions all over the peninsula. I should not say that there was any noticeable decay of character from the north to the south such as the attributive pride of the old Castilian in the Sheridan Knowlesian drama would teach; the Cordovese looked no more shiftless than the haughtiest citizens of Burgos.

They had decidedly prettier *patios* and more of them, and they had many public carriages against none whatever in that ancient capital. Rubber tires I did not expect in Cordova and certainly did not get in a city where a single course over the pavements of 850 would have worn them to tatters: but there seems a good deal of public spirit if one may judge from the fact that it is the municipality which keeps Abderrahman's mosque in repair. There are public gardens, far pleasanter than those of Valladolid, which we visited in an interval of the afternoon, and there is a very personable bull-ring to which we drove in the vain hope of seeing the people come out in a typical multitude. But there had been no feast of bulls; and we had to make what we could out of the walking and driving in the Paseo del Gran Capitan toward evening. In its long, discouraging course there were some good houses, but not many, and the promenaders of any social quality were almost as few. Some ladies in private carriages were driving out, and a great many more in public ones as well dressed as the others, but with no pretense of state in the horses or drivers. The women of the people all wore flowers in their hair, a dahlia or a marigold, whether their hair was black or gray. No ladies were walking in the Paseo, except one pretty mother, with her nice-looking children about her, who totaled the sum of her class; but men of every class rather swarmed. High or low, they all wore the kind of hat which abounds everywhere in Andalusia and is called a Cordovese: flat, stiff, squat in crown and wide in brim, and of every shade of gray, brown, and black.

I ought to have had my associations with the great Captain Gonsalvo in the promenade which the city has named after him, but I am not sure that I had, though his life was one of the Spanish books which I won my way through in the middle years of my pathless teens. A comprehensive ignorance of the countries and histories which formed the setting of his most dramatic career was not the best preparation for knowledge of the man, but it was the best I had, and now I can only look back at my struggle with him and wonder that I came off alive. It is the hard fate of the self-taught that their learning must cost them twice as much labor as it would if they were taught by others; the very books they study are grudging friends if not insidious foes. Long afterward when I came to Italy, and began to make the past part of my present, I began to untangle a little the web that the French and the Aragonese wove in the conquest and reconquest of the wretched Sicilies; but how was I to imagine in the Connecticut Western Reserve the scene of Gonsalvo's victories in Calabria? Even loath Ferdinand the Catholic said they brought greater glory to his crown than his own conquest of Granada; I dare say I took some unintelligent pride in his being Viceroy of Naples, and I may have been indignant at his recall and then his retirement from court by the jealous king. But my present knowledge of these facts, and of his helping put down the Moorish insurrection in 1500, as well as his exploits as commander of a Spanish armada against the Turks is a recent debt I owe to the *Encyclopedia Britannica* and not to my boyish researches. Of like actuality is my debt to Mr. Calvert's *Southern Spain,* where he quotes the accounting which the Great Captain gave on the greedy king's demand for a statement of his expenses in the Sicilies.

"Two hundred thousand seven hundred and thirty-six ducats and 9 reals paid to the clergy and the poor who prayed for the victory of the army of Spain.

"One hundred millions in pikes, bullets, and intrenching tools; 10,000 ducats in scented gloves, to preserve the troops from the odor of the enemies' dead left on the battle-field; 100,000 ducats, spent in the repair of the bells completely worn out by every-day announcing fresh victories gained over our enemies; 50,000 ducats in 'aguardiente' for the troops on the eve of battle. A million and a half for the safeguarding prisoners and wounded.

"One million for Masses of Thanksgiving; 700,494 ducats for secret service, etc.

"And one hundred millions for the patience with which I have listened to the king, who demands an account from the man who has presented him with a Kingdom."

It seems that Gonsalvo was one of the greatest humorists, as well as captains of his age, and the king may very well have liked his fun no better than his fame. Now that he has been dead nearly four hundred years, Ferdinand would, if he were living, no doubt join Cordova in honoring Gonzalo Hernandez de Aguila y de Cordova. After all he was not born in Cordova (as I had supposed till an hour ago), but in the little city of Montilla, five stations away on the railroad to the Malaga, and now more noted for its surpassing sherry than for the greatest soldier of his time. To have given its name to Amontillado is glory enough for Montilla, and it must be owned that Gonzalo Hernandez de Aguila y de Montilla would not sound so well as the title we know the hero by, when we know him at all. There may be some who will say that Cordova merits remembrance less because of him than because of Columbus, who first came to the Catholic kings there to offer them not a mere kingdom, but a whole hemisphere. Cordova was then the Spanish headquarters for the operations against Granada, and one reads of the fact with a luminous sense which one cannot have till one has seen Cordova.

## VIII

After our visits to the mosque and the bridge and the museum there remained nothing of our forenoon, and we gave the whole of the earlier afternoon to an excursion which strangers are expected to make into the first climb of hills to the eastward of the city. The road which reaches the Huerto de los Arcos is rather smoother for driving than the streets of Cordova, but the rain had made it heavy, and we were glad of our good horses and their owner's mercy to them. He stopped so often to breathe them when the ascent began that we had abundant time to note the features of the wayside; the many villas, piously named for saints, set on the incline, and orcharded about with orange trees, in the beginning of that measureless forest of olives which has no limit but the horizon.

From the gate to the villa which we had come to see it was a stiff ascent by terraced beds of roses, zinneas, and purple salvia beside walls heavy with jasmine and trumpet creepers, in full bloom, and orange trees, fruiting and flowering in their desultory way. Before the villa we were to see a fountain much favored by our guide who had a passion for the jets that played ball with themselves as long as the gardener let him turn the water on, and watched with joy to see how high the balls would go before slipping back. The fountain was in a grotto-like nook, where benches of cement decked with scallop shells were set round a basin with the figures of two small boys in it bestriding that of a lamb, all employed in letting the water dribble from their mouths. It was very simple-hearted, as such things seem mostly obliged to be, but nature helped art out so well with a lovely abundance of leaf and petal that a far more exacting taste than ours must have been satisfied. The garden was in fact very pretty, though whether it was worth fifteen pesetas and three hours coming to see the reader must decide for himself when he does it. I think it was, myself, and I would like to be there now, sitting in a shell-covered cement chair at the villa steps, and letting the landscape unroll itself wonderfully before me. We were on a shore of that ocean of olives which in southern Spain washes far up the mountain walls of the blue and bluer distances, and which we were to skirt more and more in bay and inlet and widening and narrowing expanses throughout Andalusia. Before we left it we wearied utterly of it, and in fact the olive of Spain is not the sympathetic olive of Italy, though I should think it a much more practical and profitable tree. It is not planted so much at haphazard as the Italian olive seems to be; its mass looks less like an old apple orchard than the Italian; its regular succession is a march of trim files as far as the horizon or the hillsides, which they often climbed to the top. We were in the season of the olive harvest, and throughout the month of October its nearer lines showed the sturdy trees weighed down by the dense fruit, sometimes very small, sometimes as large as pigeon eggs. There were vineyards and wheat-fields in that vast prospect, and certainly there were towns and villages; but what remains with me is the sense of olives and ever more olives, though this may be the cumulative effect of other such prospects as vast and as monotonous.

While we looked away and away, the gardener and a half-grown boy were about their labors that Sunday afternoon as if it were a week-day, though for that reason perhaps they were not working very hard. They seemed mostly to be sweeping up the fallen leaves from the paths, and where the leaves had not fallen from the horse-chestnuts the boy was assisting nature by climbing the trees and plucking them. We tried to find out why he was doing this, but to this day I do not know why he was doing it, and I must be content to contribute the bare fact to the science of arboriculture. Possibly it was in the interest of neatness, and was a precaution against letting the leaves drop and litter the grass. There was apparently a passion for neatness throughout, which in the villa itself mounted to ecstasy. It was in a state to be come and lived in at any moment, though I believe it was occupied only in the late spring and the early autumn; in winter the noble family went to Madrid, and in summer to some northern watering-place. It was rather small, and expressed a life of the minor hospitalities when the family was in residence. It was no place for house-parties, and scarcely for week-end visits, or even for neighborhood dinners. Perhaps on that terrace there was afternoon ice-cream or chocolate for friends who rode or drove over or out; it seemed so possible that we had to check in ourselves the cozy impulse to pull up our shell-covered cement chairs to some central table of like composition.

Within, the villa was of a spick-and-spanness which I feel that I have not adequately suggested; and may I say that the spray of a garden-hose seemed all that would be needed to put the place in readiness for occupation? Not that even this was needed for that interior of tile and marble, so absolutely apt for the climate and the use the place would be put to. In vain we conjectured, and I hope not impertinently, the characters and tastes of the absentees; the sole clue that offered itself was a bookshelf of some Spanish versions from authors scientific and metaphysical to the verge of agnosticism. I would not swear to Huxley and Herbert Spencer among the English writers, but they were such as these, not in their entire bulk, but in extracts and special essays. I recall the slightly tilted row of the neat paper copies; and I wish I knew who it was liked to read them. The Spanish have a fondness for such dangerous ground; from some of their novels it appears they feel it rather chic to venture on it.

IX

We came away from Cordova with a pretty good conscience as to its sights. Upon the whole we were glad they were so few, when once we had made up our minds about the mosque. But now I have found too late that we ought to have visited the general market in the old square where the tournaments used to take place; we ought to have seen also the Chapel of the Hospital del Cardenal, because it was part of the mosque of Al-Manssour; we ought to have verified the remains of two baths out of the nine hundred once existing in the Calle del Bagno Alta; and we ought finally to have visited the remnant of a Moorish house in the Plazuela de San Nicolas, with its gallery of jasper columns, now unhappily whitewashed. The Campo Santo has an unsatisfied claim upon my interest because it was the place where the perfervid Christian zealots used to find the martyrdom they sought at the hands of the unwilling Arabs; and where, far earlier, Julius Caesar planted a plane tree after his victory over the forces of Pompeii at Munda. The tree no longer exists, but neither does Caesar, or the thirty thousand enemies whom he slew there, or the sons of Pompeii who commanded them. These were so near beating Casar at first that he ran among his soldiers "asking them whether they were not ashamed to deliver him into the hands of boys." One of the boys escaped, but two days after the fight the head of the elder was brought to Caesar, who was not liked for the triumph he made himself after the event in Rome, where it was thought out of taste to rejoice over the calamity of his fellow-countrymen as if they had been foreign foes; the Romans do not seem to have minded his putting twenty-eight thousand Cordovese to death for their Pompeian politics. If I had remembered all this from my Plutarch, I should certainly have gone to see the place where Caesar planted that plane tree. Perhaps some kind soul will go to see it for me. I myself do not expect to return to Cordova.

# IX. FIRST DAYS IN SEVILLE

Cordova seemed to cheer up as much as we at our going. We had undoubtedly had the better night's sleep; as often as we woke we found Cordova awake, walking and talking, and coughing more than the night before, probably from fresh colds taken in the rain. From time to time there were church-bells, variously like tin pans and iron pots in tone, without sonorousness in their noise, or such wild clangor as some Italian church-bells have. But Cordova had lived through it, and at the station was lively with the arriving and departing trains. The morning was not only bright; it was hot, and the place babbled with many voices. We thought one voice crying "Agua, agua!" was a parrot's and then we thought it was a girl's, but really it was a boy with water for sale in a stone bottle. He had not a rose, white or red, in his hair, but if he had been a girl, old or young, he would have had one, white or red. Some of the elder women wore mantillas, but these wore flowers too, and were less pleasing than pathetic for it; one very massive matron was less pleasing and more pathetic than the rest. Peasant women carried bunches of chickens by the legs, and one had a turkey in a rush bag with a narrow neck to put its head out of for its greater convenience in gobbling. At the door of the station a donkey tried to bite a fly on its back; but even a Spanish donkey cannot do everything. There was no attempt to cheat us in the weight of our trunks, as there often is in Italy, and the *mozo* who put us and our hand-bags into the train was content with his reasonable fee. As for the pair of Civil Guards who were to go with us, they were of an insurpassable beauty and propriety, and we felt it a peculiar honor when one of them got into the compartment beside ours.

We were to take the mail-train to Seville; and in Spain the *correo* is next to the Sud-Express, which is the last word in the vocabulary of Peninsular railroading. Our *correo* had been up all night on the way from Madrid, and our compartment had apparently been used as a bedchamber, with moments of supper-room. It seemed to have been occupied by a whole family; there were frowsy pillows crushed into the corners of the seats, and, though a porter caught these away, the cigar stubs, and the cigarette ashes strewing the rug and fixed in it with various liquids, as well as some scattering hair-pins, escaped his care. But when it was dried and aired out by windows opened to the sunny weather, it was by no means a bad compartment. The broad cushions were certainly cleaner than the carpet; and it was something—it was a great deal—to be getting out of Cordova on any terms. Not that Cordova seems at this distance so bad as it seemed on the ground. If we could have had the bright Monday of our departure instead of the rainy Sunday of our stay there we might have wished to stay longer. But as it was the four hours' run to Seville was delightful, largely because it Was the run from Cordova.

We were running at once over a gentle ground-swell which rose and sank in larger billows now and then, and the yellow Guadalquivir followed us all the way, in a valley that sometimes widened to the blue mountains always walling the horizon. We had first entered Andalusia after dark, and the scene had now a novelty little staled by the distant view of the afternoon before. The olive orchards then seen afar were intimately realized more and more in their amazing extent. None of the trees looked so old, so world-old, as certain trees in the careless olive groves of Italy. They were regularly planted, and most were in a vigorous middle life; where they were old they were closely pollarded; and there were young trees, apparently newly set out; there were holes indefinitely waiting for others. These were often, throughout Andalusia, covered to their first fork with cones of earth; and we remained in the dramatic superstition that this was to protect them against the omnivorous hunger of the goats, till we were told that it was to save their roots from being loosened by the wind. The orchards filled the level foregrounds and the hilly backgrounds to the vanishing-points of the mountainous perspectives; but when I say this I mean the reader to allow for wide expanses of pasturage, where lordly bulls were hoarding themselves for the feasts throughout Spain which the bulls of Andalusia are happy beyond others in supplying. With their devoted families they paraded the meadows, black against the green, or stood in sharp arrest, the most characteristic accent of the scene. In the farther rather than the nearer distance there were towns, very white, very African, keeping jealously away from the stations, as the custom of most towns is in Spain, beyond the wheat-lands which disputed the landscape with the olive orchards.

One of these towns lay white at the base of a hill topped by a yellow Moorish castle against the blue sky, like a subject waiting for its painter and conscious of its wonderful adaptation to water-color. The railroad-banks were hedged with Spanish bayonet, and in places with cactus grown into trees, all knees and elbows, and of a diabolical uncouthness. The air was fresh and springlike, and under the bright sun, which we had already felt hot, men were plowing the gray fields for wheat. Other men were beginning their noonday lunch, which, with the long nap to follow, would last till three o'clock, and perhaps be rashly accounted to them for sloth by the industrious tourist who did not know that their work had begun at dawn and would not end till dusk. Indolence may be a vice of the towns in Spain, but there is no loafing in the country, if I may believe the conclusions of my note-book. The fields often looked barren enough, and large spaces of their surface were covered by a sort of ground palm, as it seemed to be, though whether it was really a ground palm or not I know no more than I know the name or nature of the wild flower which looked an autumn crocus, and which with other wild flowers fringed the whole course of the train. There was especially a small yellow flower, star-shaped, which we afterward learned was called Todos Santos, from its custom of blooming at All Saints, and which washed the sward in the childlike enthusiasm of buttercups. A fine white narcissus abounded, and clumps of a mauve flower which swung its tiny bells over the sward washed by the Todos Santos. There were other flowers, which did what they could to brighten our way, all clinging to the notion of summer, which the weather continued to flatter throughout our fortnight in Seville.

I could not honestly say that the stations or the people about them were more interesting than in La Mancha. But at one place, where some gentlemen in linen jackets dismounted with their guns, a group of men with dogs leashed in pairs and saddle-horses behind them, took me with the sense of something peculiarly native where everything was so native. They were slim, narrow-hipped young fellows, tight-jerkined, loose-trousered, with a sort of divided apron of leather facing the leg and coming to the ankle; and all were of a most masterly Velasquez coloring and drawing. As they stood smoking motionlessly, letting the smoke drift from their nostrils, they seemed somehow of the same make with the slouching hounds, and they leaned forward together, giving the hunters no visible or audible greeting, but questioning their will with one quality of gaze. The hunters moved toward them, but not as if they belonged together, or expected any sort of demonstration from the men, dogs, and horses that were of course there to meet them. As long as our train paused, no electrifying spark kindled them to a show of emotion; but it would have been interesting to see what happened after we left them behind; they could not have kept their attitude of mutual indifference much longer. These peasants, like the Spaniards everywhere, were of an intelligent and sagacious look; they only wanted a chance, one must think, to be a leading race. They have sometimes an anxiety of appeal in their apathy, as if they would like to know more than they do.

There was some livelier thronging at the station where the train stopped for luncheon, but secure with the pretty rush-basket which the head waiter at our hotel, so much better than the hotel, had furnished us at starting, we kept to our car; and there presently we were joined by a young couple who were unmistakably a new married couple. The man was of a rich brown, and the woman of a dead white with dead black hair. They both might have been better-looking than they were, but apparently not better otherwise, for at Seville the groom helped us out of the car with our hand-bags.

I do not know what polite offers from him had already brought out the thanks in which our speech bewrayed us; but at our outlandish accents they at once became easier. They became frankly at home with themselves, and talked in their Andalusian patter with no fear of being understood. I might, indeed, have been far apter in Spanish without understanding their talk, for when printed the Andalusian dialect varies as far from the Castilian as, say, the Venetian varies from the Tuscan, and when spoken, more. It may then be reduced almost wholly to vowel sounds, and from the lips of some speakers it is really no more consonantal than if it came from the beaks of birds. They do not lisp the soft *c* or the *z*, as the Castilians do, but hiss them, and lisp the *s* instead, as the reader will find amusingly noted in the Sevillian chapters of *The Sister of San Sulpice,* which are the most charming chapters of that most charming novel. At the stations there were sometimes girls and sometimes boys with water for sale from stone bottles, who walked by the cars crying it; and there were bits of bright garden, or there were flowers in pots. There were also poor little human flowers, or call them weeds, if you will, that suddenly sprang up beside our windows, and moved their petals in pitiful prayer for alms. They always sprang up on the off side of the train, so that the trainmen could not see them, but I hope no trainman in Spain would have had the heart to molest them. As a matter of taste in vegetation, however, we preferred an occasional effect of mixed orange and pomegranate trees, with their perennial green and their autumnal red. We were, in fact, so spoiled by the profusion of these little human flowers, or weeds, that we even liked the change to the dried stalk of an old man, flowering at top into a flat basket of pale-pink shrimps. He gave us our first sight of sea-fruit, when we had got, without knowing it, to Seville Junction. There was, oddly enough, no other fruit for sale there; but there was a very agreeable-looking booth at the end of the platform placarded with signs of Puerto Rico coffee, cognac, and other drinks; and outside of it there were wash-basins and clean towels. I do not know how an old woman with a blind daughter made herself effective in the crowd, which did not seem much preoccupied with the opportunities of ablution and refection at that booth; but perhaps she begged with her blind daughter's help while the crowd was busy in assorting itself for Cadiz and Seville and Malaga and Cordova and other musically syllabled mothers of history and romance.

II

A few miles and a few minutes more and we were in the embrace of the loveliest of them, which was at first the clutch on the octroi. But the octroi at Seville is not serious, and a walrus-mustached old porter, who looked like an old American car-driver of the bearded eighteen-sixties, eased us—not very swiftly, but softly—through the local customs, and then we drove neither so swiftly nor so softly to the hotel, where we had decided we would have rooms on the *patio*. We had still to learn that if there is a *patio* in a Spanish hotel you cannot have rooms in it, because they are either in repair or they are occupied. In the present case they were occupied; but we could have rooms over the street, which were the same as in the *patio*, and which were perfectly quiet, as we could perceive from the trolley-cars grinding and squealing under their windows. The manager (if that was the quality of the patient and amiable old official who received us) seemed surprised to see the cars there, perhaps because they were so inaudible; but he said we could have rooms in the annex, fronting on the adjoining plaza and siding on an inoffensive avenue where there were absolutely no cars. The interior, climbing to a lofty roof by a succession of galleries, was hushed by four silent senoras, all in black, and seated in mute ceremony around a table in chairs from which their little feet scarcely touched the marble pavement. Their quiet confirmed the manager's assurance of a pervading tranquillity, and though the only bath in the annex was confessedly on the ground floor, and we were to be two floors above, the affair was very simple: the chambermaid would always show us where the bath was.

With misgiving, lost in a sense of our helplessness, we tried to think that the avenue under us was then quieting down with the waning day; and certainly it was not so noisy as the plaza, which, resounded with the whips and quips of the cabmen, and gave no signs of quiescence. Otherwise the annex was very pleasant, and we took the rooms shown us, hoping the best and fearing the worst. Our fears were wiser than our hopes, but we did not know this, and we went as gaily as we could for tea in the *patio* of our hotel, where a fountain typically trickled amidst its water-plants and a noiseless Englishman at his separate table almost restored our lost faith in a world not wholly racket. A young Spaniard and two young Spanish girls helped out the illusion with their gentle movements and their muted gutturals, and we looked forward to dinner with fond expectation. To tell the truth, the dinner, when we came back to it, was not very good, or at least not very winning, and the next night it was no better, though the head waiter had then, made us so much favor with himself as to promise us a side-table for the rest of our stay. He was a very friendly head waiter, and the dining-room was a long glare of the encaustic tiling which all Seville seems lined with, and of every Moorish motive in the decoration. Besides, there was a young Scotch girl, very interestingly pale and delicate of face, at one of the tables, and at another a Spanish girl with the most wonderful fire-red hair, and there were several miracles of the beautiful obesity which abounds in Spain.

When we returned to the annex it did seem, for the short time we kept our windows shut, that the manager had spoken true, and we promised ourselves a tranquil night, which, after our two nights in Cordova, we needed if we did not merit. But we had counted without the spread of popular education in Spain. Under our windows, just across the way, there proved to be a school of the "Royal Society of Friends of their Country," as the Spanish inscription in its front proclaimed; and at dusk its pupils, children and young people of both sexes, began clamoring for knowledge at its doors. About ten o'clock they burst from them again with joyous exultation in their acquirements; then, shortly after, every manner of vehicle began to pass, especially heavy market wagons overladen and drawn by horses swarming with bells. Their succession left scarcely a moment of the night unstunned; but if ever a moment seemed to be escaping, there was a maniacal bell in a church near by that clashed out: "Hello! Here's a bit of silence; let's knock it on the head!"

We went promptly the next day to the gentle old manager and told him that he had been deceived in thinking he had given us rooms on a quiet street, and appealed to his invention for something, for anything, different. His invention had probably never been put to such stress before, and he showed us an excess of impossible apartments, which we subjected to a consideration worthy of the greatest promise in them. Our search ended in a suite of rooms on the top floor, where we could have the range of a flat roof outside if we wanted; but as the private family living next door kept hens, led by a lordly turkey, on their roof, we were sorrowfully forced to forego our peculiar advantage. Peculiar we then thought it, though we learned afterward that poultry-farming was not uncommon on the flat roofs of Seville, and there is now no telling how we might have prospered if we had taken those rooms and stocked our roof with Plymouth Rocks and Wyandottes. At the moment, however, we thought it would not do, and we could only offer our excuses to the manager, whose resources we had now exhausted, but not whose patience, and we parted with expressions of mutual esteem and regret.

Our own grief was sincerer in leaving behind us the enthusiastic chambermaid of the annex who had greeted us with glad service, and was so hopeful that when she said our doors should be made to latch and lock in the morning, it was as if they latched and locked already. Her zeal made the hot water she brought for the baths really hot, *"Caliente, caliente,"* and her voice would have quieted the street under our windows if music could have soothed it. At a friendly word she grew trustful, and told us how it was hard, hard for poor people in Seville; how she had three dollars a month and her husband four; and how they had to toil for it. When we could not help telling her, cruelly enough, what they singly and jointly earn in New

York, she praised rather than coveted the happier chance impossible to them. They would like to go, but they could not go! She was gay with it all, and after we had left the hotel and come back for the shawl which had been forgotten, she ran for it, shouting with laughter, as if we must see it the great joke she did; and she took the reward offered with the self-respect never wanting to the Spanish poor. Very likely if I ransacked my memory I might find instances of their abusing those advantages over the stranger which Providence puts in the reach of the native everywhere; but on the spur of the moment, I do not recall any. In Spain, where a woman earns three dollars a month, as in America where she earns thirty, the poor seem to abound in the comparative virtues which the rich demand in return for the chances of Heaven which they abandon to them. There were few of those rendering us service there whom we would not willingly have brought away with us; but very likely we should have found they had the defects of their qualities.

When we definitely turned our backs on the potential poultry-farm offered us at our hotel, we found ourselves in as good housing at another, overlooking the length and breadth of the stately Plaza San Fernando, with its parallelogram of tall palms, under a full moon swimming in a cloudless heaven by night and by day. By day, of course, we did not see it, but the sun was visibly there, rather blazing hot, even in mid-October, and showing more distinctly than the moon the beautiful tower of the Giralda from the waist up, and the shoulder of the great cathedral, besides features of other noble, though less noble, edifices. Our plaza was so full of romantic suggestion that I am rather glad now I had no association with it. I am sure I could not have borne at the time to know, as I have only now learned by recurring to my Baedeker, that in the old Franciscan cloister once there had stood the equestrian statue of the Comendador who dismounts and comes unbidden to the supper of Don Giovanni in the opera. That was a statue which, seen in my far youth, haunted my nightmares for many a year, and I am sure it would have kept me from sleep in the conditions, now so perfect, of our new housing if I had known, about it.

III

The plaza is named, of course, for King Fernando, who took Seville from the Moors six hundred years ago, and was canonized for his conquests and his virtues. But I must not enter so rashly upon the history of Seville, or forget the arrears of personal impression which I have to bring up. The very drive from the station was full of impressions, from the narrow and crooked streets, the houses of yellow, blue, and pink stucco, the flowered and fountained *patios* glimpsed passingly, the half-lengths of church-towers, and the fleeting facades of convents and palaces, all lovely in the mild afternoon light. These impressions soon became confluent, so that without the constant witness of our note-books I should now find it impossible to separate them. If they could be imparted to the reader in their complexity, that would doubtless be the ideal, though he would not believe that their confused pattern was a true reflex of Seville; so I recur to the record, which says that the morning after our arrival we hurried to see the great and beautiful cathedral. It had failed, in our approach the afternoon before, to fulfil the promise of one of our half-dozen guide-books (I forget which one) that it would seem to gather Seville about it as a hen gathers her chickens, but its vastness grew upon us with every moment of our more intimate acquaintance. Our acquaintance quickly ripened into the affectionate friendship which became a tender regret when we looked our last upon it; and vast as it was, it was never too large for our embrace. I doubt if there was a moment in our fortnight's devotion when we thought the doughty canons, its brave-spoken founders, "mad to have undertaken it," as they said they expected people to think, or any moment when we did not revere them for imagining a temple at once so beautiful and so big.

Our first visit was redeemed from the commonplace of our duty-round of the side-chapels by two things which I can remember without the help of my notes. One, and the great one, was Murillo's "Vision of St. Anthony," in which the painter has most surpassed himself, and which not to have seen, Gautier says, is not to have known the painter. It is so glorious a masterpiece, with the Child joyously running down from the clustering angels toward the kneeling saint in the nearest corner of the foreground, that it was distinctly a moment before I realized that the saint had once been cut out of his corner and sent into an incredible exile in America, and then munificently restored to it, though the seam in the canvas only too literally attested the incident. I could not well say how this fact then enhanced the interest of the painting, and then how it ceased from the consciousness, which it must always recur to with any remembrance of it. If one could envy wealth its chance of doing a deed of absolute good, here was the occasion, and I used it. I did envy the mind, along with the money, to do that great thing. Another great thing which still more swelled my American heart and made it glow with patriotic pride was the monument to Columbus, which our suffering his dust to be translated from Havana has made possible in Seville. There may be other noble results of our war on Spain for the suzerainty of Cuba and the conquest of Puerto Rico and the Philippines, but there is none which matches in moral beauty the chance it won us for this Grand Consent. I suppose those effigies of the four Spanish realms of Castile, Leon, Aragon, and Navarre, which bear the coffin of the discoverer in stateliest processional on their shoulders, may be censured for being too boldly superb, too almost swagger, but I will not be the one to censure them. They are painted the color of life, and they advance colossally, royal-robed and mail-clad, as if marching to some proud music, and would tread you down if you did not stand aside. It is perhaps not art, but it is magnificent; nothing less stupendously Spanish would have sufficed; and I felt that the magnanimity which had yielded Spain this swelling opportunity had made America her equal in it.

We went to the cathedral the first morning after our arrival in Seville, because we did not know how soon we might go away, and then we went every morning or every afternoon of our fortnight there. Habitually we entered by that Gate of Pardon which in former times had opened the sanctuary to any wickedness short of heresy; but, as our need of refuge was not pressing, we wearied of the Gate of Pardon, with its beautiful Saracenic arch converted to Christianity by the Renaissance bas-relief obliterating the texts from the Koran. We tried to form the habit of going in by other gates, but the Gate of Pardon finally prevailed; there was always a gantlet of cabmen to be run beside it, which brought our sins home to us. It led into the badly paved Court of Oranges, where the trees seem planted haphazard and where there used also to be fountains. Gate and court are remnants of the mosque, patterned upon that of Cordova by one of the proud Moorish kings of Seville, and burned by the Normans when they took and sacked his city. His mosque had displaced the early Christian basilica of San Vicente, which the still earlier temple to Venus Salambo had become. Then, after the mosque was rebuilt, the good San Fernando in his turn equipped it with a Gothic choir and chapels and turned it into the cathedral, which was worn out with pious uses when the present edifice was founded, in their *folie des grandeurs,* by those glorious madmen in the first year of the fifteenth century.

IV

Little of this learning troubled me in my visits to the cathedral, or even the fact that, next to St. Peter's, it was the largest church in the world. It was sufficient to itself by mere force of architectural presence, without the help of incidents or measurements. It was a city in itself, with a community of priests and sacristans dwelling in it, and a floating population of sightseers and worshipers always passing through it. The first morning we had submitted to make the round of the chapels, patiently paying to have each of them unlocked and wearily wondering at their wonders, but only sympathizing really with the stern cleric who showed the ceremonial vestments and jewels of the cathedral, and whose bitter face expressed, or seemed to express, abhorrence of our whole trivial tourist tribe. After that morning we took our curiosity into our own keeping and looked at nothing that did not interest us, and we were interested most in those fellow-beings who kept coming and going all day long.

Chiefly, of course, they were women. In Catholic countries women have either more sins to be forgiven than the men, or else they are sorrier for them; and here, whether there was service or not, they were dropped everywhere in veiled and motionless prayer. In Seville the law of the mantilla is rigorously enforced. If a woman drives, she may wear a hat; but if she walks, she must wear a mantilla under pain of being pointed at by the finger of scorn. If she is a young girl she may wear colors with it (a cheerful blue seems the favorite), but by far the greater number came to the cathedral in complete black. Those somber figures which clustered before chapel, or singly dotted the pavement everywhere, flitted in and out like shadows in the perpetual twilight. For far the greater number, their coming to the church was almost their sole escape into the world. They sometimes met friends, and after a moment, or an hour, of prayer they could cheer their hearts with neighborly gossip. But for the greater part they appeared and disappeared silently and swiftly, and left the spectator to helpless conjecture of their history. Many of them would have first met their husbands in the cathedral when they prayed, or when they began to look around to see who was looking at them. It might have been their trysting-place, safeguarding them in their lovers' meetings, and after marriage it had become their social world, when their husbands left them for the clubs or the cafes. They could not go at night, of course, except to some special function, but they could come by day as often as they liked. I do not suppose that the worshipers I saw habitually united love or friendship with their devotions in the cathedral, but some certainly joined business with devotion; at a high function one day an American girl felt herself sharply nudged in the side, and when she turned she found the palm of her kneeling neighbor stretched toward her. They must all have had their parish churches besides the cathedral, and a devotee might make the day a social whirl by visiting one shrine after another. But I do not think that many do. The Spanish women are of a domestic genus, and are expected to keep at home by the men who expect to keep abroad.

I do not know just how it is in the parish churches; they must each have its special rite, which draws and holds the frequenter; but the cathedral constantly offers a drama of irresistible appeal. We non-Catholics can feel this even at the distance to which our Protestantism has remanded us, and at your first visit to the Seville cathedral during mass you cannot help a moment of recreant regret when you wish that a part in the mystery enacting was your birthright. The esthetic emotion is not denied you; the organ-tide that floods the place bears you on it, too; the priests perform their rites before the altar for you; they come and go, they bow and kneel, for you; the censer swings and smokes for you; the little wicked-eyed choir-boys and mischievous-looking acolytes suppress their natures in your behalf as much as if you were a believer, or perhaps more. The whole unstinted hospitality of the service is there for you, as well as for the children of the house, and the heart must be rude and the soul ungrateful that would refuse it. For my part, I accepted it as far as I knew how, and when I left the worshipers on their knees and went tiptoeing from picture to picture and chapel to chapel, it was with shame for the unscrupulous sacristan showing me about, and I felt that he, if not I, ought to be put out and not allowed back till the function was over. I call him sacristan at a venture; but there were several kinds of guides in the cathedral, some in the livery of the place and some in civil dress, willing to supplement our hotel interpreter, or lying in wait for us when we came alone. I wish now I had taken them all, but at the time they tired me, and I denied them.

Though not a day passed but we saw it, I am not able to say what the cathedral was like. The choir was planted in the heart of it, as it might be a celestial refuge in that forest of mighty pillars, as great in girth as the giant redwoods of California, and climbing to a Gothic firmament horizoned round as with sunset light from near a hundred painted windows. The chapels on each side, the most beautiful in Spain, abound in riches of art and pious memorials, with chief among them the Royal Chapel, in the prow, as it were, of the ship which the cathedral has been likened to, keeping the bones not only of the sainted hero, King Fernando, but also, among others, the bones of Peter the Cruel, and of his unwedded love, Maria de Padilla, far too good for Peter in life, if not quite worthy of San Fernando in death. You can see the saint's body on certain dates four times a year, when, as your Baedeker will tell you, "the troops of the garrison march past and lower their colors" outside the cathedral. We were there on none of these dates, and, far more regretably, not on the day of Corpus Christi, when those boys whose effigies in sculptured and painted wood we had seen in the museum at Valladolid pace in their mystic dance before the people at the opposite portal of the cathedral. But I appoint any reader, so minded, to go and witness the rite some springtime for me. There is no hurry, for it is destined to endure through the device practised in defeating the pope who proposed to abolish it. He ordained that it should continue only as long as the boys' actual costumes lasted; but by renewing these carefully wherever they began to wear out, they have become practically imperishable.

If we missed this attraction of the cathedral, we had the high good fortune to witness another ceremony peculiar to it, but perhaps less popularly acceptable. The building had often suffered from earthquakes, and on the awful day, *dies irae*, of the great Lisbon earthquake, during mass and at the moment of the elevation of the Host, when the worshipers were on their knees, there came such a mighty shock in sympathy with the far-off cataclysm that the people started to their feet and ran out of the cathedral. If the priests ran after them, as soon as the apparent danger was past they led the return of their flock and resumed the interrupted rite. It was, of course, by a miracle that the temple was spared, and when it was realized how scarcely Seville had escaped the fate of Lisbon it was natural that the event should be dramatized in a perpetual observance. Every year now, on the 1st of November, the clergy leave the cathedral at a chosen moment of the mass, with much more stateliness than in the original event, and lead the people out of one portal, to return with them by another for the conclusion of the ceremonial.

We waited long for the climax, but at last we almost missed it through the overeagerness of the guide I had chosen out of many that petitioned. He was so politely, so forbearingly insistent in his offer to see that we were vigilantly cared for, that I must have had a heart harder than Peter the Cruel's to have denied him, and he planted us at the most favorable point for the function in the High Chapel, with instructions which portal to hurry to when the movement began, and took his peseta and went his way. Then, while we confidingly waited, he came rushing back and with a great sweep of his hat wafted us to the door which he had said the procession would go out by, but which he seemed to have learned it would come in by, and we were saved from what had almost been his fatal error. I forgave him the more gladly because I could rejoice in his returning to repair his error, although he had collected his money; and with a heart full of pride in his verification of my theory of the faithful Spanish nature, I gave myself to the shining gorgeousness of the procession that advanced chanting in the blaze of the Sevillian sun. There was every rank of clergy, from the archbishop down, in robes of ceremonial, but I am unable honestly to declare the admiration for their splendor which I would have willingly felt. The ages of faith in which those vestments were designed were apparently not the ages of taste; yet it was the shape of the vestments and not the color which troubled the eye of unfaith, if not of taste. The archbishop in crimson silk, with his train borne by two acolytes, the canons in their purple, the dean in his gold-embroidered robes, and the priests and choristers in their black robes and white surplices richly satisfied it; and if some of the clerics were a little frayed and some of the acolytes were spotted with the droppings of the candles, these were details which one remembered afterward and that did not matter at the time.

When the procession was housed again, we went off and forgot it in the gardens of the Alcazar. But I must not begin yet on the gardens of the Alcazar. We went to them every day, as we did to the cathedral, but we did not see them until our second morning in Seville. We gave what was left from the first morning in the cathedral to a random exploration of the streets and places of the city. There was, no doubt, everywhere some touch of the bravery of our square of San Fernando, where the public windows were hung with crimson tapestries and brocades in honor of St. Raphael; but his holiday did not make itself molestively felt in the city's business or pleasure. Where we could drive we drove, and where we must we walked, and we walked of course through the famous Calle de las Sierpes, because no one drives there. As a rule no woman walks there, and naturally there were many women walking there, under the eyes of the popular cafes and aristocratic clubs which principally abound in Las Sierpes, for it is also the street of the principal shops, though it is not very long and is narrower than many other streets of Seville. It has its name from so commonplace an origin as the sign over a tavern door, with some snakes painted on it; but if the example of sinuosity had been set it by prehistoric serpents, there were scores of other streets which have bettered its instruction. There were streets that crooked away everywhere, not going anywhere, and breaking from time to time into irregular angular spaces with a church or a convent or a nobleman's house looking into them.

## VI

The noblemen's houses often showed a severely simple facade to the square or street, and hid their inner glories with what could have been fancied a haughty reserve if it had not been for the frankness with which they opened their *patios* to the gaze of the stranger, who, when he did not halt his carriage before them, could enjoy their hospitality from a sidewalk sometimes eighteen inches wide. The passing tram-car might grind him against the tall grilles which were the only barriers to the *patios*, but otherwise there would be nothing to spoil his enjoyment of those marble floors and tiled walls and fountains potted round with flowering plants. In summer he could have seen the family life there; and people who are of such oriental seclusion otherwise will sometimes even suffer the admiring traveler to come as well as look within. But one who would not press their hospitality so far could reward his forbearance by finding some of the *patios* too new-looking, with rather a glare from their tiles and marbles, their painted iron pillars, and their glass roofs which the rain comes through in the winter. The ladies sit and sew there, or talk, if they prefer, and receive their friends, and turn night into day in the fashion of climates where they are so easily convertible. The *patio* is the place of that peculiarly Spanish rite, the *tertulia*, and the family nightly meets its next of kin and then its nearer and farther friends there with that Latin regularity which may also be monotony. One *patio* is often much like another, though none was perhaps of so much public interest as the *patio* of the lady who loved a bull-fighter and has made her *patio* a sort of shrine to him. The famous *espada* perished in his heroic calling, no worse if no better than those who saw him die, and now his bust is in plain view, with a fit inscription recognizing his worth and prowess, and with the heads of some of the bulls he slew.

Under that clement sky the elements do not waste the works of man as elsewhere, and many of the houses of Seville are said to be such as the Moors built there. We did not know them from the Christian houses; but there are no longer any mosques, while in our wanderings we had the pretty constant succession of the convents which, when they are still in the keeping of their sisterhoods and brotherhoods, remain monuments of the medieval piety of Spain; or, when they are suppressed and turned to secular uses, attest the recurrence of her modern moods of revolution and reform. It is to one of these that Seville owes the stately Alameda de Hercules, a promenade covering the length and breadth of aforetime convent gardens, which you reach from the Street of the Serpents by the Street of the Love of God, and are then startled by the pagan presence of two mighty columns lifting aloft the figures of Caesar and of the titular demigod. Statues and pillars are alike antique, and give you a moment of the Eternal City the more intense because the promenade is of an unkempt and broken surface, like the Cow-field which the Roman Forum used to be. Baedeker calls it shady, and I dare say it is shady, but I do not remember the trees—only those glorious columns climbing the summer sky of the Andalusian autumn, and proclaiming the imperishable memory of the republic that conquered and the empire that ruled the world, and have never loosed their hold upon it. We were rather newly from the grass-grown ruin of a Roman town in Wales, and in this other Iberian land we were always meeting the witnesses of the grandeur which no change short of some universal sea change can wholly sweep from the earth. Before it Goth and Arab shrink, with all their works, into the local and provisional; Rome remains for all time imperial and universal.

To descend from this high-horsed reflection, as I must, I have to record that there did not seem to be so many small boys in Seville as in the Castillian capitals we had visited; in the very home of the bull-feast we did not see one mimic *corrida* given by the *torreros* of the future. Not even in the suburb of Triana, where the small boys again consolingly superabounded, was the great national game played among the wheels and hoofs of the dusty streets to which we crossed the Guadalquivir that afternoon. To be sure, we were so taken with other things that a boyish bull-feast might have rioted unnoticed under our horses' very feet, especially on the long bridge which gives you the far upward and downward stretch of the river, so simple and quiet and empty above, so busy and noisy and thronged with shipping below. I suppose there are lovelier rivers than that—we ourselves are known to brag of our Pharpar and Abana—but I cannot think of anything more nobly beautiful than the Guadalquivir resting at peace in her bed, where she has had so many bad dreams of Carthaginian and Roman and Gothic and Arab and Norman invasion. Now her waters redden, for the time at least, only from the scarlet hulls of the tramp steamers lying in long succession beside the shore where the gardens of the Delicias were waiting to welcome us that afternoon to our first sight of the pride and fashion of Seville. I never got enough of the brave color of those tramp steamers; and in thinking of them as English, Norse, French, and Dutch, fetching or carrying their cargoes over those war-worn, storied waters, I had some finer thrills than in dwelling on the Tower of Gold which rose from the midst of them. It was built in the last century of the Moorish dominion to mark the last point to which the gardens of the Moorish palace of the Alcazar could stretch, but they were long ago obliterated behind it; and though it was so recent, no doubt it would have had its pathos if I could ever have felt pity for the downfall of the Moslem power in Spain. As it was, I found the tramp steamers more moving, and it was these that my eye preferably sought whenever I crossed the Triana bridge.

## VII

We were often crossing it on one errand or other, but now we were especially going to see the gipsy quarter of Seville, which disputes with that of Granada the infamy of the loathsomest purlieu imaginable. Perhaps because it was so very loathsome, I would not afterward visit the gipsy quarter in Granada, and if such a thing were possible I would willingly unvisit the gipsy quarter of Seville. All Triana is pretty squalid, though it has merits and charms to which I will try eventually to be just, and I must even now advise the reader to visit the tile potteries there. If he has our good-fortune he may see in the manager of one a type of that fusion of races with which Spain long so cruelly and vainly struggled after the fall of the last Moorish kingdom. He was beautifully lean and clean of limb, and of a grave gentleness of manner; his classically regular face was as swarthy as the darkest mulatto's, but his quiet eyes were gray. I carried the sense of his fine decency with me when we drove away from his warerooms, and suddenly whirled round the corner of the street into the gipsy quarter, and made it my prophylactic against the human noisomeness which instantly beset our course. Let no Romany Rye romancing Barrow, or other fond fibbing sentimentalist, ever pretend to me hereafter that those persistent savages have even the ridiculous claim of the North American Indians to the interest of the civilized man, except as something to be morally and physically scoured and washed up, and drained and fumigated, and treated with insecticides and put away in mothballs. Our own settled order of things is not agreeable at all points; it reeks and it smells, especially in Spain, when you get down to its lower levels; but it does not assail the senses with such rank offense as smites them in the gipsy quarter with sights and sounds and odors which to eye and ear, as well as nose, were all stenches.

Low huts lined the street, which swarmed at our coming with ragged children running beside us and after us and screaming, "Minny, niooney, *money!*" in a climax of what they wanted. Men leaned against the door-posts and stared motionless, and hags, lean and fat, sat on the thresholds and wished to tell our fortunes; younger women ranged the sidewalks and offered to dance. They all had flowers in their hair, and some were of a horrible beauty, especially one in a green waist, with both white and red flowers in her dusky locks. Down the middle of the road a troop of children, some blond, but mostly black, tormented a hapless ass colt; and we hurried away as fast as our guide could persuade our cabman to drive. But the gipsy quarter had another street in reserve which made us sorry to have left the first. It paralleled the river, and into the center of it every manner of offal had been cast from the beginning of time to reek and fester and juicily ripen and rot in unspeakable corruption. It was such a thoroughfare as Dante might have imagined in his Hell, if people in his time had minded such horrors; but as it was we could only realize that it was worse than infernal, it was medieval, and that we were driving in such putrid foulness as the gilded carriages of kings and queens and the prancing steeds and palfreys of knights and ladies found their way through whenever they went abroad in the picturesque and romantic Middle Ages. I scarcely remember now how we got away and down to the decent waterside, and then by the helpful bridge to the other shore of the Guadalquivir, painted red with the reflections of those consoling tramp steamers.

After that abhorrent home of indolence, which its children never left except to do a little fortune-telling and mule and donkey trading, eked out with theft in the country round, any show of honest industry looked wholesome and kind. I rejoiced almost as much in the machinery as in the men who were loading the steamers; even the huge casks of olives, which were working from the salt-water poured into them and frothing at the bung in great white sponges of spume, might have been examples of toil by which those noisome vagabonds could well have profited. But now we had come to see another sort of leisure—the famous leisure of fortune and fashion driving in the Delicias, but perhaps never quite fulfilling the traveler's fond ideal of it. We came many times to the Delicias in hope of it, with decreasing disappointment, indeed, but to the last without entire fruition. For our first visit we could not have had a fitter evening, with its pale sky reddening from a streak of sunset beyond Triana, and we arrived in appropriate circumstance, round the immense circle of the bull-ring and past the palace which the Duc de Montpensier has given the church for a theological seminary, with long stretches of beautiful gardens. Then we were in the famous Paseo, a drive with footways on each side, and on one side dusky groves widening to the river. The paths were lit with gleaming statues, and among the palms and the eucalyptuses were orange trees full of their golden globes, which we wondered were not stolen till we were told they were of that bitter sort which are mostly sent to Scotland, not because they are in accord with the acrid nature of man there, but that they may be wrought into marmalade. On the other hand stretched less formal woods, with fields for such polite athletics as tennis, which the example of the beloved young English Queen of Spain is bringing into reluctant favor with women immemorially accustomed to immobility. The road was badly kept, like most things in Spain, where when a thing is done it is expected to stay done. Every afternoon it is a cloud of dust and every evening a welter of mud, for the Iberian idea of watering a street is to soak it into a slough. But nothing can spoil the Paseo, and that evening we had it mostly to ourselves, though there were two or three carriages with ladies in hats, and at one place other ladies dismounted and courageously walking, while their carriages followed. A magnate of some sort was shut alone in a brougham, in the care of footman and coachman with deeply silver-banded hats; there were a few military and civil riders, and there was distinctly a young man in a dog-cart with a groom, keeping abreast the landau of three ladies in mantillas, with whom he was improving what seemed a chance acquaintance. Along the course the public park gave way at times to the grounds of private villas; before one of these a boy did what he could for us by playing ball with a priest. At other points there were booths with chairs and tables, where I am sure interesting parties of people would have been sitting if they could have expected us to pass.

VIII

The reader, pampered by the brilliant excitements of our American promenades, may think this spectacle of the gay world of Seville dull; but he ought to have been with us a colder, redder, and sadder evening when we had the Delicias still more to ourselves. Afterward the Delicias seemed to cheer up, and the place was fairly frequented on a holiday, which we had not suspected was one till our cabman convinced us from his tariff that we must pay him double, because you must always do that in Seville on holidays. By this time we knew that most of the Sevillian rank and riches had gone to Madrid for the winter, and we were the more surprised by some evident show of them in the private turnouts where by far most of the turnouts were public. But in Spain a carriage is a carriage, and the Sevillian cabs are really very proper and sometimes even handsome, and we felt that our own did no discredit to the Delicias. Many of the holiday-makers were walking, and there were actually women on foot in hats and hobble-skirts without being openly mocked. On the evening of our last resort to the Delicias it was quite thronged far into the twilight, after a lemon sunset that continued to tinge the east with pink and violet. There were hundreds of carriages, fully half of them private, with coachmen and footmen in livery. With them it seemed to be the rule to stop in the circle at a turning-point a mile off and watch the going and coming. It was a serious spectacle, but not solemn, and it had its reliefs, its high-lights. It was always pleasant to see three Spanish ladies on a carriage seat, the middle one protruding because of their common bulk, and oftener in umbrella-wide hats with towering plumes than in the charming mantilla. There were no top-hats or other formality in the men's dress; some of them were on horseback, and there were two women riding.

Suddenly, as if it had come up out of the ground, I perceived a tram-car keeping abreast of the riding and walking and driving, and through all I was agreeably aware of files of peasants bestriding their homing donkeys on the bridle-path next the tram. I confess that they interested me more than my social equals and superiors; I should have liked to talk with those fathers and mothers of toil, bestriding or perched on the cruppers of their donkeys, and I should have liked especially to know what passed in the mind of one dear little girl who sat before her father with her bare brown legs tucked into the pockets of the pannier.

# X. SEVILLIAN ASPECTS AND INCIDENTS

It is always a question how much or little we had better know about the history of a strange country when seeing it. If the great mass of travelers voted according to their ignorance, the majority in favor of knowing next to nothing would be overwhelming, and I do not say they would be altogether unwise. History itself is often of two minds about the facts, or the truth from them, and when you have stored away its diverse conclusions, and you begin to apply them to the actual conditions, you are constantly embarrassed by the misfits. What did it avail me to believe that when the Goths overran the north of Spain the Vandals overran the south, and when they swept on into Africa and melted away in the hot sun there as a distinctive race, they left nothing but the name Vandalusia, a letter less, behind them? If the Vandals were what they are reported to have been, the name does not at all characterize the liveliest province of Spain. Besides, the very next history told me that they took even their name with them, and forbade me the simple and apt etymology which I had pinned my indolent faith to.

I

Before I left Seville I convinced a principal bookseller, much against his opinions, that there must be some such brief local history of the city as I was fond of finding in Italian towns, and I took it from his own reluctant shelf. It was a very intelligent little guide, this *Seville in the Hand*, as it calls itself, but I got it too late for use in exploring the city, and now I can turn to it only for those directions which will keep the reader from losing his way in the devious past. The author rejects the fable which the chroniclers delight in, and holds with historians who accept the Phoenicians as the sufficiently remote founders of Seville. This does not put out of commission those Biblical "ships of Tarshish" which Dr. Edward Everett Hale, in his graphic sketch of Spanish history, has sailing to and from the neighboring coasts. Very likely they came up the Guadalquivir, and lay in the stream where a few thousand years later I saw those cheerful tramp-steamers lying. At any rate, the Phoenicians greatly flourished there, and gave their colony the name of Hispalis, which it remained content with till the Romans came and called the town Julia Romula, and Julius Caesar fenced it with the strong walls which the Moorish conquerors, after the Goths, reinforced and have left plain to be seen at this day. The most casual of wayfaring men must have read as he ran that the Moorish power fell before the sword of San Fernando as the Gothic fell before their own, and the Roman before the Gothic. But it is more difficult to realize that earlier than the Gothic, somewhere in between the Vandals and the Romans, had been the Carthaginians, whose great general Hamilcar fancied turning all Spain into a Carthaginian province. They were a branch of the Phoenicians as even the older, unadvertised edition of the *Encyclopedia Britannica* will tell, and the Phoenicians were a sort of Hebrews. Whether they remained to flourish with the other Jews under the Moors, my *Sevilla en la Mano* does not say; and I am not sure whether they survived to share the universal exile into which Islam and Israel were finally driven. What is certain is, that the old Phoenician name of Hispalis outlived the Roman name of Julia Romula and reappeared in the Arabic as Ishbiliya (I know it from my Baedeker) and is now permanently established as Seville.

Under the Moors the city was subordinate to Cordova, though I can hardly bear to think so in my far greater love of Seville. But it was the seat of schools of science, art, and agriculture, and after the Christians had got it back, Alfonso the Learned founded other schools there for the study of Latin and Arabic. But her greatest prosperity and glory came to Seville with the discovery of America. Not Columbus only, but all his most famous contemporaries, sailed from the ports of her coasts; she was the capital of the commerce with the new world, ruling and regulating it by the oldest mercantile tribunal in the world, and becoming the richest city of Spain. Then riches flowered in the letters and arts, especially the arts, and Herrera, Pacheco, Velasquez, Murillo, and Zurburan were born and flourished in Seville. In modern times she has taken a prominent part in political events. She led in the patriotic war to drive out the armies of Napoleon, and she seems to have been on both sides in the struggle for liberal and absolutist principles, the establishment of the brief republic of 1868, and the restoration of the present monarchy.

Through all the many changes from better to Worse, from richer to poorer, Seville continued faithful to the ideal of religious unity which the wise Isabel and the shrewd Ferdinand divined was the only means of consolidating the intensely provincial kingdoms of Spain into one nation of Spaniards. Andalusia not being Gothic had never been Aryan, and it was one of her kings who carried his orthodoxy to Castile and established it inexpugnably at Toledo after he succeeded his heretical father there. When four or five hundred years later it became a political necessity of the Catholic Kings to expel their Jewish and Moorish subjects and convert their wealth to pious and patriotic uses, Andalusia was one of the most zealous provinces in the cause. When presently the inquisitions of the Holy Office began, some five hundred heretics were burned alive at Seville before the year was out; many others, who were dead and buried, paid the penalty of their heresy in effigy; in all more than two thousand suffered in the region round about. Before he was in Valladolid, Torquemada was in Seville, and there he drew up the rules that governed the procedure of the Inquisition throughout Spain. A magnificent *quemadero,* or crematory, second only to that of Madrid, was built: a square stone platform where almost every day the smoke of human sacrifice ascended. This crematory for the living was in the meadow of San Sebastian, now a part of the city park system which we left on the right that first evening when we drove to the Delicias. I do not know why I should now regret not having visited the place of this dreadful altar and offered my unavailing pity there to the memory of those scores of thousands of hapless martyrs who suffered there to no end, not even to the end of confirming Spain in the faith one and indivisible, for there are now, after so many generations of torment, two Protestant churches in Seville. For one thing I did not know where the place of the *quemadero* was; and I do not yet know where those Protestant churches are.

II

If I went again to Seville I should try to visit them—but, as it was, we gave our second day to the Alcazar, which is merely the first in the series of palaces and gardens once stretching from the flank of the cathedral to the Tower of Gold beside the Guadalquivir. A rich sufficiency is left in the actual Alcazar to suggest the splendor of the series, and more than enough in the gardens to invite our fatigue, day after day, to the sun and shade of its quiet paths and seats when we came spent with the glories and the bustling piety of the cathedral. In our first visit we had the guidance of a patriotic young Granadan whose zeal for the Alhambra would not admit the Alcazar to any comparison, but I myself still prefer it after seeing the Alhambra. It is as purely Moorish as that and it is in better repair if not better taste. The taste in fact is the same, and the Castilian kings consulted it as eagerly as their Arabic predecessors in the talent of the Moslem architects whom they had not yet begun to drive into exile. I am not going to set up rival to the colored picture postals, which give a better notion than I could give of the painted and gilded stucco decoration, the ingenious geometrical designs on the walls, and the cloying sweetness of the honeycombing in the vaulted roofs. Every one will have his feeling about Moorish architecture; mine is that a little goes a great way, and that it is too monotonous to compete with the Gothic in variety, while it lacks the dignity of any form of the Greek or the Renaissance. If the phrase did not insult the sex which the faith of the Moslem insufferably insults, one might sum up one's slight for it in the word effeminate.

The Alcazar gardens are the best of the Alcazar. But I would not ignore the homelike charm of the vast court by which you enter from the street outside to the palace beyond. It is planted casually about with rather shabby orange trees that children were playing under, and was decorated with the week's wash of the low, simple dwellings which may be hired at a rental moderate even for Seville, where a handsome and commodious house in a good quarter rents for sixty dollars a year. One of those two-story cottages, as we should call them, in the ante-court of the Alcazar had for the student of Spanish life the special advantage of a lover close to a ground-floor window dropping tender nothings down through the slats of the shutter to some maiden lurking within. The nothings were so tender that you could not hear them drop, and, besides, they were Spanish nothings, and it would not have served any purpose for the stranger to listen for them. Once afterward we saw the national courtship going on at another casement, but that was at night, and here the precious first sight of it was offered at ten o'clock in the morning. Nobody seemed to mind the lover stationed outside the shutter with which the iron bars forbade him the closest contact; and it is only fair to say that he minded nobody; he was there when we went in and there when we came out, and it appears that when it is a question of love-making time is no more an object in Spain than in the United States. The scene would have been better by moonlight, but you cannot always have it moonlight, and the sun did very well; at least, the lover did not seem to miss the moon.

He was only an incident, and I hope the most romantic reader will let me revert from him to the Alcazar gardens. We were always reverting to them on any pretext or occasion, and we mostly had them to ourselves in the gentle afternoons when we strayed or sat about at will in them. The first day we were somewhat molested by the instruction of our patriotic Granadan guide, who had a whopper-jaw and grayish blue eyes, but coal-black hair for all his other blondness. He smoked incessant cigarettes, and he showed us especially the pavilion of Charles the Fifth, whom, after that use of all English-speaking Spanish guides, he called Charley Fift. It appeared that the great emperor used this pavilion for purposes of meditation; but he could not always have meditated there, though the frame of a brazier standing in the center intimated that it was tempered for reflection. The first day we found a small bird in possession, flying from one bit of the carved wooden ceiling to another, and then, taking our presence in dudgeon, out into the sun. Another day there was a nursery-girl there with a baby that cried; on another, still more distractingly, a fashionable young French bride who went kodaking round while her husband talked with an archaeological official, evidently Spanish. In his own time, Charley probably had the place more to himself, though even then his thoughts could not have been altogether cheerful, whether he recalled what he had vainly done to keep out of Spain and yet to take the worst of Spain with him into the Netherlands, where he tried to plant the Inquisition among his Flemings; he was already much soured with a world that had cloyed him, and was perhaps considering even then how he might make his escape from it to the cloister.

III

We did not know as yet how almost entirely dramatic the palace of the Alcazar was, how largely it was representative of what the Spanish successors of the Moorish kings thought those kings would have made it if they had made it; and it was probably through an instinct for the genuine that we preferred the gardens after our first cries of wonder. What remains to me of our many visits is the mass of high borders of box, with roses, jasmine, and orange trees, palms, and cypresses. The fountains dribbled rather than gushed, and everywhere were ranks and rows of plants in large, high earthen pots beside or upon the tiled benching that faced the fountains and would have been easier to sit on if you had not had to supply the back yourself. The flowers were not in great profusion, and chiefly we rejoiced in the familiar quaintness of clumps of massive blood-red coxcombs and strange yellow ones. The walks were bordered with box, and there remains distinctly the impression of marble steps and mosaic seats inlaid with tiles; all Seville seems inlaid with tiles. One afternoon we lingered longer than usual because the day was so sunnily warm in the garden paths and spaces, without being hot. A gardener whom we saw oftenest hung about his flowers in a sort of vegetable calm, and not very different from theirs except that they were not smoking cigarettes. He did not move a muscle or falter in his apparently unseeing gaze; but when one of us picked a seed from the ground and wondered what it was he said it was a magnolia seed, and as if he could bear no more went away. In one wilding place which seemed set apart for a nursery several men were idly working with many pauses, but not so many as to make the spectator nervous. As the afternoon waned and the sun sank, its level rays dwelt on the galleries of the palace which Peter the Cruel built himself and made so ugly with harsh brown stucco ornament that it set your teeth on edge, and with gigantic frescos exaggerated from the Italian, and very coarse and rank.

It was this savage prince who invented much of the Alcazar in the soft Moorish taste; but in those hideous galleries he let his terrible nature loose, though as for that some say he was no crueler than certain other Spanish kings of that period. This is the notion of my unadvertised *Encyclopaedia Britannica*, and perhaps we ought to think of him leniently as Peter the Ferocious. He was kind to some people and was popularly known as the Justiciary; he especially liked the Moors and Jews, who were gratefully glad, poor things, of being liked by any one under the new Christian rule. But he certainly killed several of his half-brothers, and notably he killed his half-brother Don Fadrique in the Alcazar. That is, if he had no hand in the butchery himself he had him killed after luring him to Seville for the tournaments and forgiving him for all their mutual injuries with every caressing circumstance. One reads that after the king has kissed him he sits down again to his game of backgammon and Don Fadrique goes into the next room to Maria do Padilla, the lovely and gentle lady whom Don Pedro has married as much as he can with a wedded wife shut up in Toledo. She sits there in terror with her damsels and tries with looks and signs to make Don Fadrique aware of his danger. But he imagines no harm till the king and his companions, with their daggers drawn, come to the curtains, which the king parts, commanding, "Seize the Master of Santiago!" Don Fadrique tries to draw his sword, and then he turns and flies through the halls of the Alcazar, where he finds every door bolted and barred. The king's men are at his heels, and at last one of them fells him with a blow of his mace. The king goes back with a face of sympathy to Maria, who has fallen to the floor.

The treacherous keeping is all rather in the taste of the Italian Renaissance, but the murder itself is more Roman, as the Spanish atrocities and amusements are apt to be. Murray says it was in the beautiful Hall of the Ambassadors that Don Fadrique was killed, but the other manuals are not so specific. Wherever it was, there is a blood-stain in the pavement which our Granadan guide failed to show us, possibly from a patriotic pique that there are no blood-stains in the Alhambra with personal associations. I cannot say that much is to be made of the vaulted tunnel where poor Maria de Padilla used to bathe, probably not much comforted by the courtiers afterward drinking the water from the tank; she must have thought the compliment rather nasty, and no doubt it was paid her to please Don Pedro.

We found it pleasanter going and coming through the corridor leading to the gardens from the public court. This was kept at the outer end by an "old rancid Christian" smoking incessant cigarettes and not explicitly refusing to sell us picture postals after taking our entrance fee; the other end was held by a young, blond, sickly-looking girl, who made us take small nosegays at our own price and whom it became a game to see if we could escape. I have left saying to the last that the king and queen of Spain have a residence in the Alcazar, and that when they come in the early spring they do not mind corning to it through that plebeian quadrangle. I should not mind it myself if I could go back there next spring.

IV

We had refused with loathing the offer of those gipsy jades to dance for us in their noisome purlieu at Triana, but we were not proof against the chance of seeing some gipsy dancing in a cafe-theater one night in Seville. The decent place was filled with the "plain people," who sat with their hats on at rude tables smoking and drinking coffee from tall glasses. They were apparently nearly all working-men who had left nearly all their wives to keep on working at home, though a few of these also had come. On a small stage four gipsy girls, in unfashionably and untheatrically decent gowns of white, blue, or red, with flowers in their hair, sat in a semicircle with one subtle, silent, darkling man among them. One after another they got up and did the same twisting and posturing, without dancing, and while one posed and contorted the rest unenviously joined the spectators in their clapping and their hoarse cries of "Ole!" It was all perfectly proper except for one high moment of indecency thrown in at the end of each turn, as if to give the house its money's worth. But the real, overflowing compensation came when that little, lithe, hipless man in black jumped to his feet and stormed the audience with a dance of hands and arms, feet and legs, head, neck, and the whole body, which Mordkin in his finest frenzy could not have equaled or approached. Whatever was fiercest and wildest in nature and boldest in art was there, and now the house went mad with its hand-clappings and table-hammerings and deep-throated "Oles!"

Another night we went to the academy of the world-renowned Otero and saw the instruction of Sevillian youth in native dances of the *haute ecole*. The academy used to be free to a select public, but now the chosen, who are nearly always people from the hotels, must pay ten pesetas each for their pleasure, and it is not too much for a pleasure so innocent and charming. The academy is on the ground floor of the *maestro's* unpretentious house, and in a waiting-room beyond the shoemaker's shop which filled the vestibule sat, patient in their black mantillas, the mothers and nurses of the pupils. These were mostly quite small children in their every-day clothes, but there were two or three older girls in the conventional dancing costume which a lady from one of the hotels had emulated. Everything was very simple and friendly; Otero found good seats among the *aficionados* for the guests presented to him, and then began calling his pupils to the floor of the long, narrow room with quick commands of "*Venga!*" A piano was tucked away in a corner, but the dancers kept time now with castanets and now by snapping their fingers. Two of the oldest girls, who were apparently graduates, were "differently beautiful" in their darkness and fairness, but alike picturesquely Spanish in their vivid dresses and the black veils fluttering from their high combs. A youth in green velvet jacket and orange trousers, whose wonderful dancing did him credit as Otero's prize pupil, took part with them; he had the square-jawed, high-cheek-boned face of the lower-class Spaniard, and they the oval of all Spanish women. Here there was no mere posturing and contortioning among the girls as with the gipsies; they sprang like flames and stamped the floor with joyous detonations of their slippers. It was their convention to catch the hat from the head of some young spectator and wear it in a figure and then toss it back to him. One of them enacted the part of a *torero* at a bull-fight, stamping round first in a green satin cloak which she then waved before a man's felt hat thrown on the ground to represent the bull hemmed about with *banderillas* stuck quivering into the floor. But the prettiest thing was the dancing of two little girl pupils, one fair and thin and of an angelic gracefulness, and the other plump and dark, who was as dramatic as the blond was lyrical. They accompanied themselves with castanets, and, though the little fatling toed in and wore a common dress of blue-striped gingham, I am afraid she won our hearts from her graceful rival. Both were very serious and gave their whole souls to the dance, but they were not more childishly earnest than an older girl in black who danced with one of the gaudy graduates, panting in her anxious zeal and stopping at last with her image of the Virgin she resembled flung wildly down her back from the place where it had hung over her heart.

V

We preferred walking home from Senor Otero's house through the bright, quiescing street, because in driving there we had met with an adventure which we did not care to repeat. We were driving most unaggressively across a small plaza, with a driver and a friend on the box beside him to help keep us from harm, when a trolley-car came wildly round a corner at the speed of at least two miles an hour and crossed our track. Our own speed was such that we could not help striking the trolley in a collision which was the fault of no one apparently. The front of the car was severely banged, one mud-guard of our victoria was bent, and our conversation was interrupted. Immediately a crowd assembled from the earth or the air, but after a single exchange of reproaches between the two drivers nothing was said by any one. No policeman arrived to *constater* the facts, and after the crowd had silently satisfied or dissatisfied itself that no one was hurt it silently dispersed. The car ambled grumbling off and we drove on with some vague murmurs from our driver, whose nerves seemed shaken, but who was supported in a somewhat lurching and devious progress by the caressing arm of the friend on the seat beside him.

All this was in Seville, where the popular emotions are painted in travel and romance as volcanic as at Naples, where no one would have slept the night of our accident and the spectators would be debating it still. In our own surprise and alarm we partook of the taciturnity of the witnesses, which I think was rather fine and was much decenter than any sort of utterance. On our way home we had occasion to practise a like forbearance toward the lover whom we passed as he stood courting through the casement of a ground floor. The soft air was full of the sweet of jasmine and orange blossoms from the open *patios*. Many people besides ourselves were passing, but in a well-bred avoidance of the dark figure pressed to the grating and scarcely more recognizable than the invisible figure within. I confess I thought it charming, and if at some period of their lives people must make love I do not believe there is a more inoffensive way of doing it.

By the sort of echo notable in life's experience we had a reverberation of the orange-flower perfume of that night in the orange-flower honey at breakfast next morning. We lived to learn that our own bees gather the same honey from the orange flowers of Florida; but at the time we believed that only the bees of Seville did it, and I still doubt whether anywhere in America the morning wakes to anything like the long, rich, sad calls of the Sevillian street hucksters. It is true that you do not get this plaintive music without the accompanying note of the hucksters' donkeys, which, if they were better advised, would not close with the sort of inefficient sifflication which they now use in spoiling an otherwise most noble, most leonine roar. But when were donkeys of any sort ever well advised in all respects? Those of Seville, where donkeys abound, were otherwise of the superior intelligence which throughout Spain leaves the horse and even the mule far behind, and constitutes the donkeys, far beyond the idle and useless dogs, the friends of man. They indefinitely outnumber the dogs, and the cats are of course nowhere in the count. Yet I would not misprize the cats of Seville, which apparently have their money price. We stopped to admire a beautiful white one, on our way to see the market one day, praising it as intelligibly as we could, and the owner caught it up, when we had passed and ran after us, and offered to sell it to us.

That might have been because it was near the market where we experienced almost the only mercantile zeal we had known in Spain. Women with ropes and garlands of onions round their necks invited us to buy, and we had hopeful advances from the stalls of salads and fruits, where there was a brave and beautiful show of lettuces and endives, grapes, medlars, and heaps of melons, but no oranges; I do not know why, though there were shining masses of red peppers and green, peppers, and vast earthen bowls with yellow peas soaking in them. The flowers were every gay autumnal sort, especially dahlias, sometimes made into stiff bouquets, perhaps for church offerings. There were mounds of chestnuts, four or five feet high and wide; and these flowers and fruits filled the interior of the market, while the stalls for the flesh and fish were on the outside. There seemed more sellers than buyers; here and there were ladies buying, but it is said that the mistresses commonly send their maids for the daily provision.

Ordinarily I should say you could not go amiss for your profit and pleasure in Seville, but there are certain imperative objects of interest like the Casa de Pilatos which you really have to do. Strangely enough, it is very well worth doing, for, though it is even more factitiously Moorish than the Alcazar, it is of almost as great beauty and of greater dignity. Gardens, galleries, staircases, statues, paintings, all are interesting, with a mingled air of care and neglect which is peculiarly charming, though perhaps the keener sensibilities, the morbider nerves may suffer from the glare and hardness of the tiling which render the place so wonderful and so exquisite. One must complain of something, and I complain of the tiling; I do not mind the house being supposed like the house of Pontius Pilate in Jerusalem.

It belongs to the Duke of Medina-Celi, who no more comes to it from Madrid than the Duke of Alva comes to his house, which I somehow perversely preferred. For one thing, the Alva palace has eleven *patios,* all far more forgotten than the four in the House of Pilate, and I could fully glut my love of *patios* without seeing half of them. Besides, it was in the charge of a typical Spanish family: a lean, leathery, sallow father, a fat, immovable mother, and a tall, silent daughter. The girl showed us darkly about the dreary place, with its fountains and orange trees and palms, its damp, Moresque, moldy walls, its damp, moldy, beautiful wooden ceilings, and its damp, moldy staircase leading to the family rooms overhead, which we could not see. The family stays for a little time only in the spring and fall, but if ever they stay so late as we had come the sunlight lying so soft and warm in the *patio* and the garden out of it must have made them as sorry to leave it as we were.

I am not sure but I valued the House of Alva somewhat for the chance my visit to it gave me of seeing a Sevillian tenement-house such as I had hoped I might see. One hears that such houses are very scrupulously kept by the janitors who compel the tenants to a cleanliness not perhaps always their nature. At any rate, this one, just across the way from the Alva House, was of a surprising neatness. It was built three stories high, with galleries looking into an open court and doors giving from these into the several tenements. As fortune, which does not continually smile on travel, would have it that morning, two ladies of the house were having a vivid difference of opinion on an upper gallery. Or at least one was, for the other remained almost as silent as the spectators who grouped themselves about her or put their heads out of the windows to see, as well as hear, what it was about. I wish I knew and I would tell the reader. The injured party, and I am sure she must have been deeply injured, showered her enemy with reproaches, and each time when she had emptied the vials of her wrath with much shaking of her hands in the wrong-doer's face she went away a few yards and filled them up again and then returned for a fresh discharge. It was perfectly like a scene of Goldoni and like many a passage of real life in his native city, and I was rapt in it across fifty years to the Venice I used to know. But the difference in Seville was that there was actively only one combatant in the strife, and the witnesses took no more part in it than the passive resistant.

VI

As a contrast to this violent scene which was not so wholly violent but that it was relieved by a boy teasing a cat with his cap in the foreground, and the sweet singing of canaries in the windows of the houses near, I may commend the Casa de los Venerables, ecclesiastics somehow related to the cathedral and having their tranquil dwelling not far from it. The street we took from the Duke of Alva's palace was so narrow and crooked that we scraped the walls in passing, and we should never have got by one heavily laden donkey if he had not politely pushed the side of his pannier into a doorway to make room for us. When we did get to the Casa de los Venerables we found it mildly yellow-washed and as beautifully serene and sweet as the house of venerable men should be. Its distinction in a world of *patios* was a *patio* where the central fountain was sunk half a story below the entrance floor, and encircled by a stairway by which the humble neighbor folk freely descended to fill their water jars. I suppose that gentle mansion has other merits, but the fine staircase that ended under a baroque dome left us facing a bolted door, so that we had to guess at those attractions, which I leave the reader to imagine in turn.

I have kept the unique wonder of Seville waiting too long already for my recognition, though in its eight hundred years it should have learned patience enough for worse things. From its great antiquity alone, if from nothing else, it is plain that the Giralda at Seville could not have been studied from the tower of the Madison Square Garden in New York, which the American will recall when he sees it. If the case must be reversed and we must allow that the Madison Square tower was studied from the Giralda, we must still recognize that it is no servile copy, but in its frank imitation has a grace and beauty which achieves originality. Still, the Giralda is always the Giralda, and, though there had been no Saint-Gaudens to tip its summit with such a flying-footed nymph as poises on our own tower, the figure of Faith which crowns it is at least a good weather-vane, and from its office of turning gives the mighty bell-tower its name. Long centuries before the tower was a belfry it served the mosque, which the cathedral now replaces, as a minaret for the muezzin to call the faithful to prayer, but it was then only two-thirds as high. The Christian belfry which continues it is not in offensive discord with the structure below; its other difference in form and spirit achieves an impossible harmony. The Giralda, however, chiefly works its enchantment by its color, but here I must leave the proof of this to the picture postal which now everywhere takes the bread out of the word-painter's mouth. The time was when with a palette full of tinted adjectives one might hope to do an unrivaled picture of the Giralda; but that time is gone; and if the reader has not a colored postal by him he should lose no time in going to Seville and seeing the original. For the best view of it I must advise a certain beautifully irregular small court in the neighborhood, with simple houses so low that you can easily look up over their roofs and see the mighty bells of the Giralda rioting far aloft, flinging themselves beyond the openings of the belfry and deafeningly making believe to leap out into space. If the traveler fails to find this court (for it seems now and then to be taken in and put away), he need not despair of seeing the Giralda fitly. He cannot see Seville at all without seeing it, and from every point, far or near, he sees it grand and glorious.

I remember it especially from beyond the Guadalquivir in the drive we took through Triana to the village of Italica, where three Roman emperors were born, as the guide-books will officiously hasten to tell, and steal away your chance of treating your reader with any effect of learned research. These emperors (I will not be stopped by any guide-book from saying) were Trajan, Hadrian, and Theodosius; and Triana is named for the first of them. Fortunately, we turned to the right after crossing the bridge and so escaped the gipsy quarter, but we paused through a long street so swarming with children that we wondered to hear whole schoolrooms full of them humming and droning their lessons as we made our way among the tenants. Fortunately, they played mostly in the gutters, the larger looking after the smaller when their years and riches were so few more, with that beautiful care which childhood bestows on babyhood everywhere in Europe. To say that those Spanish children were as tenderly watchful of these Spanish babies as English children is to say everything. Now and then a mother cared for a babe as only a mother can in an office which the pictures and images of the Most Holy Virgin consecrate and endear in lands where the sterilized bottle is unknown, but oftenest it was a little sister that held it in her arms and crooned whatever was the Spanish of—

> *Rack back, baby, daddy shot a b'ar;*
>
> *Rack back, baby, see it hangin' thar.*

For there are no rocking-chairs in Triana, as there were none in our backwoods, and the little maids tilted to and fro on the fore legs and hind legs of their chairs and lulled their charges to sleep with seismic joltings. When the street turned into a road it turned into a road a hundred feet wide; one of those roads which Charles III., when he came to the Spanish throne from Naples, full of beneficent projects and ideals, bestowed upon his unwilling and ungrateful subjects. These roads were made about the middle of the eighteenth century, and they have been gathering dust ever since, so that the white powder now lies in the one beyond Triana five or six inches deep. Along the sides occasional shade-trees stifled, and beyond these gaunt, verdureless fields widened away, though we were told that in the spring the fields were red with flowers and green with young wheat. There were no market-gardens, and the chief crop seemed brown pigs and black goats. In some of the foregrounds, as well as the backgrounds, were olive orchards with olives heaped under them and peasants still resting from their midday breakfast. A mauve bell-shaped flower plentifully fringed the wayside; our driver said it had no name, and later an old peasant said it was "bad."

VII

We passed a convent turned into a prosperous-looking manufactory and we met a troop of merry priests talking gayly and laughing together, and very effective in their black robes against the white road. When we came to the village that was a *municipium* under Augustus and a *colonia* under Hadrian, we found it indeed scanty and poor, but very neat and self-respectful-looking, and not unworthy to have been founded by Scipio Africanus two hundred years before Christ. Such cottage interiors as we glimpsed seemed cleaner and cozier than some in Wales; men in wide flat-brimmed hats sat like statues at the doors, absolutely motionless, but there were women bustling in and out in their work, and at one place a little girl of ten had been left to do the family wash, and was doing it joyously and spreading the clothes in the dooryard to dry. We did not meet with universal favor as we drove by; some groups of girls mocked our driver; when we said one of them was pretty he answered that he had seen prettier.

At the entrance to the ruins of the amphitheater which forms the tourist's chief excuse for visiting Italica the popular manners softened toward us; the village children offered to sell us wild narcissus flowers and were even willing to take money in charity. They followed us into the ruins, much forbidden by the fine, toothless old custodian who took possession of us as his proper prey and led us through the moldering caverns and crumbling tiers of seats which form the amphitheater. Vast blocks, vast hunks, of the masonry are broken off from the mass and lie detached, but the mass keeps the form and dignity of the original design; and in the lonely fields there it had something august and proud beyond any quality of the Arena at Verona or the Colosseum at Rome. It is mostly stripped of the marble that once faced the interior, and is like some monstrous oval shaped out of the earth, but near the imperial box lay some white slabs with initials cut in them which restored the vision of the "grandeur that was Rome" pretty well over the known world when this great work was in its prime.

Our custodian was qualified by his toothlessness to lisp like any old Castilian the letters that other Andalusians hiss, but my own Spanish was so slight and his *patois* was so dense that the best we could do was to establish a polite misunderstanding. On this his one word of English, repeated as we passed through the subterranean doors, "Lion, lion, lion," cast a gleam of intelligence which brightened into a vivid community of ideas when we ended in his cottage, and he prepared to sell us some of the small Roman coins which formed his stock in trade. The poor place was beautifully neat, and from his window he made us free of a sight of Seville, signally the cathedral and the Giralda, such as could not be bought for money in New York.

Then we set out on our return, leaving unvisited to the left the church of San Isidore de Campo, with its tombs of Guzman the Good and that Better Lady Dona Urraca Osorio, whom Peter the Cruel had burned. I say better, because I hold it nobler in Urraca to have rejected the love of a wicked king than in Guzman to have let the Moors slay his son rather than surrender a city to them. But I could only pay honor to her pathetic memory and the memory of that nameless handmaid of hers who rushed into the flames to right the garments on the form which the wind had blown them away from, and so perished with her. We had to take on trust from the guide-books all trace of the Roman town where the three emperors were born, and whose "palaces, aqueducts, and temples and circus were magnificent." We had bought some of the "coins daily dug up," but we intrusted to the elements those "vestiges of vestiges" left of Trajan's palaces after an envious earthquake destroyed them so lately as 1755.

The one incident of our return worthy of literature was the dramatic triumph of a woman over a man and a mule as we saw it exhibited on the parapet of a culvert over a dry torrent's bed. It was the purpose of this woman, standing on the coping in statuesque relief and showing against the sky the comfortable proportions of the Spanish housewife, to mount the mule behind the man. She waited patiently while the man slowly and as we thought faithlessly urged the mule to the parapet; then, when she put out her hands and leaned forward to take her seat, the mule inched softly away and left her to recover her balance at the risk of a fall on the other side. We were too far for anything but the dumb show, but there were, no doubt, words which conveyed her opinions unmistakably to both man and mule. With our hearts in our mouths we witnessed the scene and its repetitions till we could bear it no longer, and we had bidden our cabman drive on when with a sudden spring the brave woman launched herself semicircularly forward and descended upon the exact spot which she had been aiming at. There solidly established on the mule, with her arms fast round the man, she rode off; and I do not think any reader of mine would like to have been that mule or that man for the rest of the way home.

We met many other mules, much more exemplary, in teams of two, three, and four, covered with bells and drawing every kind of carryall and stage and omnibus. These vehicles were built when the road was, about 1750, and were, like the road, left to the natural forces for keeping themselves in repair. The natural forces were not wholly adequate in either case, but the vehicles were not so thick with dust as the road, because they could shake it off. They had each two or four passengers seated with the driver; passengers clustered over the top and packed the inside, but every one was in the joyous mood of people going home for the day. In a plaza not far from the Triana bridge you may see these decrepit conveyances assembling every afternoon for their suburban journeys, and there is no more picturesque sight in Seville, more homelike, more endearing. Of course, when I say this I leave out of the count the bridge over the Guadalquivir at the morning or evening hour when it is covered with brightly caparisoned donkeys, themselves covered with men needing a shave, and gay-kerchiefed women of every age, with boys and dogs underfoot, and pedestrians of every kind, and hucksters selling sea-fruit and land-fruit and whatever else the stranger would rather see than eat. Very little outcry was needed for the sale of these things, which in Naples or even in Venice would have been attended by such vociferation as would have sufficed to proclaim a city in flames.

On a day not long after our expedition to Italica we went a drive with a young American friend living in Seville, whom I look to for a book about that famous city such as I should like to write myself if I had the time to live it as he has done. He promised that he would show us a piece of the old Roman wall, but he showed us ever so much more, beginning with the fore court of the conventual church of Santa Paula, where we found the afternoon light waiting to illumine for us with its tender caress the Luca della Robbia-like colored porcelain figures of the portal and the beautiful octagon tower staying a moment before taking flight for heaven: the most exquisite moment of our whole fortnight in Seville. Tall pots of flowers stood round, and the grass came green through the crevices of the old footworn pavement. When we passed out a small boy scuffled for our copper with the little girl who opened the gate for us, but was brought to justice by us, and joined cheerfully in the chorus of children chanting "Mo-ney, mo-ney!" round us, but no more expecting an answer to their prayer than if we had been saints off the church door.

We passed out of the city by a gate where in a little coign of vantage a cobbler was thoughtfully hammering away in the tumult at a shoe-sole, and then suddenly on our right we had the Julian wall: not a mere fragment, but a good long stretch of it. The Moors had built upon it and characterized it, but had not so masked it as to hide the perdurable physiognomy of the Roman work. It was vastly more Roman wall than you see at Rome; but far better than this heroic image of war and waste was the beautiful old aqueduct, perfectly Roman still, with no visible touch from Moor, or from Christian, before or after the Moor, and performing its beneficent use after two thousand years as effectively as in the years before Christ came to bless the peacemakers. Nine miles from its mountain source the graceful arches bring the water on their shoulders; and though there is now an English company that pipes other streams to the city through its underground mains, the Roman aqueduct, eternally sublime in its usefulness, is constant to the purpose of the forgotten men who imagined it. The outer surfaces of the channel which it lifted to the light and air were tagged with weeds and immemorial mosses, and dripped as with the sweat of its twenty-centuried toil.

We followed it as far as it went on our way to a modern work of peace and use which the ancient friend and servant of man would feel no unworthy rival. Beyond the drives and gardens of the Delicias, where we lingered our last to look at the pleasurers haunting them, we drove far across the wheat-fields where a ship-canal five miles long is cutting to rectify the curve of the Guadalquivir and bring Seville many miles nearer the sea than it has ever been before; hitherto the tramp steamers have had to follow the course of the ships of Tarshish in their winding approach. The canal is the notion of the young king of Spain, and the work on it goes forward night and day. The electric lights were shedding their blinding glare on the deafening clatter of the excavating machinery, and it was an unworthy relief to escape from the intense modernity of the scene to that medieval retreat nearer the city where the *aficionados* night-long watch the bulls coming up from their pastures for the fight or the feast, whichever you choose to call it, of the morrow. These amateurs, whom it would be rude to call sports, lurk in the wayside cafe over their cups of chocolate and wait till in that darkest hour before dawn, with irregular trampling and deep bellowing, these hapless heroes of the arena pass on to their doom. It is a great thing for the *aficionados* who may imagine in that bellowing the the gladiator's hail of *Morituri salutant.* At any rate, it is very chic; it gives a man standing in Seville, which disputes with Madrid the primacy in bull-feasting. If the national capital has bull-feasting every Sunday of the year, all the famous *torreros* come from Andalusia, with the bulls, their brave antagonists, and in the great provincial capital there are bull-feasts of insurpassable, if not incomparable, splendor.

Before our pleasant drive ended we passed, as we had already passed several times, the scene of the famous Feria of Seville, the cattle show which draws tens of thousands to the city every springtime for business and pleasure, but mostly pleasure. The Feria focuses in its greatest intensity at one of the entrances to the Delicias, where the street is then so dense with every sort of vehicle that people can cross it only by the branching viaduct, which rises in two several ascents from each footway, intersecting at top and delivering their endless multitudes on the opposite sidewalk. Along the street are gay pavilions and cottages where the nobility live through the Feria with their families and welcome the public to the sight of their revelry through the open doors and windows. Then, if ever, the stranger may see the dancing, and hear the singing and playing which all the other year in Seville disappoints him of.

## VIII

On the eve of All Saints, after we had driven over the worst road in the world outside of Spain or America, we arrived at the entrance of the cemetery where Baedeker had mysteriously said "some sort of fair was held." Then we perceived that we were present at the preparations for celebrating one of the most affecting events of the Spanish year. This was the visit of kindred and friends bringing tokens of remembrance and affection to the dead. The whole long, rough way we had passed them on foot, and at the cemetery gate we found them arriving in public cabs, as well as in private carriages, with the dignity and gravity of smooth-shaven footmen and coachmen. In Spain these functionaries look their office more solemnly even than in England and affect you as peculiarly correct and eighteenth-century. But apart from their looks the occasion seemed more a festivity than a solemnity. The people bore flowers, mostly artificial, as well as lanterns, and within the cemetery they were furbishing up the monuments with every appliance according to the material, scrubbing the marble, whitewashing the stucco, and repainting the galvanized iron. The lanterns were made to match the monuments and fences architecturally, and the mourners were attaching them with a gentle satisfaction in their fitness; I suppose they were to be lighted at dark and to burn through the night. There were men among the mourners, but most of them were women and children; some were weeping, like a father leading his two little ones, and an old woman grieving for her dead with tears. But what prevailed was a community of quiet resignation, almost to the sort of cheerfulness which bereavement sometimes knows. The scene was tenderly affecting, but it had a tremendous touch of tragic setting in the long, straight avenue of black cypresses which slimly climbed the upward slope from the entrance to the farther bound of the cemetery. Otherwise there was only the patience of entire faith in this annually recurring visit of the living to the dead: the fixed belief that these should rise from the places where they lay. and they who survived them for yet a little more of time should join them from whatever end of the earth in the morning of the Last Day.

All along I have been shirking what any right-minded traveler would feel almost his duty, but I now own that there is a museum in Seville, the Museo Provincial, which was of course once a convent and is now a gallery, with the best, but not the very best, Murillos in it, not to speak of the best Zurburans. I will not speak at all of those pictures, because I could in no wise say what they were, or were like, and because I would not have the reader come to them with any opinions of mine which he might bring away with him in the belief that they were his own. Let him not fail to go to the museum, however; he will be the poorer beyond calculation if he does not; but he will be a beggar if he does not go to the Hospital de la Caridad, where in the church he will find six Murillos out-Murilloing any others excepting always the incomparable "Vision of St. Anthony" in the cathedral. We did not think of those six Murillos when we went to the hospital; we knew nothing of the peculiar beauty and dignity of the church; but we came because we wished to see what the repentance of a man could do for others after a youth spent in wicked riot. The gentle, pensive little Mother who received us carefully said at once that the hospital was not for the sick, but only for the superannuated and the poor and friendless who came to pass a night or an indefinite time in it, according to the pressure of their need; and after showing us the rich little church, she led us through long, clean corridors where old men lay in their white beds or sat beside them eating their breakfasts, very savory-looking, out of ample white bowls. Some of them saluted us, but the others we excused because they were so preoccupied. In a special room set apart for them were what we brutally call tramps, but who doubtless are known in Spain for indigent brethren overtaken on their wayfaring without a lodging for the night. Here they could come for it and cook their supper and breakfast at the large circular fireplace which filled one end of their room. They rose at our entrance and bowed; and how I wish I could have asked them, every one, about their lives!

There was nothing more except the doubt of that dear little Mother when I gave her a silver dollar for her kindness. She seemed surprised and worried, and asked, "Is it for the charity or for me?" What could I do but answer, "Oh, for your Grace," and add another for the charity. She still looked perplexed, but there was no way out of our misunderstanding, if it was one, and we left her with her sweet, troubled face between the white wings of her cap, like angel's wings mounting to it from her shoulders. Then we went to look at the statue of the founder bearing a hapless stranger in his arms in a space of flowers before the hospital, where a gardener kept watch that no visitor should escape without a bunch worth at least a peseta. He had no belief that the peseta could possibly be for the charity, and the poverty of the poor neighborhood was so much relieved by the mere presence of the hospital that it begged of us very little as we passed through.

IX

We had expected to go to Granada after a week in Seville, but man is always proposing beyond his disposing in strange lands as well as at home, and we were fully a fortnight in the far lovelier capital. In the mean time we had changed from our rooms in the rear of the hotel to others in the front, where we entered intimately into the life of the Plaza San Fernando as far as we might share it from our windows. It was not very active life; even the cabmen whose neat victorias bordered the place on three sides were not eager for custom; they invited the stranger, but they did not urge; there was a continual but not a rapid passing through the ample oblong; there was a good deal of still life on the benches where leisure enjoyed the feathery shadow of the palms, for the sun was apt to be too hot at the hour of noon, though later it conduced to the slumber which in Spain accompanies the digestion of the midday meal in all classes. As the afternoon advanced numbers of little girls came into the plaza and played children's games which seemed a translation of games familiar to our own country. One evening a small boy was playing with them, but after a while he seemed to be found unequal to the sport; he was ejected from the group and went off gloomily to grieve apart with his little thumb in his mouth. The sight of his dignified desolation was insupportable, and we tried what a copper of the big-dog value would do to comfort him. He took it without looking up and ran away to the peanut-stand which is always steaming at the first corner all over Christendom. Late in the evening—in fact, after the night had fairly fallen—we saw him making his way into a house fronting on the plaza. He tried at the door with one hand and in the other he held an unexhausted bag of peanuts. He had wasted no word of thanks on us, and he did not now. When he got the door open he backed into the interior still facing us and so fading from our sight and knowledge.

He had the touch of comedy which makes pathos endurable, but another incident was wholly pathetic. As we came out of an antiquity shop near the cathedral one afternoon we found on the elevated footway near the Gate of Pardon a mother and daughter, both of the same second youth, who gently and jointly pronounced to us the magical word *encajes*. Rather, they questioned us with it, and they only suggested, very forbearingly, that we should come to their house with them to see those laces, which of course were old laces; their house was quite near. But that one of us twain who was singly concerned in *encajes* had fatigued and perhaps overbought herself at the antiquity shop, and she signified a regret which they divined too well was dissent. They looked rather than expressed a keen little disappointment; the mother began a faint insistence, but the daughter would not suffer it. Here was the pride of poverty, if not poverty itself, and it was with a pang that we parted from these mutely appealing ladies. We could not have borne it if we had not instantly promised ourselves to come the next day and meet them and go home with them and buy all their *encajes* that we had money for. We kept our promise, and we came the next day and the next and every day we remained in Seville, and lingered so long that we implanted in the cabmen beside the curbing the inextinguishable belief that we were in need of a cab; but we never saw those dear ladies again.

These are some of the cruel memories which the happiest travel leaves, and I gratefully recall that in the case of a custodian of the Columbian Museum, which adjoins the cathedral, we did not inflict a pang that rankled in our hearts for long. I gave him a handful of copper coins which I thought made up a peseta, but his eyes were keener, and a sorrow gloomed his brow which projected its shadow so darkly over us when we went into the cathedral for one of our daily looks that we hastened to return and make up the full peseta with another heap of coppers; a whole sunburst of smiles illumined his face, and a rainbow of the brightest colors arched our sky and still arches it whenever we think of that custodian and his rehabilitated trust in man.

This seems the crevice where I can crowd in the fact that bits of family wash hung from the rail of the old pulpit in the Court of Oranges beside the cathedral, and a pumpkin vine lavishly decorated an arcade near a doorway which perhaps gave into the dwelling of that very custodian. At the same time I must not fail to urge the reader's seeing the Columbian Museum, which is richly interesting and chiefly for those Latin and Italian authors annotated by the immortal admiral's own hand. These give the American a sense of him as the discoverer of our hemisphere which nothing else could, and insurpassably render the New World credible. At the same time they somehow bring a lump of pity and piety into the throat at the thought of the things he did and suffered. They bring him from history and make him at home in the beholder's heart, and there seems a mystical significance in the fact that the volume most abounding in marginalia should be *Seneca's Prophecies*.

The frequent passing of men as well as women and children through our Plaza San Fernando and the prevalence of men asleep on the benches; the immense majority of boys everywhere; the moralized *abattoir* outside the walls where the humanity dormant at the bull-feast wakes to hide every detail of slaughter for the market; a large family of cats basking at their ease in a sunny doorway; trains of milch goats with wicker muzzles, led by a milch cow from door to door through the streets; the sudden solemn beauty of the high altar in the cathedral, seen by chance on a brilliant day; the bright, inspiriting air of Seville; a glorious glimpse of the Giralda coming home from a drive; the figure of a girl outlined in a lofty window; a middle-aged Finnish pair trying to give themselves in murmured talk to the colored stucco of the Hall of the Ambassadors in what seems their wedding journey; two artists working near with sketches tilted against the wall; a large American lady who arrives one forenoon in traveling dress and goes out after luncheon in a mantilla with a fan and high comb; another American lady who appears after dinner in the costume of a Spanish dancing-girl; the fact that there is no Spanish butter and that the only good butter comes from France and the passable butter from Denmark; the soft long veils of pink cloud that trail themselves in the sky across our Plaza, and then dissolve in the silvery radiance of the gibbous moon; the yellowish-red electric Brush lights swinging from palm to palm as in the decoration of some vast ballroom; a second drive through Triana, and a failure to reach the church we set out for; the droves of brown pigs and flocks of brown sheep; the goatherds unloading olive boughs in the fields for the goats to browse; a dirty, kind, peaceful village, with an English factory in it, and a mansion of galvanized iron with an automobile before it; a pink villa on a hillside and a family group on the shoulder of a high-walled garden; a girl looking down from the wall, and a young man resting his hand on the masonry and looking up at her; the good faces of the people, men and women; boys wrestling and frolicking in the village streets; the wide dust-heap of a road, full of sudden holes; the heat of the sun in the first November week after touches of cold; the tram-cars that wander from one side of the city street to the other, and then barely miss scraping the house walls; in our drive home from our failure for that church, men with trains of oxen plowing and showing against the round red rayless sun; a stretch of the river with the crimson-hulled steamers, and a distant sail-boat seen across the fields; the gray moon that burnishes itself and rides bright and high for our return; people in balconies, and the air full of golden dust shot with bluish electric lights; here is a handful of suggestions from my note-book which each and every one would expand into a chapter or a small volume under the intensive culture which the reader may well have come to dread. But I fling them all down here for him to do what he likes with, and turn to speak at more length of the University, or, rather the University Church, which I would not have any reader of mine fail to visit.

X

With my desire to find likeness rather than difference in strange peoples, I was glad to have two of the students loitering in the *patio* play just such a trick on a carter at the gate as school-boys might play in our own land. While his back was turned they took his whip and hid it and duly triumphed in his mystification and dismay. We did not wait for the catastrophe, but by the politeness of another student found the booth of the custodian, who showed us to the library. A noise of recitation from the windows looking into the *patio* followed us up-stairs; but maturer students were reading at tables in the hushed library, and at a large central table a circle of grave authorities of some sort were smoking the air blue with their cigarettes. One, who seemed chief among them, rose and bowed us into the freedom of the place, and again rose and bowed when we went out. We did not stay long, for a library is of the repellent interest of a wine-cellar; unless the books or bottles are broached it is useless to linger. There are eighty thousand volumes in that library, but we had to come away without examining half of them. The church was more appreciable, and its value was enhanced to us by the reluctance of the stiff old sacristan to unlock it. We found it rich in a most wonderful *retablo* carved in wood and painted. Besides the excellent pictures at the high altar, there are two portrait brasses which were meant to be recumbent, but which are stood up against the wall, perhaps to their surprise, without loss of impressiveness. Most notable of all is the mural tomb of Pedro Enriquez de Ribera and his wife: he who built the Casa de Pilatos, and as he had visited the Holy Land was naturally fabled to have copied it from the House of Pilate. Now, as if still continuing his travels, he reposes with his wife in a sort of double-decker monument, where the Evil One would have them suggest to the beholder the notion of passengers in the upper and lower berths of a Pullman sleeper.

Of all the Spanish cities that I saw, Seville was the most charming, not for those attributive blandishments of the song and dance which the tourist is supposed to find it, but which we quite failed of, but for the simpler and less conventional amiabilities which she was so rich in. I have tried to hint at these, but really one must go to Seville for them and let them happen as they will. Many happened in our hotel where we liked everybody, from the kindly, most capable Catalonian head waiter to the fine-headed little Napoleonic-looking waiter who had identified us at San Sebastian as Americans, because we spoke "quicklier" than the English, and who ran to us when we came into the hotel and shook hands with its as if we were his oldest and dearest friends. There was a Swiss concierge who could not be bought for money, and the manager was the mirror of managers. Fancy the landlord of the Waldorf-Astoria, or the St. Regis, coming out on the sidewalk and beating down a taxicabman from a charge of fifteen pesetas to six for a certain drive! It is not thinkable, and yet the like of it happened to xis in Seville from our manager. It was not his fault, when our rear apartment became a little too chill, and we took a parlor in the front and came back on the first day hoping to find it stored full of the afternoon sun's warmth, but found that the *camerera* had opened the windows and closed the shutters in our absence so that our parlor was of a frigidity which no glitter of the electric light could temper. The halls and public rooms were chill in anticipation and remembrance of any cold outside, but in otir parlor there was a hole for the sort of stove which we saw in the reading-room, twice as large as an average teakettle, with a pipe as big around as the average rain-pipe. I am sure this apparatus would have heated us admirably, but the weather grew milder and milder and we never had occasion to make the successful experiment. Meanwhile the moral atmosphere of the hotel was of a blandness which would have gone far to content us with any meteorological perversity. When we left it we were on those human terms with every one who ruled or served in it which one never attains in an American hotel, and rarely in an English one.

At noon on the 4th of November the sun was really hot in our plaza; but we were instructed that before the winter was over there would be cold enough, not of great frosty severity, of course, but nasty and hard to bear in the summer conditions which prevail through the year. I wish I could tell how the people live then in their beautiful, cool houses, but I do not know, and I do not know how they live at any season except from the scantiest hearsay. The women remain at home except when they go to church or to drive in the Delicias—that is to say, the women of society, of the nobility. There is no society in our sense among people of the middle classes; the men when they are not at business are at the cafe; the women when they are not at mass are at home. That is what we were told, and yet at a moving-picture show we saw many women of the middle as well as the lower classes. The frequent holidays afford them an outlet, and indoors they constantly see their friends and kindred at their *tertulias*.

The land is in large holdings which are managed by the factors or agents of the noble proprietors. These, when they are not at Madrid, are to be found at their clubs, where their business men bring them papers to be signed, often unread. This sounds a little romantic, and perhaps it is not true. Some gentlemen take a great interest in the bull-feasts and breed the bulls and cultivate the bull-fighters; what other esthetic interests they have I do not know. All classes are said to be of an Oriental philosophy of life; they hold that the English striving and running to and fro and seeing strange countries comes in the end to the same thing as sitting still; and why should they bother? There is something in that, but one may sit still too much; the Spanish ladies, as I many times heard, do overdo it. Not only they do not walk abroad; they do not walk at home; everything is carried to and from them; they do not lift hand or foot. The consequence is that they have very small hands and feet; Gautier, who seems to have grown tired when he reached Seville, and has comparatively little to say of it, says that a child may hold a Sevillian lady's foot in its hand; he does not say he saw it done. What is true is that no child could begin to clasp with both hands the waist of an average Sevillian lady. But here again the rule has its exceptions and will probably have more. Not only is the English queen-consort stimulating the Andalusian girls to play tennis by her example when she comes to Seville, but it has somehow become the fashion for ladies of all ages to leave their carriages in the Delicias and walk up and down; we saw at least a dozen doing it.

Whatever flirting and intriguing goes on, the public sees nothing of it. In the street there is no gleam of sheep's-eying or any manner of indecorum. The women look sensible and good, and I should say the same of the men; the stranger's experience must have been more unfortunate than mine if he has had any unkindness from them. One heard that Spanish women do not smoke, unless they are *cigarreras* and work in the large tobacco factory, where the "Carmen" tradition has given place to the mother-of-a-family type, with her baby on the floor beside her. Even these may prefer not to set the baby a bad example and have her grow up and smoke like those English and American women. The strength of the Church is, of course, in the women's faith, and its strength is unquestionable, if not quite unquestioned. In Seville, as I have said, there are two Spanish Protestant churches, and their worship, is not molested. Society does not receive their members; but we heard that with most Spanish people Protestantism is a puzzle rather than offense. They know we are not Jews, but Christians; yet we are not Catholics; and what, then, are we? With the Protestants, as with the Catholics, there is always religious marriage. There is civil marriage for all, but without the religious rite the pair are not well seen by either sect.

It is said that the editor of the ablest paper in Madrid, which publishes a local edition at Seville, is a Protestant. The queen mother is extremely clerical, though one of the wisest and best women who ever ruled; the king and queen consort are as liberal as possible, and the king is notoriously a democrat, with a dash of Haroun al Rashid, he likes to take his governmental subordinates unawares, and a story is told of his dropping in at the post-office on a late visit to Seville, and asking for the chief. He was out, and so were all the subordinate officials down to the lowest, whom the king found at his work. The others have since been diligent at theirs. The story is characteristic of the king, if not of the post-office people.

Political freedom is almost grotesquely unrestricted. In our American republic we should scarcely tolerate a party in favor of a monarchy, but in the Spanish monarchy a republican party is recognized and represented. It holds public meetings and counts among its members many able and distinguished men, such as the novelist Perez Galdos, one of the most brilliant novelists not only in Spain but in Europe. With this unbounded liberty in Andalusia, it is said that the Spaniards of the north are still more radical.

Though the climate is most favorable for consumptives, the habits of the people are so unwholesome that tuberculosis prevails, and there are two or three deaths a day from it in Seville. There is no avoidance of tuberculous suspects; they cough, and the men spit everywhere in the streets and on the floors and carpets of the clubs. The women suffer for want of fresh air, though now with the example of the English queen before them and the young girls who used to lie abed till noon getting up early ta play tennis, it will be different. Their mothers and aunts still drive to the Delicias to prove that they have carriages, but when there they alight and walk up and down by their doctor's advice.

I only know that during our fortnight in Seville I suffered no wound to a sensibility which has been kept in full repair for literary, if not for humanitarian purposes. The climate was as kind as the people. It is notorious that in summer the heat is that of a furnace, but even then it is bearable because it is a dry heat, like that of our indoor furnaces. The 5th of November was our last day, and then it was too hot for comfort in the sun, but one is willing to find the November sun too hot; it is an agreeable solecism; and I only wish that we could have found the sun too hot during the next three days in Granada. If the 5th of November had been worse for heat than it was it must still remain dear in our memory, because in the afternoon we met once more these Chilians of our hearts whom we had met in San Sebastian and Burgos and Valladolid and Madrid. We knew we should meet them in Seville and were not the least surprised. They were as glad and gay as ever, and in our common polyglot they possessed us of the fact that they had just completed the eastern hemicycle of their Peninsular tour. They were latest from Malaga, and now they were going northward. It was our last meeting, but better friends I could not hope to meet again, whether in the Old World or the New, or that Other World which we hope will somehow be the summation of all that is best in both.

# XI. TO AND IN GRANADA

The train which leaves Seville at ten of a sunny morning is supposed to arrive in Granada at seven of a moonlight evening. This is a mistake; the moonlight is on time, but the train arrives at a quarter of nine. Still, if the day has been sunny the whole way and the moonlight is there at the end, no harm has really been done; and measurably the promise of the train has been kept.

I

There was not a moment of the long journey over the levels of Andahisia which was not charming; when it began to be over the uplands of the last Moorish kingdom, it was richly impressive. The only thing that I can remember against the landscape is the prevalence of olive orchards. I hailed as a relief the stubble-fields immeasurably spread at times, and I did not always resent the roadside planting of some sort of tall hedges which now and then hid the olives. But olive orchards may vary their monotony by the spectacle of peasants on ladders gathering their fruit into wide-mouthed sacks, and occasionally their ranks of symmetrical green may be broken by the yellow and red of poplars and pomegranates around the pleasant farmsteads. The nearer we drew to Granada the pleasanter these grew, till in the famous Vega they thickly dotted the landscape with their brown roofs and white walls.

We had not this effect till we had climbed the first barrier of hills and began to descend on the thither side; but we had incident enough to keep us engaged without the picturesqueness. The beggars alone, who did not fail us at any station, were enough; for what could the most exacting tourist ask more than to be eating his luncheon under the eyes of the children who besieged his car windows and protested their famine in accents which would have melted a heart of stone or of anything less obdurate than travel? We had always our brace of Civil Guards, who preserved us from bandits, but they left the beggars unmolested by getting out on the train next the station and pacing the platform, while the rabble of hunger thronged us on the other side. There was especially a hoy who, after being compassionated in money for his misfortune, continued to fling his wooden leg into the air and wave it at our window by some masterly gymnastics; and there was another boy who kept lamenting that he had no mother, till, having duly feed and fed him, I suggested, "But you have a father?" Then, as if he had never seen the case in that light before, he was silent, and presently went away without further insistence on his bereavement.

The laconic fidelity of my note-book enables me to recall here that the last we saw of Seville was the Cathedral and the Giralda, which the guide-books had promised us we should see first; that we passed some fields of alfalfa which the Moors had brought from Africa and the Spanish have carried to America; that in places men were plowing and that the plowed land was red; that the towns on the uplands in the distance were white and not gray, or mud-colored, as in Castile; that the morning sky was blue, with thin, pale clouds; that the first station out was charmingly called Two Brothers, and that the loungers about it were plain, but kind-looking menfolk with good faces, some actually clean-shaven, and a woman with a white rose in her hair; that Two Brothers is a suburb of Seville, frequented in the winter, and has orange orchards about it; that farther on at one place the green of the fields spread up to the walls of a white farm with a fine sense of color; that there were hawks sailing in the blue air; that there were grotesque hedges of cactus and piles of crooked cactus logs; that there were many eucalyptus trees; that there were plantations of young olives, as if never to let that all-pervading industry perish; that there were irregular mountain ranges on the right, but never the same kind of scenery on both sides of the track; that there was once a white cottage on a yellow hill and a pink villa with two towers; that there was a solitary fig tree near the road, and that there were vast lonely fields when there were not olive orchards.

Taking breath after one o'clock, much restored by our luncheon, my note-book remembers a gray-roofed, yellow-walled town, very suitable for a water-color, and just beyond it the first vineyard we had come to. Then there were pomegranate trees, golden-leaved, and tall poplars pollarded plume fashion as in southern France; and in a field a herd of brown pigs feeding, which commended itself to observance, doubtless, as color in some possible word-painting. There now abounded pomegranates, figs, young corn, and more and more olives; and as if the old olives and young olives were not enough, the earth began to be pitted with holes dug for the olives which had not yet been planted.

II

At Bobadilla, the junction where an English railway company begins to get in its work and to animate the Spanish environment to unwonted enterprise, there was a varied luncheon far past our capacity. But when a Cockney voice asked over my shoulder, "Tea, sir?" I gladly closed with the proposition. "But you've put hot milk into it!" I protested. "I know it, sir. We 'ave no cold milk at Bobadilla," and instantly a baleful suspicion implanted itself which has since grown into a upas tree of poisonous conviction: goat's milk does not keep well, and it was not only hot milk, but hot *goat's* milk which they were serving us at Bobadilla. However, there were admirable ham sandwiches, not of goat's flesh, at the other end of the room, and with these one could console oneself. There was also a commendable pancake whose honored name I never knew, but whose acquaintance I should be sorry not to have made; and all about Bobadilla there was an agreeable bustle, which we enjoyed the more when we had made sure that we had changed into the right train for Granada and found in our compartment the charming young Swedish couple who had come with us from Seville.

Thoroughly refreshed by the tea with hot goat's milk in it, by the genuine ham sandwiches and the pancakes, my note-book takes up the tale once more. It dwells upon the rich look of the land and the comfort of the farms contrasting with the wild irregularity of the mountain ranges which now began to serrate the horizon; and I have no doubt that if I had then read that most charming of all Washington Irving's Spanish studies, the story, namely, of his journey over quite the same way we had come seventy-five years later, my note-book would abound in lively comment on the changed aspect of the whole landscape. Even as it is, I find it exclamatory over the wonder of the mountain coloring which it professes to have found green, brown, red, gray, and blue, but whether all at once or not it does not say. It is more definite as to the plain we were traversing, with its increasing number of white cottages, cheerfully testifying to the distribution of the land in small holdings, so different from the vast estates abandoned to homeless expanses of wheat-fields and olive orchards which we had been passing through. It did not appear on later inquiry that these small holdings were of peasant ownership, as I could have wished; they were tenant farms, but their neatness testified to the prosperity of the tenants, and their frequency cheered our way as the evening waned and the lamps began to twinkle from their windows. At a certain station, I am reminded by my careful mentor, the craggy mountain-tops were softened by the sunset pink, and that then the warm afternoon air began to grow cooler, and the dying day to empurple the uplands everywhere, without abating the charm of the blithe cottages. It seems to have been mostly a very homelike scene, and where there was a certain stretch of woodland its loneliness was relieved by the antic feat of a goat lifting itself on its hind legs to browse the olive leaves on their native bough. The air was thinner and cooler, but never damp, and at times it relented and blew lullingly in at our window. We made such long stops that the lights began to fade out of the farm-windows, but kept bright in the villages, when at a station which we were so long in coming to that we thought it must be next to Granada, a Spanish gentleman got in with us; and though the prohibitory notice of *No Fumadores* stared him in the face, it did not stare him out of countenance; for he continued to smoke like a locomotive the whole way to our journey's end. From time to time I meditated a severe rebuke, but in the end I made him none, and I am now convinced that this was wise, for he probably would not have minded it, and as it was, when I addressed him some commonplace as to the probable time of our arrival he answered in the same spirit, and then presently grew very courteously communicative. He told me for one thing, after we had passed the mountain gates of the famous Vega and were making our way under the moonlight over the storied expanse, drenched with the blood of battles long ago, that the tall chimneys we began to see blackening the air with their volumed fumes were the chimneys of fourteen beet-root sugar factories belonging to the Duke of Wellington. Then I divined, as afterward I learned, that the lands devoted to this industry were part of the rich gift which Spain bestowed upon the Great Duke in gratitude for his services against the Napoleonic invasion. His present heir has imagined a benevolent use of his heritage by inviting the peasantry of the Vega to the culture of the sugar-beet; but whether the enterprise was prospering I could not say; and I do not suppose any reader of mine will care so much for it as I did in the pour of the moonlight over the roofs and towers that were now becoming Granada, and quickening my slow old emotions to a youthful glow. At the station, which, in spite of Boabdil el Chico and Ferdinand and Isabel, was quite like every other railway station of southern Europe, we parted friends with our Spanish fellow-traveler, whom we left smoking and who is probably smoking still. Then we mounted with our Swedish friends into the omnibus of the hotel we had chosen and which began, after discreet delays, to climb the hill town toward the Alhambra through a commonplace-looking town gay with the lights of cafes and shops, and to lose itself in the more congenial darkness of narrower streets barred with moonlight. It was drawn by four mules, covered with bells and constantly coaxed and cursed by at least two drivers on the box, while a vigorous boy ran alongside and lashed their legs without ceasing till we reached the shelf where our hotel perched.

III

I had taken the precaution to write for rooms, and we got the best in the house, or if not that then the best we could wish at a price which I could have wished much less, till we stepped out upon our balcony, and looked down and over the most beautiful, the most magnificent scene that eyes, or at least my eyes, ever dwelt on. Beside us and before us the silver cup of the Sierra Nevada, which held the city in its tiled hollow, poured it out over the immeasurable Vega washed with moonshine which brightened and darkened its spread in a thousand radiances and obscurities of windows and walls and roofs and trees and lurking gardens. Because it was unspeakable we could not speak, but I may say now that this was our supreme moment of Granada. There were other fine moments, but none unmixed with the reservations which truth obliges honest travel to own. Now, when from some secret spot there rose the wild cry of a sentinel, and prolonged itself to another who caught it dying up and breathed new life into it and sent it echoing on till it had made the round of the whole fairy city, the heart shut with a pang of pure ecstasy. One could bear no more; we stepped within, and closed the window behind us. That is, we tried to close it, but it would not latch, and we were obliged to ring for a *camerero* to come and see what ailed it.

THE GATE OF JUSTICE, PRINCIPAL ENTRANCE

The infirmity of the door-latch was emblematic of a temperamental infirmity in the whole hotel. The promises were those of Madrid, but the performances were those of Segovia. There was a glitter, almost a glare, of Ritz-like splendor, and the rates were Ritz-like, but there the resemblance ceased. The porter followed us to our rooms on our arrival and told us in excellent English (which excelled less and less throughout our stay) that he was the hall porter and that we could confidently refer all our wants to him; but their reference seemed always to close the incident. There was a secretary who assured us that our rooms were not dear, and who could not out of regard to our honor and comfort consider cheaper ones; and then ceased to be until he receipted our bill when we went away. There was a splendid dining-room with waiters of such beauty and dignity, and so purple from clean shaving, that we scarcely dared face them, and there were luncheons and dinners of rich and delicate superabundance in the menu, but of an exquisite insipidity on the palate, and of a swiftly vanishing Barmecide insubstantiality, as if they were banquets from the *Arabian Nights* imagined under the rule of the Moors. Everywhere shone silver-bright radiators, such as we had not seen since we left their like freezing in Burgos; but though the weather presently changed from an Andalusian softness to a Castilian severity after a snowfall in the Sierra, the radiators remained insensible to the difference and the air nipped the nose and fingers wherever one went in the hotel. The hall porter, who knew everything, said the boilers were out of order, and a traveler who had been there the winter before confirmed him with the testimony that they were out of order even in January. There may not have been any fire under them then, as there was none now; but if they needed repairing now it was clearly because they needed repairing then. In the corner of one of our rooms the frescoed plastering had scaled off, and we knew that if we came back a year later the same spot would offer us a familiar welcome.

But why do I gird at that hotel in Granada as if I knew of no faults in American hotels? I know of many and like faults, and I do not know of a single hotel of ours with such a glorious outlook and downlook as that hotel in Granada. The details which the sunlight of the morrow revealed to us when we had mastered the mystery of our window-catch and stood again on our balcony took nothing from the loveliness of the moonlight picture, but rather added to it, and, besides a more incredible scene of mountain and plain and city, it gave us one particular tree in a garden almost under us which my heart clings to still with a rapture changing to a fond regret. At first the tree, of what name or nature I cannot tell, stood full and perfect, a mass of foliage all yellow as if made up of "patines of bright gold." Then day by day, almost hour by hour, it darkened and the tree shrank as if huddling its leaves closer about it in the cold that fell from the ever-snowier Sierra. On the last morning we left its boughs shaking in the rain against the cold,

> *Bare, ruined choir where late the sweet birds sang.*

## IV

But we anticipate, as I should say if I were still a romantic novelist. Many other trees in and about Granada were yellower than that one, and the air hung dim with a thin haze as of Indian summer when we left our hotel in eager haste to see the Alhambra such as travelers use when they do not want some wonder of the world to escape them. Of course there was really no need of haste, and we had to wait till our guide could borrow a match to light the first of the cigarettes which he never ceased to smoke. He was commended to us by the hall porter, who said he could speak French, and so he could, to the extreme of constantly saying, with a wave of his cigarette, *"N'est ce pas?"* For the rest he helped himself out willingly with my small Spanish. At the end he would have delivered us over to a dealer in antiquities hard by the gate of the palace if I had not prevented him, as it were, by main force; he did not repine, but we were not sorry that he should be engaged for the next day.

Our way to the gate, which was the famous Gate of Justice and was lovely enough to be the Gate of Mercy, lay through the beautiful woods, mostly elms, planted there by the English early in the last century. The birds sang in their tops, and the waters warbled at their feet, and it was somewhat thrillingly cold in their dense shade, so that we were glad to get out of it, and into the sunshine where the old Moorish palace lay basking and dreaming. At once let me confide to the impatient reader that the whole Alhambra, by which he must understand a citadel, and almost a city, since it could, if it never did, hold twenty thousand people within its walls, is only historically and not artistically more Moorish than the Alcazar at Seville. Far nobler and more beautiful than its Arabic decorativeness in tinted stucco is the palace begun by Charles V., after a design in the spirit of the supreme hour of the Italian Renaissance. It is not a ruin in its long arrest, and one hears with hopeful sympathy that the Spanish king means some day to complete it. To be sure, the world is, perhaps, already full enough of royal palaces, but since they return sooner or later to the people whose pockets they come out of, one must be willing to have this palace completed as the architect imagined it.

We were followed into the Moorish palace by the music of three blind minstrels who began to tune their guitars as soon as they felt us: see us they could not. Then presently we were in the famous Court of the Lions, where a group of those beasts, at once archaic and puerile in conception, sustained the basin of a fountain in the midst of a graveled court arabesqued and honeycombed round with the wonted ornamentation of the Moors.

The place was disappointing to the boy in me who had once passed so much of his leisure there, and had made it all marble and gold. The floor is not only gravel, and the lions are not only more like sheep, but the environing architecture and decoration are of a faded prettiness which cannot bear comparison with the fresh rougeing, equally Moorish, of the Alcazar at Seville. Was this indeed the place where the Abencerrages were brought in from supper one by one and beheaded into the fountain at the behest of their royal host? Was it here that the haughty Don Juan de Vera, coming to demand for the Catholic kings the arrears of tribute due them from the Moor, "paused to regard its celebrated fountain" and "fell into discourse with the Moorish courtiers on certain mysteries of the Christian faith"? So Washington Irving says, and so I once believed, with glowing heart and throbbing brow as I read how "this most Christian knight and discreet ambassador restrained himself within the limits of lofty gravity, leaning on the pommel of his sword and looking down with ineffable scorn upon the weak casuists around him. The quick and subtle Arabian witlings redoubled their light attacks on the stately Spaniard, but when one of them, of the race of the Abencerrages dared to question, with a sneer, the immaculate conception of the blessed Virgin, the Catholic knight could no longer restrain his ire. Elevating his voice of a sudden, he told the infidel he lied, and raising his arm at the same time he smote him on the head with his sheathed sword. In an instant the Court of Lions glistened with the flash of arms," insomuch that the American lady whom we saw writing a letter beside a friend sketching there must have been startled from her opening words, "I am sitting here with my portfolio on my knees in the beautiful Court of the Lions," and if Muley Aben Hassan had not "overheard the tumult and forbade all appeal to force, pronouncing the person of the ambassador sacred," she never could have gone on.

V

I did not doubt the fact when I read of it under the level boughs of the beechen tree with J. W., sixty years ago, by the green woodland light of the primeval forest which hemmed our village in, and since I am well away from the Alhambra again I do not doubt it now. I doubt nothing that Irving says of the Alhambra; he is the gentle genius of the place, and I could almost wish that I had paid the ten pesetas extra which the custodian demanded for showing his apartment in the palace. On the ground the demand of two dollars seemed a gross extortion; yet it was not too much for a devotion so rich as mine to have paid, and I advise other travelers to buy themselves off from a vain regret by giving it. If ever a memory merited the right to levy tribute on all comers to the place it haunts, Washington Irving's is that memory. His *Conquest of Granada* is still the history which one would wish to read; his *Tales of the Alhambra* embody fable and fact in just the right measure for the heart's desire in the presence of the monuments they verify or falsify. They belong to that strange age of romance which is now so almost pathetic and to which one cannot refuse his sympathy without sensible loss. But for the eager make-believe of that time we should still have to hoard up much rubbish which we can now leave aside, or accept without bothering to assay for the few grains of gold in it. Washington Irving had just the playful kindness which sufficed best to deal with the accumulations of his age; if he does not forbid you to believe, he does not oblige you to disbelieve, and he has always a tolerant civility in his humor which comports best with the duty of taking leniently a history impossible to take altogether seriously. Till the Spaniards had put an end to the Moorish misrule, with its ruthless despotism and bloody civil brawls, the Moors deserved to be conquered; it was not till their power was broken forever that they became truly heroic in their vain struggles and their unavailing sorrows. Then their pathetic resignation to persecution and exile lent dignity even to their ridiculous religion; but it was of the first and not the second period that Irving had to treat.

VI

The Alhambra is not so impressive by its glory or grandeur as by the unparalleled beauty of its place. If it is not very noble as an effect of art, the inspiration of its founders is affirmed by their choice of an outlook which commands one of the most magnificent panoramas in the whole world. It would be useless to rehearse the proofs by name. Think of far-off silver-crested summits and of a peopled plain stretching away from them out of eye-shot, dense first with roofs and domes and towers, and then freeing itself within fields and vineyards and orchards and forests to the vanishing-point of the perspective; think of steep and sudden plunges into chasms at the foot of the palace walls, and one crooked stream stealing snakelike in their depths; think of whatever splendid impossible dramas of topography that you will, of a tremendous map outstretched in colored relief, and you will perhaps have some notion of the prospect from the giddy windows of the Alhambra; and perhaps not. Of one thing we made memorably sure beyond the gulf of the Darro, and that was the famous gipsy quarter which the traveler visits at the risk of his life in order to have his fortune told. At the same moment we made sure that we should not go nearer it, for though we knew that it was insurpassably dirty as well as dangerous, we remembered so distinctly the loathsomeness of the gipsy quarter at Seville that we felt no desire to put it to the comparison.

We preferred rather the bird's-eye study of the beautiful Generalife which our outlook enabled us to make, and which we supplemented by a visit the next day. We preferred, after the Barmecide lunch at our hotel, taking the tram-car that noisily and more noisily clambers up and down, and descending into the town by it. The ascent is so steep that at a certain point the electric current no longer suffices, and the car bites into the line of cogs with its sort of powerful under-jaw and so arrives. Yet it is a kindly little vehicle, with a conductor so affectionately careful in transporting the stranger that I felt after a single day we should soon become brothers, or at least step-brothers. Whenever we left or took his car, after the beginning or ending of the cogway, he was alert to see that we made the right change to or from it, and that we no more overpaid than underpaid him. Such homely natures console the traveler for the thousand inhospitalities of travel, and bind races and religions together in spite of patriotism and piety.

We were going first to the Cartuja, and in the city, which we found curiously much more modern, after the Latin notion, than Seville, with freshly built apartment-houses and business blocks, we took a cab, not so modern as to be a taxicab, and drove through the quarter said to have been assigned to the Moors after the fall of Granada. The dust lay thick in the roadway where filthy children played, but in the sunny doorways good mothers of families crouched taking away the popular reproach of vermin by searching one another's heads. Men bestriding their donkeys rode fearlessly through the dust, and one cleanly-looking old peasant woman, who sat hers plumply cushioned and framed in with a chair-back and arms, showed a patience with the young trees planted for future shade along the desperate avenue which I could wish we had emulated. When we reached the entrance of the old Carthusian Convent, long since suppressed and its brothers exiled, a strong force of beggarmen waited for us, but a modest beggar-woman, old and sad, had withdrawn to the church door, where she shared in our impartial alms. We were admitted to the cloister, rather oddly, by a young girl, who went for one of the remaining monks to show us the church. He came with a newspaper (I hope of clerical politics) in his hand, and distracted himself from it only long enough to draw a curtain, or turn on a light, and point out a picture or statue from time to time. But he was visibly anxious to get back to it, and sped us more eagerly than he welcomed us in a church which upon the whole is richer in its peculiar treasures of painting, sculpture, especially in wood, costly marble, and precious stones than any other I remember. According to my custom, I leave it to the guide-books to name these, and to the abounding critics of Spanish art to celebrate the pictures and statues; it is enough for me that I have now forgotten them all except those scenes of the martyrdom inflicted by certain Protestants on members of the Carthusian brotherhood at the time when all sorts of Christians felt bound to correct the opinions of all other sorts by the cruelest tortures they could invent. When the monk had put us to shame by the sight of these paintings (bad as their subjects), he put us out, letting his eyes fall back upon his newspaper before the door had well closed upon us.

The beggarmen had waited in their places to give us another chance of meriting heaven; and at the church door still crouched the old beggarwoman. I saw now that the imploring eyes she lifted were sightless, and I could not forbear another alms, and as I put my copper big-dog in her leathern palm I said, *"Adios, madre."* Then happened something that I had long desired. I had heard and read that in Spain people always said at parting, "Go with God," but up to that moment nobody had said it to me, though I had lingeringly given many the opportunity. Now, at my words and at the touch of my coin this old beggarwoman smiled beneficently and said, "Go with God," or, as she put it in her Spanish, *"Vaya vested con Dios."* Immediately I ought to have pressed another coin in her palm, with a *"Gracias, madre; muchas gracias,"* out of regard to the literary climax; but whether I really did so I cannot now remember; I can only hope I did.

VII

I think that it was while I was still in this high satisfaction that we went a drive in the promenade, which in all Spanish cities is the Alameda, except Seville, where it so deservedly is the Delicias. It was in every way a contrast to the road we had come from the Cartuja: an avenue of gardened paths and embowered driveways, where we hoped to join the rank and fashion of Granada in their afternoon's outing. But there was only one carriage besides our own with people in it, who looked no greater world than ourselves, and a little girl riding with her groom. On one hand were pretty villas, new-looking and neat, which I heard could sometimes be taken for the summer at rents so low that I am glad I have forgotten the exact figures lest the reader should doubt my word. Nothing but the fact that the winter was then hanging over us from the Sierras prevented my taking one of them for the summer that had passed, the Granadan summer being notoriously the most delightful in the world. On the other hand stretched the wonderful

Vega, which covers so many acres in history and romance, and there, so near that we look down into them at times were "the silvery windings of the Xenil," which glides through so many descriptive passages of Irving's page; only now, on account of recent rain, its windings were rather coppery.

At the hotel on the terrace under our balcony we found on our return a party of Spanish ladies and gentlemen taking tea, or whatever drink stood for it in their custom: no doubt chocolate; but it was at least the afternoon-tea hour. The women's clothes were just from Paris, and the men's from London, but their customs, I suppose, were national; the women sat on one side of the table and talked across it to the men, while they ate and drank, and then each sex grouped itself apart and talked to its kind, the women in those hardened vowels of a dialect from which the Andalusians for conversational purposes have eliminated all consonants. The sun was setting red and rayless, with a play of many lights and tints, over the landscape up to the snow-line on the Sierra. The town lay a stretch of gray roofs and white walls, intermixed with yellow poplars and black cypresses, and misted over with smoke from the chimneys of the sugar factories. The mountains stood flat against the sky, purple with wide stretches of brown, and dark, slanting furrows. The light became lemon-yellow before nightfall, and then a dull crimson under pale violet.

The twitter of the Spanish women was overborne at times by the voices of an American party whose presence I was rather proud of as another American. They were all young men, and they were making an educational tour of the world in the charge of a professor who saw to it that they learned as much of its languages and history and civilization as possible on the way. They ranged in their years from about fifteen to twenty and even more, and they were preparing for college, or doing what they could to repair the loss of university training before they took up the work of life. It seemed to me a charming notion, and charming the seriousness with which they were fulfilling it. They were not so serious in everything as to miss any incidental pleasure; they had a large table to themselves in our Barmecide banquet-hall, where they seemed always to be having a good time, and where once they celebrated the birthday of one of them with a gaiety which would have penetrated, if anything could, the shining chill of the hostelry. In the evening we heard them in the billiard-room below lifting their voices in the lays of our college muse, and waking to ecstasy the living piano in the strains of our national ragtime. They were never intrusively cheerful; one might remain, in spite of them, as dispirited as the place would have one; but as far as the *genius loci* would let me, I liked them; and so far as I made their acquaintance I thought that they were very intelligently carrying out the enterprise imagined for them.

VIII

I wish now that I had known them well enough to ask them what they candidly thought of the city of which I felt the witchery under the dying day I have left celebrating for the moment in order to speak of them. It seems to me at this distance of time and space that I did not duly reflect that in places it was a city which smelled very badly and was almost as dirty as New York in others, and very ill paved. The worst places are in the older quarters, where the streets are very crooked and very narrow, so narrow that the tram-car can barely scrape through them. They are old enough to be streets belonging to the Moorish city, like many streets in Cordova and Seville, but no fond inquiry of our guides could identify this lane or that alley as of Moorish origin. There is indeed a group of picturesque shops clearly faked to look Moorish, which the lover of that period may pin his faith to, and for a moment I did so, but upon second thought I unpinned it.

We visited this plated fragment of the old Moorish capital when we descended from our hotel with a new guide to see the great, the stupendous cathedral, where the Catholic kings lie triumphantly entombed in the heart of their conquest. It is altogether unlike the other Spanish cathedrals of my knowledge; for though the cathedral of Valladolid is of Renaissance architecture in its austere simplicity, it is somehow even less like that of Granada than the Gothic fanes of Burgos or Toledo or Seville. All the detail at Granada is classicistic, but the whole is often of Gothic effect, especially in the mass of those clustered Corinthian columns that lift its domes aloof on their prodigious bulk, huge as that of the grouped pillars in the York Minster. The white of the marble walls, the gold of altars, the colors of painted wooden sculpture form the tones of the place, subdued to one bizarre richness which I may as well leave first as last to the reader's fancy; though, let his fancy riot as it will, it never can picture that gorgeousness. Mass was saying at a side altar as we entered, and the music of stringed instruments and the shrill voices of choir-boys pierced the spaces here and there, but no more filled them than the immemorial plastic and pictorial facts: than a certain very lively bishop kneeling on his tomb and looking like George Washington; or than a St. Jerome in the Desert, outwrinkling age, with his lion curled cozily up in his mantle; or than the colossal busts of Adam and Eve and the praying figures of Ferdinand and Isabel, richly gilded in the exquisite temple forming the high altar; or than the St. James on horseback, with his horse's hoof planted on the throat of a Moor; or than the Blessed Virgins in jeweled crowns and stomachers and brocaded skirts; or than that unsparing decapitation of John the Baptist bloodily falling forward with his severed gullet thrusting at the spectator. Nothing has ever been too terrible in life for Spanish art to represent; it is as ruthlessly veracious as Russian literature; and of all the painters and sculptors who have portrayed the story of Christianity as a tale of torture and slaughter, the Spaniards seem to have studied it closest from the fact; perhaps because for centuries the Inquisition lavished the fact upon them.

The supreme interest of the cathedral is, of course, the Royal Chapel, where in a sunken level Ferdinand and Isabel lie, with their poor mad daughter Joan and her idolized unfaithful husband Philip the Fair, whose body she bore about with her while she lived. The picture postal has these monuments in its keeping and can show them better than my pen, which falters also from the tremendous *retablo* of the chapel dense with the agonies of martyrdom and serene with the piety of the Catholic Kings kneeling placidly amid the horrors. If the picture postal will not supply these, or reproduce the many and many relics and memorials which abound there and in the sacristy—jewels and vestments and banners and draperies of the royal camp-altar—there is nothing for the reader but to go himself and see. It is richly worth his while, and if he cannot believe in a box which will be shown him as the box Isabel gave Columbus her jewels in merely because he has been shown a reliquary as her hand-glass, so much the worse for him. He will not then merit the company of a small choir-boy who efficiently opens the iron gate to the crypt and gives the custodian as good as he sends in back-talk and defiantly pockets the coppers he has earned. Much less will he deserve to witness the homely scene in an area outside of the Royal Chapel, where many milch goats are assembled, and when a customer comes, preferably a little girl with a tin cup, one of the mothers of the flock is pinioned much against her will by a street boy volunteering for the office, and her head held tight while the goatherdess milks the measure full at the other end.

IX

Everywhere about the cathedral beggars lay in wait, and the neighboring streets were lively with bargains of prickly pears spread open on the ground by old women who did not care whether any one bought or not. There were also bargains in palmistry; and at one place a delightful humorist was selling clothing at auction. He allured the bidders by having his left hand dressed as a puppet and holding a sparkling dialogue with it; when it did not respond to his liking he beat it with his right hand, and every now and then he rang a little bell. He had a pleased crowd about him in the sunny square; but it seemed to me that all the newer part of Granada was lively with commerce in ample, tram-trodden streets which gave the shops, larger than any we had seen out of Madrid, a chance uncommon in the narrow ways of other Spanish cities. Yet when I went to get money on my letter of credit, I found the bank withdrawn from the modernity in a seclusion reached through a lovely *patio*. We were seated in old-fashioned welcome, such as used to honor a banker's customers in Venice, and all comers bowed and bade us good day. The bankers had no such question of the different signatures as vexed those of Valladolid, and after no more delay than due ceremony demanded, I went away with both my money and my letter, courteously seen to the door.

The guide, to whom we had fallen in the absence of our French-speaking guide of the day before, spoke a little English, and he seemed to grow in sympathetic intelligence as the morning passed. He made our sightseeing include visits to the church of St. John of God, and the church of San Geronimo, which was built by Gonsalvo de Cordova, the Great Captain, and remains now a memorial to him. We rang at the door, and after long delay a woman came and let us into an interior stranger ever than her being there as custodian. It was frescoed from floor to ceiling everywhere, except the places of the altars now kept by the painted *retablos* and the tombs and the statues of the various saints and heroes. The *retablo* of the high altar is almost more beautiful than wonderful, but the chief glory of the place is in the kneeling figures of the Great Captain and his wife, one on either side of the altar, and farther away the effigies of his famous companions-in-arms, and on the walls above their heraldic blazons and his. The church Was unfinished when the Great Captain died in the displeasure of his ungrateful king, and its sumptuous completion testifies to the devotion of his wife and her taste in choosing the best artists for the work.

I have still the sense of a noonday quiet that lingered with us after we left this church and which seemed to go with us to the Hospital of St. John of God, founded, with other hospitals, by the pious Portuguese, who, after a life of good works, took this name on his well-merited canonization. The hospital is the monument of his devotion to good works, and is full of every manner of religious curio. I cannot remember to have seen so many relics under one roof, bones of both holy men and women, with idols of the heathen brought from Portuguese possessions in the East which are now faded from the map, as well as the body of St. John of God shrined in silver in the midst of all.

I do not know why I should have brought away from these two places a peacefulness of mind such as seldom follows a visit to show-places, but the fact is so; perhaps it was because we drove to and from them, and were not so tired as footworn sight-seers are, or so rebellious. One who had seen not only the body of St. John of God, but his cane with a whistle in it to warn the charitable of his coming and attune their minds to alms-giving, and the straw basket in which he collected food for the poor, now preserved under an embroidered satin covering, and an autograph letter of his framed in glass and silver, might even have been refreshed by his experience. At any rate, we were so far from tired that after luncheon we walked to the Garden of the Generalife, and then walked all over it. The afternoon was of the very mood for such a visit, and we passed it there in these walks and bowers, and the black cypress aisles, and the trees and vines yellowing to the fall of their leaves. The melancholy laugh of water chasing down the steep channels and gurgling through the stone rails of stairways was everywhere, and its dim smile gleamed from pools and tanks. In the court where it stretched in a long basin an English girl was painting and another girl was sewing, to whom I now tardily offer my thanks for adding to the charm of the place. Not many other people were there to dispute our afternoon's ownership. I count a peasant family, the women in black shawls and the men wearing wide, black sashes, rather as our guests than as strangers; and I am often there still with no sense of molestation. Even the reader who does not conceive of a garden being less flowers and shrubs than fountains and pavilions and porches and borders of box and walls of clipped evergreens, will scarcely follow me to the Generalife or outstay me there.

The place is probably dense with history and suffocating with association, but I prefer to leave all that to the imagination where my own ignorance found it. A painter had told me once of his spending a summer in it, and he showed some beautiful pieces of color in proof, but otherwise I came to it with a blank surface on which it might photograph itself without blurring any earlier record. This, perhaps, is why I love so much to dwell there on that never-ending afternoon of late October. It was long past the hour of its summer bloom, but the autumnal air was enriching it beyond the dreams of avarice with the gold which prevails in the Spanish landscape wherever the green is gone, and we could look out of its yellowing bowers over a landscape immeasurable in beauty. Of course, we tried to master the facts of the Generalife's past, but we really did not care for them and scarcely believed that Charles V. had doubted the sincerity of the converted Moor who had it from Ferdinand of Aragon, and so withheld it from his heirs for four generations until they could ripen to a genuine Christianity at Genoa, whither they withdrew and became the patrician family now its proprietors. The arms of this family decorate the roof and walls of the colonnaded belvedere from which you look out over the city and the plain and the mountains; and there are remnants of Moorish decoration in many places, but otherwise the Generalife is now as Christian as the noble Pallavicini who possess it. There were plenty of flower-beds, box-bordered, but there were no flowers in them; the flowers preferred standing about in tall pots. There was an arbor overhung with black forgotten grapes before the keeper's door and in the corner of it dangled ropes of fire-red peppers.

This detail is what, with written help, I remember of the Generalife, but no loveliness of it shall fade from, my soul. From its embowered and many-fountained height it looks over to the Alhambra, dull red, and the city wall climbing the opposite slope across the Darro to a church on the hilltop which was once a mosque. The precipice to which the garden clings plunges sheer to the river-bed with a downlook insurpassably thrilling; but the best view of the city is from the flowery walk that runs along the side of the Alcazaba, which was once a fortress and is now a garden, long forgetful of its office of defending the Alhambra palace. From this terrace Granada looks worthy of her place in history and romance. We visited the Alcazaba after the Generalife, and were very critical, but I must own the supremacy of this prospect. I should not mind owning its supremacy among all the prospects in the world.

## XI

Meanwhile our shining hotel had begun to thrill with something besides the cold which nightly pierced it from the snowy Sierra. This was the excitement pending from an event promised the next day, which was the production of a drama in verse, of peculiar and intense interest for Granada, where the scene of it was laid in the Alhambra at one of the highest moments of its history, and the persons were some of those dearest to its romance. Not only the company to perform it (of course the first company in Spain) had been in the hotel overnight, and the ladies of it had gleamed and gloomed through the cold corridors, but the poet had been conspicuous at dinner, with his wife, young and beautiful and blond, and powdered so white that her blondness was of quite a violet cast. There was not so much a question of whether we should take tickets as whether we could get them, but for this the powerful influence of our guide availed, and he got tickets providentially given up in the morning for a price so exorbitant I should be ashamed to confess it. They were for the afternoon performance, and at three o'clock we went with the rest of the gay and great world of Granada to the principal theater.

The Latin conception of a theater is of something rather more barnlike than ours, but this theater was of a sufficiently handsome presence, and when we had been carried into it by the physical pressure exerted upon us by the crowd at the entrance we found its vastness already thronged. The seats in the orchestra were mostly taken; the gallery under the roof was loud with the impatience for the play which the auditors there testified by cries and whistlings and stampings until the curtain lifted; the tiers of boxes rising all round the theater were filled with family parties. The fathers and mothers sat in front with the children between them of all ages down to babies in their nurses' arms. These made themselves perfectly at home, in one case reaching over the edge of the box and clawing the hair of a gentleman standing below and openly enjoying the joke. The friendly equality of the prevailing spirit was expressed in the presence of the family servants at the back of the family boxes, from which the latest fashions showed themselves here and there, as well as the belated local versions of them. In the orchestra the men had promptly lighted their cigars and the air was blue with smoke. Friends found one another, to their joyful amaze, not having met since morning; and especially young girls were enraptured to recognize young men; one girl shook hands twice with a young man, and gurgled with laughter as long as he stood near her.

As a lifelong lover of the drama and a boyish friend of Granadan romance, I ought to have cared more for the play than the people who had come to it, but I did not. The play was unintentionally amusing enough; but after listening for two hours to the monotonous cadences of the speeches which the persons of it recited to one another, while the ladies of the Moorish world took as public a part in its events as if they had been so many American Christians, we came away. We had already enjoyed the first entr'acte, when the men all rose and went out, or lighted fresh cigars and went to talk with the Paris hats and plumes or the Spanish mantillas and high combs in the boxes. The curtain had scarcely fallen when the author of the play was called before it and applauded by the generous, the madly generous, spectators. He stood bowing and bowing on tiptoe, as if the wings of his rapture lifted him to them and would presently fly away with him. He could not drink deep enough of the delicious draught, put brimming to his lips, and the divine intoxication must have lasted him through the night, for after breakfast the next morning I met him in our common corridor at the hotel smiling to himself, and when I could not forbear smiling in return he smiled more; he beamed, he glowed upon me as if I were a crowded house still cheering him to the echo. It was a beautiful moment and I realized even better than the afternoon before what it was to be a young poet and a young Spanish poet, and to have had a first play given for the first time in the city of Granada, where the morning papers glowed with praise so ardent that the print all but smoked with it. We were alone in the corridor where we met, and our eyes confessed us kindred spirits, and I hope he understood me better than if I had taken him in my arms and kissed him on both cheeks.

I really had no time for that; I was on my way down-stairs to witness the farewell scene between the leading lady and the large group of young Granadans who had come up to see her off. When she came out to the carriage with her husband, by a delicate refinement of homage they cheered him, and left him to deliver their devotion to her, which she acknowledged only with a smile. But not so the leading lady's lady's-maid, when her turn came to bid good-by from our omnibus window to the assembled upper servants of the hotel. She put her head out and said in a voice hoarse with excitement and good-fellowship, *"Adios, hombres!"* ("Good-by, men!"), and vanished with us from their applausive presence.

With us, I say, for we, too, were leaving Granada in rain which was snow on the Sierra and so cold that we might well have seemed leaving Greenland. The brave mules which had so gallantly, under the lash of the running foot-boy beside them, galloped uphill with us the moonlight night of our coming, now felt their anxious way down in the dismal drizzle of that last morning, and brought us at last to the plaza before the station. It was a wide puddle where I thought our craft should have floundered, but it made its way to the door, and left us dry shod within and glad to be quitting the city of my young dreams.

## XII. THE SURPRISES OF RONDA

The rain that pelted sharply into the puddle before the station at Granada was snow on the Sierra, and the snow that fell farther and farther down the mountainsides resolved itself over the Vega into a fog as white and almost as cold. Half-way across the storied and fabled plain the rain stopped and the fog lifted, and then we saw by day, as we had already seen by night, how the Vega was plentifully dotted with white cottages amid breadths of wheat-land where the peasants were plowing. Here and there were fields of Indian corn, and in a certain place there was a small vineyard; in one of the middle distances there spread a forest of Lombardy poplars, yellow as gold, and there was abundance of this autumn coloring in the landscape, which grew lonelier as we began to mount from the level. Olives, of course, abounded, and there were oak woods and clumps of wild cherry trees. The towns were far from the stations, which we reached at the rate of perhaps two miles an hour as we approached the top of the hills; and we might have got out and walked without fear of being left behind by our train, which made long stops, as if to get its breath for another climb. Before this the sole companion of our journey, whom we decided to be a landed proprietor coming out in his riding-gear to inspect his possessions, had left us, but at the first station after our descent began other passengers got in, with a captain of Civil Guards among them, very loquacious and very courteous, and much deferred to by the rest of us. At Bobadilla, where again we had tea with hot goat's milk in it, we changed cars, and from that on we had the company of a Rock-Scorpion pair whose name was beautifully Italian and whose speech was beautifully English, as the speech of those born at Gibraltar should rightfully be.

I

It was quite dark at Ronda when our omnibus drove into the gardened grounds of one of those admirable inns which an English company is building in Spain, and put us down at the door of the office, where a typical English manageress and her assistant appointed us pleasant rooms and had fires kindled in them while we dined. There were already fires in the pleasant reading-room, which did not diffuse a heat too great for health but imparted to the eye a sense of warmth such as we had experienced nowhere else in Spain. Over all was spread a quiet and quieting British influence; outside of the office the nature of the service was Spanish, but the character of it was English; the Spanish waiters spoke English, and they looked English in dress and manner; superficially the chambermaid was as English as one could have found her in the United Kingdom, but at heart you could see she was as absolutely and instinctively a Spanish *camerera* as any in a hotel of Madrid or Seville. In the atmosphere of insularity the few Spanish guests were scarcely distinguishable from Anglo-Saxons, though a group of magnificent girls at a middle table, quelled by the duenna-like correctness of their mother, looked with their exaggerated hair and eyes like Spanish ladies made up for English parts in a play.

We had our breakfast in the reading-room where all the rest were breakfasting and trying not to see that they were keeping one another from the fire. It was very cold, for Ronda is high in the mountains which hem it round and tower far above it. We had already had our first glimpse of their summits from our own windows, but it was from the terrace outside the reading-room that we felt their grandeur most after we had drunk our coffee: we could scarcely have borne it before. In their presence, we could not realize at once that Ronda itself was a mountain, a mere mighty mass of rock, cleft in twain, with chasmal depths where we saw pygmy men and mules creeping out upon the valley that stretched upward to the foot of the Sierra. Why there should ever have been a town built there in the prehistoric beginning, except that the rock was so impossible to take, and why it should have therefore been taken by that series of invaders who pervaded all Spain—by the Phoenicians, by the Carthaginians, by the Romans, by the Goths, by the Moors, by the Christians, and after many centuries by the French, and finally by the Spaniards again—it would not be easy to say. Among its many conquerors, the Moors left their impress upon it, though here as often as elsewhere in Spain their impress is sometimes merely a decoration of earlier Roman work. There remains a Roman bridge which the Moors did not make over into the likeness of their architecture, but built a bridge of their own which also remains and may be seen from the magnificent structure with which the Spaniards have arched the abyss where the river rushes writhing and foaming through the gorge three hundred feet below. There on the steps that lead from the brink, the eye of pity may still see the files of Christian captives bringing water up to their Moslem masters; but as one cannot help them now, even by the wildest throe, it is as well to give a vain regret to the architect of the Spanish bridge, who fell to his death from its parapet, and then push on to the market hard by.

II

You have probably come to see that market because you have read in your guide-books that the region round about Ronda is one of the richest in Spain for grapes and peaches and medlars and melons and other fruits whose names melt in the mouth. If you do not find in the market the abundance you expect of its picturesqueness you must blame the lateness of the season, and go visit the bull-ring, one of the most famous in the world, for Ronda is not less noted for its *toreros* and *aficionados* than for its vineyards and orchards. But here again the season will have been before you with the glory of those *corridas* which you have still hoped not to witness but to turn from as an example to the natives before the first horse is disemboweled or the first bull slain, or even the first *banderillero* tossed over the barrier.

The bull-ring seemed fast shut to the public when we approached it, but we found ourselves smilingly welcomed to the interior by the kindly mother in charge. She made us free of the whole vast place, where eight thousand people could witness in perfect comfort the dying agonies of beasts and men, but especially she showed us the chamber over the gate, full of bullfighting properties: the pikes, the little barbed pennons, the long sword by which the bull suffers and dies, as well as the cumbrous saddles and bridles and spears for the unhappy horses and their riders. She was especially compassionate of the horses, and she had apparently no pleasure in any of the cruel things, though she was not critical of the sport. The King of Spain is president of the Ronda bull-fighting association, and she took us into the royal box, which is the worthier to be seen because under it the bulls are shunted and shouted into the ring from the pen where they have been kept in the dark. Before we escaped her husband sold us some very vivid postal cards representing the sport; so that with the help of a large black cat holding the center of the ring, we felt that we had seen as much of a bull-fight as we could reasonably wish.

We were seeing the wonders of the city in the guidance of a charming boy whom we had found in wait for us at the gate of the hotel garden when we came out. He offered his services in the best English he had, and he had enough of it to match my Spanish word for word throughout the morning. He led us from the bull-ring to the church known to few visitors, I believe, where the last male descendant of Montezuma lies entombed, under a fit inscription, and then through the Plaza past the college of Montezuma, probably named for this heir of the Aztec empire. I do not know why the poor prince should have come to die in Ronda, but there are many things in Ronda which I could not explain: especially why a certain fruit is sold by an old woman on the bridge. Its berries are threaded on a straw and look like the most luscious strawberries but taste like turpentine, though they may be avoided under the name of *madrones*. But on no account would I have the reader avoid the Church of Santa Maria Mayor. It is so dark within that he will not see the finely carved choir seats without the help of matches, or the pictures at all; but it is worth realizing, as one presently may, that the hither part of the church is a tolerably perfect mosque of Moorish architecture, through which you must pass to the Renaissance temple of the Christian faith.

Near by is the Casa de Mondragon which he should as little miss if he has any pleasure in houses with two *patios* perching on the gardened brink of a precipice and overlooking one of the most beautiful valleys in the whole world, with donkey-trains climbing up from it over the face of the cliff. The garden is as charming as red geraniums and blue cabbages can make a garden, and the house is fascinatingly quaint and unutterably Spanish, with the inner *patio* furnished in bright-colored cushions and wicker chairs, and looked into by a brown wooden gallery. A stately lemon-colored elderly woman followed us silently about, and the whole place was pervaded by a smell that was impossible at the time and now seems incredible.

III

I here hesitate before a little adventure which I would not make too much of nor yet minify: it seems to me so gentle and winning. I had long meant to buy a donkey, and I thought I could make no fitter beginning to this end than by buying a donkey's head-stall in the country where donkeys are more respected and more brilliantly accoutred than anywhere else in the whole earth. When I ventured to suggest my notion, or call it dream, to our young guide, he instantly imagined it in its full beauty, and he led us directly to a shop in the principal street which for the richness and variety of the coloring in its display might have been a florist's shop. Donkeys' trappings in brilliant yellow, vermillion, and magenta hung from the walls, and head-stalls, gorgeously woven and embroidered, dangled from the roof. Among them and under them the donkeys' harness-maker sat at his work, a short, brown, handsome man with eyes that seemed the more prominent because of his close-shaven head. We chose a headstall of such splendor that no heart could have resisted it, and while he sewed to it the twine muzzle which Spanish donkeys wear on their noses for the protection of the public, our guide expatiated upon us, and said, among other things to our credit, that we were from America and were going to take the head-stall back with us.

The harness-maker lifted his head alertly. "Where, in America?" and we answered for ourselves, "From New York."

Then the harness-maker rose and went to an inner doorway and called through it something that brought out a comely, motherly woman as alert as himself. She verified our statement for herself, and having paved the way firmly for her next question she asked, "Do you know the Escuela Mann?"

As well as our surprise would let us, we said that we knew the Mann School, both where and what it was.

She waited with a sort of rapturous patience before saying, "My son, our eldest son, was educated at the Escuela Mann, to be a teacher, and now he is a professor in the Commercial College in Puerto Rico."

If our joint interest in this did not satisfy her expectation I for my part can never forgive myself; certainly I tried to put as much passion into my interest as I could, when she added that his education at the Escuela Mann was without cost to him. By this time, in fact, I was so proud of the Escuela Mann that I could not forbear proclaiming that a member of my own family, no less than the father of the grandson for whose potential donkey I was buying that headstall, was one of the architects of the Escuela Mann building.

She now vanished within, and when she came out she brought her daughter, a gentle young girl who sat down and smiled upon us through the rest of the interview. She brought also an armful of books, the Spanish-English Ollendorff which her son had used in studying our language, his dictionary, and the copy-book where he had written his exercises, with two photographs of him, not yet too Americanized; and she showed us not only how correctly but how beautifully his exercises were done. If I did not admire these enough, again I cannot forgive myself, but she seemed satisfied with what I did, and she talked on about him, not too loquaciously, but lovingly and lovably as a mother should, and proudly as the mother of such a boy should, though without vainglory; I have forgotten to say that she had a certain distinction of face, and was appropriately dressed in black. By this time we felt that a head-stall for such a donkey as I was going to buy was not enough to get of such people, and I added a piece of embroidered leather such as goes in Spain on the front of a donkey's saddle; if we could not use it so, in final defect of the donkey, we could put it on a veranda chair. The saddler gave it at so low a price that we perceived he must have tacitly abated something from the visual demand, and when we did not try to beat him down, his wife went again into that inner room and came out with an iron-holder of scarlet flannel backed with canvas, and fringed with magenta, and richly inwrought with a Moorish design, in white, yellow, green, and purple. I say Moorish, because one must say something, but if it was a pattern of her own invention the gift was the more precious when she bestowed it on the sister of one of the architects of the Escuela Mann. That led to more conversation about the Escuela Mann, and about the graduate of it who was now a professor in Puerto Rico, and we all grew such friends, and so proud of one another, and of the country so wide open to the talents without cost to them, that when I asked her if she would not sometime be going to America, her husband answered almost fiercely in his determination, "I am going when I have learned English!" and to prove that this was no idle boast, he pronounced some words of our language at random, but very well. We parted in a glow of reciprocal esteem and I still think of that quarter-hour as one of my happiest; and whatever others may say, I say that to have done such a favor to one Spanish family as the Escuela Mann had been the means of our nation doing this one was a greater thing than to have taken Cuba from Spain and bought the Philippines when we had seized them already and had led the Filipinos to believe that we meant to give their islands to them.

IV

Suddenly, on the way home to our very English hotel, the air of Ronda seemed charged with English. We were already used to the English of our young guide, which so far as it went, went firmly and courageously after forethought and reflection for each sentence, but we were not quite prepared for the English of two polite youths who lifted their hats as they passed us and said, "Good afternoon." The general English lasted quite overnight and far into the next day when we found several natives prepared to try it on us in the pretty Alameda, and learned from one, who proved to be the teacher of it in the public school, that there were some twenty boys studying it there: heaven knows why, but the English hotel and its success may have suggested it to them as a means of prosperity. The students seem each prepared to guide strangers through Ronda, but sometimes they fail of strangers. That was the case with the pathetic young hunchback whom we met in Alameda, and who owned that he had guided none that day. In view of this and as a prophylactic against a course of bad luck, I made so bold as to ask if I might venture to repair the loss of the peseta which he would otherwise have earned. He smiled wanly, and then with the countenance of the teacher, he submitted and thanked me in English which I can cordially recommend to strangers knowing no Spanish.

All this was at the end of another morning when we had set out with the purpose of seeing the rest of Ronda for ourselves. We chose a back street parallel to the great thoroughfare leading to the new bridge, and of a squalor which we might have imagined but had not. The dwellers in the decent-looking houses did not seem to mind the sights and scents of their street, but these revolted us, and we made haste out of it into the avenue where the greater world of Ronda was strolling or standing about, but preferably standing about. In the midst of it, at the entrance of the new bridge we heard ourselves civilly saluted and recognized with some hesitation the donkey's harness-maker who, in his Sunday dress and with his hat on, was not just the work-day presence we knew. He held by the hand a pretty boy of eleven years, whom he introduced as his second son, self-destined to follow the elder brother to America, and duly take up the profession of teaching in Puerto Rico after experiencing the advantages of the Escuela Mann. His father said that he already knew some English, and he proposed that the boy should go about with us and practise it, and after polite demur and insistence the child came with us, to our great pleasure. He bore himself with fit gravity, in his cap and long linen pinafore as he went before us, and we were personally proud of his fine, long face and his serious eyes, dark and darkened yet more by their long lashes. He knew the way to just such a book store as we wanted, where the lady behind the desk knew him and willingly promised to get me some books in the Andalusian dialect, and send them to our hotel by him at half past twelve. Naturally she did not do so, but he came to report her failure to get them. We had offered to pay him for his trouble, but he forbade us, and when we had overcome his scruple he brought the money back, and we had our trouble over again to make him keep it. To this hour I do not know how we ever brought ourselves to part with him; perhaps it was his promise of coming to America next year that prevailed with us; his brother was returning on a visit and then they were going back together.

V

Our search for literature in Ronda was not wholly a failure. At another bookstore, I found one of those local histories which I was always vainly trying for in other Spanish towns, and I can praise the *Historia de Ronda par Federico Lozano Gutierrez* as well done, and telling all that one would ask to know about that famous city. The author's picture is on the cover, and with his charming letter dedicating the book to his father goes far to win the reader's heart. Outside the bookseller's a blind minstrel was playing the guitar in the care of a small boy who was selling, not singing, the ballads. They celebrated the prowess of Spain in recent wars, and it would not be praising them too highly to say that they seemed such as might have been written by a drum-major. Not that I think less of them for that reason, or that I think I need humble myself greatly to the historian of Ronda for associating their purchase with that of his excellent little book. If I had bought some of the blind minstrel's almanacs and jest-books I might indeed apologize, but ballads are another thing.

After we left the bookseller's, our little guide asked us if we would like to see a church, and we said that we would, and he took us into a white and gold interior, with altar splendors out of proportion to its simplicity, all in the charge of a boy no older than himself, who was presently joined by two other contemporaries. They followed us gravely about, and we felt that it was an even thing between ourselves and the church as objects of interest equally ignored by Baedeker. Then we thought we would go home and proposed going by the Alameda.

That is a beautiful place, where one may walk a good deal, and drive, rather less, but not sit down much unless indeed one likes being swarmed upon by the beggars who have a just priority of the benches. There seemed at first to be nobody walking in the Alameda except a gentleman pacing to and from the handsome modern house at the first corner, which our guide said was this cavalier's house. He interested me beyond any reason I could give; he looked as if he might represent the highest society in Ronda, but did not find it an adequate occupation, and might well have interests and ambitions beyond it. I make him my excuses for intruding my print upon him, but I would give untold gold if I had it to know all about such a man in such a city, walking up and down under the embrowning trees and shrinking flowers of its Alameda, on a Sunday morning like that.

Our guide led us to the back gate of our hotel garden, where we found ourselves in the company of several other students of English. There was our charming young guide of the day before and there was that sad hunchback already mentioned, and there was their teacher who seemed so few years older and master of so little more English. Together we looked into the valley into which the vision makes its prodigious plunge at Ronda before lifting again over the fertile plain to the amphitheater of its mighty mountains; and there we took leave of that nice boy who would not follow us into our garden because, as he showed us by the sign, it was forbidden to any but guests. He said he was going into the country with his family for the afternoon, and with some difficulty he owned that he expected to play there; it was truly an admission hard to make for a boy of his gravity. We shook hands at parting with him, and with our yesterday's guide, and with the teacher and with the hunchback; they all offered it in the bond of our common English; and then we felt that we had parted with much, very much of what was sweetest and best in Ronda.

VI

The day had been so lovely till now that we said we would stay many days in Ronda, and we loitered in the sun admiring the garden; the young landlady among her flowers said that all the soil had to be brought for it in carts and panniers, and this made us admire its autumn blaze the more. That afternoon we had planned taking our tea on the terrace for the advantage of looking at the sunset light on the mountains, but suddenly great black clouds blotted it out. Then we lost courage; it appeared to us that it would be both brighter and, warmer by the sea and that near Gibraltar we could more effectually prevent our steamer from getting away to New York without us. We called for our bill, and after luncheon the head waiter who brought it said that the large black cat which had just made friends with us always woke him if he slept late in the morning and followed him into the town like a dog when he walked there.

It was hard to part with a cat like that, but it was hard to part with anything in Ronda. Yet we made the break, and instead of ruining over the precipitous face of the rock where the city stands, as we might have expected, we glided smoothly down the long grade into the storm-swept lowlands sloping to the sea. They grew more fertile as we descended and after we had left a mountain valley where the mist hung grayest and chillest, we suddenly burst into a region of mellow fruitfulness, where the haze was all luminous, and where the oranges hung gold and green upon the trees, and the women brought grapes and peaches and apples to the train. The towns seemed to welcome us southward and the woods we knew instantly to be of cork trees, with Don Quixote and Sancho Panza under their branches anywhere we chose to look.

Otherwise, the journey was without those incidents which have so often rendered these pages thrilling. Just before we left Ronda a couple, self-evidently the domestics of a good family, got into our first-class carriage though they had unquestionably only third-class tickets. They had the good family's dog with them, and after an unintelligible appeal to us and to the young English couple in the other corner, they remained and banished any misgivings they had by cheerful dialogue. The dog coiled himself down at my feet and put his nose close to my ankles, so that without rousing his resentment I could not express in Spanish my indignation at what I felt to be an outrageous intrusion: servants, we all are, but in traveling first class one must draw the line at dogs, I said as much to the English couple, but they silently refused any part in the demonstration. Presently the conductor came out to the window for our fares, and he made the Spanish pair observe that they had third-class tickets and their dog had none. He told them they must get out, but they noted to him the fact that none of us had objected to their company, or their dog's, and they all remained, referring themselves to us for sympathy when the conductor left. After the next station the same thing happened with little change; the conductor was perhaps firmer and they rather more yielding in their disobedience. Once more after a stop the conductor appeared and told them that when the train halted again, they and their dog must certainly get out. Then something surprising happened: they really got out, and very amiably; perhaps it was the place where they had always meant to get out; but it was a great triumph for the railway company, which owed nothing in the way of countenance to the young English couple; they had done nothing but lunch from their basket and bottle. We ourselves arrived safely soon after nightfall at Algeciras, just in time for dinner in the comfortable mother-hotel whose pretty daughter had made us so much at home in Ronda.

# XIII. ALGECIRAS AND TARIFA

When we walked out on the terrace of our hotel at Algeciras after breakfast, the first morning, we were greeted by the familiar form of the Rock of Gibraltar still advertising, as we had seen it three years before, a well-known American insurance company. It rose beyond five miles of land-locked water, which we were to cross every other day for three weeks on many idle and anxious errands, until we sailed from it at last for New York.

Meanwhile Algeciras was altogether delightful not only because of our Kate-Greenaway hotel, embowered in ten or twelve acres of gardened ground, with walks going and coming under its palms and eucalyptuses, beside beds of geraniums and past trellises of roses and jasmines, all in the keeping of a captive stork which was apt unexpectedly to meet the stranger and clap its formidable mandibles at him, and then hop away with half-lifted wings. Algeciras had other claims which it urged day after day more winningly upon us as the last place where we should feel the charm of Spain unbroken in the tradition which reaches from modern fact far back into antique fable. I will not follow it beyond the historic clue, for I think the reader ought to be satisfied with knowing that the Moors held it as early as the seven hundreds and as late as the thirteen hundreds, when the Christians definitively recaptured it and their kings became kings of Algeciras as well as kings of Spain, and remain so to this day. At the end of the eighteenth century one of these kings made it his lookout for watching the movements of the inimical English fleets, and then Algeciras slumbered again, haunted only by "a deep dream of peace" till the European diplomats, rather unexpectedly assisted by an American envoy, made it the scene of their famous conference for settling the Morocco question in. 1906.

I think this is my whole duty to the political interest of Algeciras, and until I come to our excursion to Tarifa I am going to give myself altogether to our pleasure in the place unvexed by any event of history. I disdain even to note that the Moors took the city again from the Christians, after twenty-five years, and demolished it, for I prefer to remember it as it has been rebuilt and lies white by its bay, a series of red-tiled levels of roof with a few church-towers topping them. It is a pretty place, and remarkably clean, inhabited mostly by beggars, with a minority of industrial, commercial, and professional citizens, who live in agreeable little houses, with *patios* open to the passer, and with balconies overhanging him. It has of course a bull-ring, enviously closed during our stay, and it has one of the pleasantest Alamedas and the best swept in Spain, where some nice boys are playing in the afternoon sun, and a gentleman, coming out of one of the villas bordering on it, is courteously interested in the two strangers whom he sees sitting on a bench beside the walk, with the leaves of the plane trees dropping round them in the still air.

The Alameda is quite at the thither end of Algeciras. At the end next our hotel, but with the intervention of a space of cliff, topped and faced by summer cottages and gardens, is the station with a train usually ready to start from it for Ronda or Seville or Malaga, I do not know which, and with the usual company of freight-cars idling about, empty or laden with sheets of cork, as indifferent to them as if they were so much mere pine or spruce lumber. There is a sufficiently attractive hotel here for transients, and as an allurement to the marine and military leisure of Gibraltar, "The Picnic Restaurant," and "The Cabin Tea Room," where no doubt there is something to be had beside sandwiches and tea. Here also is the pier for the Gibraltar boats, with the Spanish custom-house which their passengers must pass through and have their packages and persons searched for contraband. One heard of wild caprices on the part of the inspectors in levying duties which were sometimes made to pass the prime cost of the goods in Gibraltar. I myself only carried in books which after the first few declarations were recognized as of no imaginable value and passed with a genial tolerance, as a sort of joke, by officers whom I saw feeling the persons of their fellow-Spaniards unsparingly over.

We had, if anything, less business really in Algeciras than in Gibraltar, but we went into the town nearly every afternoon, and wantonly bought things. By this means we proved that the Andalusian shopmen had not the proud phlegm of the Castilians across their counters. In the principal dry-goods store two salesmen rivaled each other in showing us politeness, and sent home our small purchases as promptly as if we had done them a favor in buying. We were indeed the wonder of our fellow-customers who were not buying; but our pride was brought down in the little shop where the proprietress was too much concerned in cooking her dinner (it smelled delicious) to mind our wish for a very cheap green vase, inestimably Spanish after we got it home. However, in another shop where the lady was ironing her week's wash on the counter, a lady friend who was making her an afternoon call got such a vase down for us and transacted the negotiation out of pure good will for both parties to it.

Parallel with the railway was a channel where small fishing-craft lay, and where a leisurely dredging-machine was stirring up the depths in a stench so dire that I wonder we do not smell it across the Atlantic. Over this channel a bridge led into the town, and offered the convenient support of its parapet to the crowd of spectators who wished to inhale that powerful odor at their ease, and who hung there throughout the working-day; the working-day of the dredging-machine, that is. The population was so much absorbed in this that when we first crossed into the town, we found no beggar children even, though there were a few blind beggarmen, but so few that a boy who had one of them in charge was obliged to leave off smelling the river and run and hunt him up for us. Other boys were busy in street-sweeping and b-r-r-r-r-ing to the donkeys that carried off the sweepings in panniers; and in the fine large plaza before the principal church of Algeciras there was a boy who had plainly nothing but mischief to do, though he did not molest us farther than to ask in English, "Want to see the cathedral?" Then he went his way swiftly and we went into the church, which we found very whitewashed and very Moorish in architecture, but very Spanish in the Blessed Virgins on most of the altars, dressed in brocades and jewels. A sacristan was brushing and dusting the place, but he did not bother us, and we went freely about among the tall candles standing on the floor as well as on the altars, and bearing each a placard attached with black ribbon, and dedicated in black letters on silver "To the Repose of This or That" one among the dead.

The meaning was evident enough, but we sought something further of the druggist at the corner, who did his best for us in such English as he had. It was not quite the English of Ronda; but he praised his grammar while he owned that his vocabulary was in decay from want of practise. In fact, he well-nigh committed us to the purchase of one of those votive candles, which he understood we wished to buy; he all but sent to the sacristan to get one. There were several onlookers, as there always are in Latin pharmacies, and there was a sad young mother waiting for medicine with a sick baby in her arms. The druggist said it had fever of the stomach; he seemed proud of the fact, and some talk passed between him and the bystanders which related to it. We asked if he had any of the quince jelly which we had learned to like in Seville, but he could only refer us to the confectioner's on the other corner. Here was not indeed quince jelly, but we compromised on quince cheese, as the English call it; and we bought several boxes of it to take to America, which I am sorry to say moulded before our voyage began, and had to be thrown away. Near this confectioner's was a booth where boiled sweet-potatoes were sold, with oranges and joints of sugar-cane, and, spitted on straws, that terrible fruit of the strawberry tree which we had tasted at Honda without wishing to taste it ever again. Yet there was a boy boldly buying several straws of it and chancing the intoxication which over-indulgence in it is said to cause. Whether the excitement of these events was too great or not, we found ourselves suddenly unwilling, if not unable, to walk back to our hotel, and we took a cab of the three standing in the plaza. One was without a horse, another without a driver, but the third had both, as in some sort of riddle, and we had no sooner taken it than a horse was put into the first and a driver ran out and got on the box of the second, as if that was the answer to the riddle.

II

It was then too late for them to share our custom, but I am not sure that it was not one of these very horses or drivers whom we got another day for our drive about the town and its suburbs, and an excursion to a section of the Moorish aqueduct which remains after a thousand years. You can see it at a distance, but no horse or driver in our employ could ever find the way to it; in fact, it seemed to vanish on approach, and we were always bringing up in our hotel gardens without having got to it; I do not know what we should have done with it if we had. We were not able to do anything definite with the new villas built or building around Algeciras, though they looked very livable, and seemed proof of a prosperity in the place for which I can give no reason except the great natural beauty of the nearer neighborhood, and the magnificence of the farther, mountain-walled and skyed over with a September blue in November. I think it would be a good place to spend the winter if one liked each day to be exactly like every other. I do not know whether it is inhabited by English people from Gibraltar, where there are of course those resources of sport and society which an English colony always carries with it.

The popular amusements of Algeciras in the off season for bull-feasts did not readily lend themselves to observance. Chiefly we noted two young men with a graphophone on wheels which, being pushed about, wheezed out the latest songs to the acceptance of large crowds. We ourselves amused a large crowd when one of us attempted to sketch the yellow facade of a church so small that it seemed all facade; and another day when that one of us who held the coppers, commonly kept sacred to blind beggars, delighted an innumerable multitude of mendicants having their eyesight perfect. They were most of them in the vigor of youth, and they were waiting on a certain street for the monthly dole with which a resident of Algeciras may buy immunity for all the other days of the month. They instantly recognized in the stranger a fraudulent tax-dodger, and when he attempted tardily to purchase immunity they poured upon him; in front, behind, on both sides, all round, they boiled up and bubbled about him; and the exhaustion of his riches alone saved him alive. It must have been a wonderful spectacle, and I do not suppose the like of it was ever seen in Algeciras before. It was a triumph over charity, and left quite out of comparison the organized onsets of the infant gang which always beset the way to the hotel under a leader whose battle-cry, at once a demand and a promise, was "Penny-go-way, Penny-go-way!"

Along that pleasant shore bare-legged fishermen spread their nets, and going and coming by the Gibraltar boats were sometimes white-hosed, brown-cloaked, white-turbaned Moors, who occasionally wore Christian boots, but otherwise looked just such Moslems as landed at Algeciras in the eighth century; people do not change much in Africa. They were probably hucksters from the Moorish market in Gibraltar, where they had given their geese and turkeys the holiday they were taking themselves. They were handsome men, tall and vigorous, but they did not win me to sympathy with their architecture or religion, and I am not sure but, if there had been any concerted movement against them on the landing at Algeciras, I should have joined in driving them out of Spain. As it was I made as much Africa as I could of them in defect of crossing to Tangier, which we had firmly meant to do, but which we forbore doing till the plague had ceased to rage there. By this time the boat which touched at Tangier on the way to Cadiz stopped going to Cadiz, and if we could not go to Cadiz we did not care for going to Tangier. It was something like this, if not quite like it, and it ended in our seeing Africa only from the southernmost verge of Europe at Tarifa. At that little distance across it looked dazzlingly white, like the cotton vestments of those Moorish marketmen, but probably would have been no cleaner on closer approach.

III

As a matter of fact, we were very near not going even to Tarifa, though we had promised ourselves going from the first. But it was very charming to linger in the civilization of that hotel; to wander through its garden paths in the afternoon after a forenoon's writing and inhale the keen aromatic odors of the eucalyptus, and when the day waned to have tea at an iron table on the seaward terrace. Or if we went to Gibraltar, it was interesting to wonder why we had gone, and to be so glad of getting back, and after dinner joining a pleasant international group in the long reading-room with the hearth-fires at either end which, if you got near them, were so comforting against the evening chill. Sometimes the pleasure of the time was heightened by the rain pattering on the glass roof of the *patio*, where in the afternoon a bulky Spanish mother sat mute beside her basket of laces which you could buy if you would, but need not if you would rather not; in either case she smiled placidly.

At last we did get together courage enough to drive twelve miles over the hills to Tarifa, but this courage was pieced out of the fragments of the courage we had lost for going to Cadiz by the public automobile which runs daily from Algeciras. The road after you passed Tarifa was so bad that those who had endured it said nobody could endure it, and in such a case I was sure I could not, but now I am sorry I did not venture, for since then I have motored over some of the roads in the state of Maine and lived. If people in Maine had that Spanish road as far as Tarifa they would think it the superb Massachusetts state road gone astray, and it would be thought a good road anywhere, with the promise of being better when the young eucalyptus trees planted every few yards along it grew big enough to shade it. But we were glad of as much sun as we could get on the brisk November morning when we drove out of the hotel garden and began the long climb, with little intervals of level and even of lapse. We started at ten o'clock, and it was not too late in that land of anomalous hours to meet peasants on their mules and donkeys bringing loads of stuff to market in Algeciras. Men were plowing with many yoke of oxen in the wheat-fields; elsewhere there were green pastures with herds of horses grazing in them, an abundance of brown pigs, and flocks of sheep with small lambs plaintively bleating. The pretty white farmhouses, named each after a favorite saint, and gathering at times into villages, had grapes and figs and pomegranates in their gardens; and when we left them and climbed higher, we began passing through long stretches of cork woods.

The trees grew wild, sometimes sturdily like our oaks, and sometimes gnarled and twisted like our seaside cedars, and in every state of excoriation. The bark is taken from them each seventh year, and it begins to be taken long before the first seventh. The tender saplings and the superannuated shell wasting to its fall yield alike their bark, which is stripped from the roots to the highest boughs. Where they have been flayed recently they look literally as if they were left bleeding, for the sap turns a red color; but with time this changes to brown, and the bark begins to renew itself and grows again till the next seventh year. Upon the whole the cork-wood forest is not cheerful, and I would rather frequent it in the pages of *Don Quixote* than out; though if the trees do not mind being barked it is mere sentimentality in me to pity them.

The country grew lonelier and drearier as we mounted, and the wind blew colder over the fields blotched with that sort of ground-palm, which lays waste so much land in southern Spain. When we descended the winding road from the summit we came in sight of the sea with Africa clearly visible beyond, and we did not lose sight of it again. Sometimes we met soldiers possibly looking out for smugglers but, let us hope, not molesting them; and once we met a brace of the all-respected Civil Guards, marching shoulder to shoulder, with their cloaks swinging free and their carbines on their arms, severe, serene, silent. Now and then a mounted wayfarer came toward us looking like a landed proprietor in his own equipment and that of his steed, and there were peasant women solidly perched on donkeys, and draped in long black cloaks and hooded in white kerchiefs.

IV

The landscape softened again, with tilled fields and gardened spaces around the cottages, and now we had Tarifa always in sight, a stretch of white walls beside the blue sea with an effect of vicinity which it was very long in realizing. We had meant when we reached the town at last to choose which *fonda* we should stop at for our luncheon, but our driver chose the Fonda de Villanueva outside the town wall, and I do not believe we could have chosen better if he had let us. He really put us down across the way at the *venta* where he was going to bait his horses; and in what might well have seemed the custody of a little policeman with a sword at his side, we were conducted to the *fonda* and shown up into the very neat icy cold parlor where a young girl with a yellow flower in her hair received us. We were chill and stiff from our drive and we hoped for something warmer from the dining-room, which we perceived must face southward, and must be full of sun. But we reckoned without the ideal of the girl with the yellow flower in her hair: in the little saloon, shining round with glazed tiles where we next found ourselves, the sun had been carefully screened and scarcely pierced the scrim shades. But this was the worst, this was all that was bad, in that *fonda*. When the breakfast or the luncheon, or whatever corresponds in our usage to the Spanish *almuerzo*, began to come, it seemed as if it never would stop. An original but admirable omelette with potatoes and bacon in it was followed by fried fish flavored with saffron. Then there was brought in fried kid with a dish of kidneys; more fried fish came after, and then boiled beef, with a dessert of small cakes. Of course there was wine, as much as you would, such as it was, and several sorts of fruit. I am sorry to have forgotten how little all this cost, but at a venture I will say forty cents, or fifty at the outside; and so great kindness and good will went with it from the family who cooked it in the next room and served it with such cordial insistence that I think it was worth quite the larger sum. It would not have been polite to note how much of this superabundance was consumed by the three Spanish gentlemen who had so courteously saluted us in sitting down at table with us. I only know that they made us the conventional acknowledgment in refusing our conventional offer of some things we had brought with us from our hotel to eat in the event of famine at Tarifa.

When we had come at last to the last course, we turned our thoughts somewhat anxiously to the question of a guide for the town which we felt so little able to explore without one; and it seemed to me that I had better ask the policeman who had brought us to our *fonda*. He was sitting at the head of the stairs where we had left him, and so far from being baffled by my problem, he instantly solved it by offering himself to be our guide. Perhaps it was a profession which he merely joined to his civic function, but it was as if we were taken into custody when he put himself in charge of us and led us to the objects of interest which I cannot say Tarifa abounds in. That is, if you leave out of the count the irregular, to and fro, up and down, narrow lanes, passing the blank walls of low houses, and glimpsing leafy and flowery *patios* through open gates, and suddenly expanding into broader streets and unexpected plazas, with shops and cafes and churches in them.

Tarifa is perhaps the quaintest town left in the world, either in or out of Spain, but whether it is more Moorish than parts of Cordova or Seville I could not say. It is at least pre-eminent in a feature of the women's costume which you are promised at the first mention of the place, and which is said to be a survival of the Moslem civilization. Of course we were eager for it, and when we came into the first wide street, there at the principal corner three women were standing, just as advertised, with black skirts caught up from their waists over their heads and held before their faces so that only one eye could look out at the strangers. It was like the women's costume at Chiozza on the Venetian lagoon, but there it is not claimed for Moorish and here it was authenticated by being black. "Moorish ladies," our guide proudly proclaimed them in his scanty English, but I suspect they were Spanish; if they were really Orientals, they followed us with those eyes single as daringly as if they had been of our own Christian Occident.

The event was so perfect in its way that it seemed as if our guiding policeman might have especially ordered it; but this could not have really been, and was no such effect of his office as the immunity from beggars which we enjoyed in his charge. The worst boy in Tarifa (we did not identify him) dared not approach for a big-dog or a little, and we were safe from the boldest blind man, the hardiest hag, however pockmarked. The lanes and the streets and the plazas were clean as though our guide had them newly swept for us, and the plaza of the principal church (no guide-book remembers its name) is perhaps the cleanest in all Spain.

## VI

The church itself we found very clean, and of an interest quite beyond the promise of the rather bare outside. A painted window above the door cast a glare of fresh red and blue over the interior, and over the comfortably matted floor; and there was a quite freshly carved and gilded chapel which the pleasant youth supplementing our policeman for the time said was done by artists still living in Tarifa. The edifice was of a very flamboyant Gothic, with clusters of slender columns and a vault brilliantly swirled over with decorations of the effect of peacock feathers. But above all there was on a small side altar a figure of the Child Jesus dressed in the corduroy suit and felt hat of a Spanish shepherd, with a silver crook in one hand and leading a toy lamb by a string in the other. Our young guide took the image down for us to look at, and showed its shepherd's dress with peculiar satisfaction; and then he left it on the ground while he went to show us something else. When we came back we found two small boys playing with the Child, putting its hat off and on, and feeling of its clothes. Our guide took it from them, not unkindly, and put it back on the altar; and whether the reader will agree with me or not, I must own that I did not find the incident irreverent or without a certain touchingness, as if those children and He were all of one family and they were at home with Him there.

Rather suddenly, after we left the church, by way of one of those unexpectedly expanding lanes, we found ourselves on the shore of the purple sea where the Moors first triumphed over the Goths twelve hundred years before, and five centuries later the Spaniards beat them back from their attempt to reconquer the city. There were barracks, empty of the Spanish soldiers gone to fight the same old battle of the Moors on their own ground in Africa, and there was the castle which Alfonso Perez de Guzman held against them in 1292, and made the scene of one of those acts of self-devotion which the heart of this time has scarcely strength for. The Moors when they had vainly summoned him to yield brought out his son whom they held captive, and threatened to kill him. Guzman drew his knife and flung it down to them, and they slew the boy, but Tarif a was saved. His king decreed that thereafter the father should be known as Guzman the Good, and the fact has gone into a ballad, but the name somehow does not seem quite to fit, and one wishes that the father had not won it that way.

We were glad to go away from the dreadful place, though Tangier was so plain across the strait, and we were almost in Africa there, and hard by, in the waters tossing free, the great battle of Trafalgar was fought. From the fountains of my far youth, when I first heard of Guzman's dreadful heroism, I endeavored to pump up an adequate emotion; I succeeded somewhat better with Nelson and his pathetic prayer of "Kiss me, Hardy," as he lay dying on his bloody deck; but I did not much triumph with either, and I was grateful when our good little policeman comfortably questioned the deed of Guzman which he said some doubted, though he took us to the very spot where the Moors had parleyed with Guzman, and showed us the tablet over the castle gate affirming the fact.

We liked far better the pretty Alameda rising in terraces from it with beds of flowers beside the promenade, and boys playing up and down, and old men sitting in the sun, and trying to ignore the wind that blew over them too freshly for us. Our policeman confessed that there was nothing more worth seeing in Tarifa, and we entreated of him the favor of showing us a shop where we could buy a Cordovese hat; a hat which we had seen nourishing on the heads of all men in Cordova and Seville and Granada and Ronda, and had always forborne to buy because we could get it anywhere; and now we were almost leaving Spain without it. We wanted one brown in color, as well as stiff and flat of brim, and slightly conical in form; and our policeman promptly imagined it, and took us to a shop abounding solely in hats, and especially in Cordoveses. The proprietor came out wiping his mouth from an inner room, where he had left his family visibly at their *almuerzo;* and then we were desolated together that he should only have Cordoveses that were black. But passing a *patio* where there was a poinsettia in brilliant bloom against the wall, we found ourselves in a variety store where there were Cordoveses of all colors; and we chose one of the right brown, with the picture of a beautiful Spanish girl, wearing a pink shawl, inside the crown which was fluted round in green and red ribbon. Seven pesetas was the monstrous asking price, but we beat it down to five and a half, and then came a trying moment: we could not carry a Cordovese in tissue-paper through the streets of Tarifa, but could we ask our guide, who was also our armed escort, to carry it? He simplified the situation by taking it himself and bearing it back to the *fonda* as proudly as if he had not also worn a sword at his side; and we parted there in a kindness which I should like to think he shared equally with us.

He was practically the last of those Spaniards who were always winning my heart (save in the bank at Valladolid where they must have misunderstood me), and whom I remember with tenderness for their courtesy and amiability. In little things and large, I found the Spaniards everywhere what I heard a Piedmontese commercial traveler say of them in Venice fifty years ago: "They are the honestest people in Europe." In Italy I never began to see the cruelty to animals which English tourists report, and in Spain I saw none at all. If the reader asks how with this gentleness, this civility and integrity, the Spaniards have contrived to build up their repute for cruelty, treachery, mendacity, and every atrocity; how with their love of bull-feasts and the suffering to man and brute which these involve, they should yet seem so kind to both, I answer frankly, I do not know. I do not know how the Americans are reputed good and just and law-abiding, although they often shoot one another, and upon mere suspicion rather often burn negroes alive.

Milton Keynes UK
Ingram Content Group UK Ltd.
UKHW022155250224
438379UK00006B/757

Milton Keynes UK
Ingram Content Group UK Ltd.
UKHW022155250224
438379UK00006B/757